THE REVOLUTION WILL BE HILARIOUS

POSTMILLENNIAL POP

General Editors: Karen Tongson and Henry Jenkins

Puro Arte: Filipinos on the Stages of Empire
Lucy Mae San Pablo Burns

Spreadable Media: Creating Value and Meaning in a Networked Culture
Henry Jenkins, Sam Ford, and Joshua Green

Media Franchising: Creative License and Collaboration in the Culture Industries
Derek Johnson

Your Ad Here: The Cool Sell of Guerrilla Marketing
Michael Serazio

Looking for Leroy: Illegible Black Masculinities
Mark Anthony Neal

From Bombay to Bollywood: The Making of a Global Media Industry
Aswin Punathambekar

A Race So Different: Performance and Law in Asian America
Joshua Takano Chambers-Letson

Surveillance Cinema
Catherine Zimmer

Modernity's Ear: Listening to Race and Gender in World Music
Roshanak Kheshti

The New Mutants: Superheroes and the Radical Imagination of American Comics
Ramzi Fawaz

Restricted Access: Media, Disability, and the Politics of Participation
Elizabeth Ellcessor

The Sonic Color-Line: Race and the Cultural Politics of Listening
Jennifer Lynn Stoever

Diversión: Play and Popular Culture in Cuban America
Albert Sergio Laguna

Antisocial Media: Anxious Labor in the Digital Economy
Greg Goldberg

Open TV: Innovation beyond Hollywood and the Rise of Web Television
Aymar Jean Christian

Missing More Than Meets the Eye: Special Effects and the Fantastic Transmedia Franchise
Bob Rehak

Playing to the Crowd: Musicians, Audiences, and the Intimate Work of Connection
Nancy K. Baym

Old Futures: Speculative Fiction and Queer Possibility
Alexis Lothian

Anti-Fandom: Dislike and Hate in the Digital Age
Edited by Melissa A. Click

Social Media Entertainment: The New Industry at the Intersection of Hollywood and Silicon Valley
Stuart Cunningham and David Craig

Video Games Have Always Been Queer
Bonnie Ruberg

The Power of Sports: Media and Spectacle in American Culture
Michael Serazio

The Dark Fantastic: Race and the Imagination from Harry Potter to the Hunger Games
Ebony Elizabeth Thomas

The Race Card: From Gaming Technologies to Model Minorities
Tara Fickle

Open World Empire: Race, Erotics, and the Global Rise of Video Games
Christopher B. Patterson

The Content of Our Caricature: African American Comic Art and Political Belonging
Rebecca Wanzo

Stories of the Self: Life Writing after the Book
Anna Poletti

Hip Hop Heresies: Queer Aesthetics in New York City
Shanté Paradigm Smalls

The Revolution Will Be Hilarious: Comedy for Social Change and Civic Power
Caty Borum

The Revolution Will Be Hilarious

Comedy for Social Change and Civic Power

Caty Borum

NEW YORK UNIVERSITY PRESS

New York

NEW YORK UNIVERSITY PRESS
New York
www.nyupress.org

© 2023 by New York University

References to Internet websites (URLs) were accurate at the time of writing. Neither the author nor New York University Press is responsible for URLs that may have expired or changed since the manuscript was prepared.

Please contact the Library of Congress for Cataloging-in-Publication data.

ISBN: 9781479810826 (hardback)
ISBN: 9781479810833 (paperback)
ISBN: 9781479810840 (library ebook)
ISBN: 9781479810857 (consumer ebook)

New York University Press books are printed on acid-free paper, and their binding materials are chosen for strength and durability. We strive to use environmentally responsible suppliers and materials to the greatest extent possible in publishing our books.

Manufactured in the United States of America

10 9 8 7 6 5 4 3 2 1

Also available as an ebook

For Elias and Simone, my favorite funny people

Humanity has advanced, when it has advanced, not because it has been sober, responsible, and cautious, but because it has been playful, rebellious, and immature.
—Tom Robbins

CONTENTS

List of Figures   xiii

Preface   xv

Introduction: "It's like Taking Your Vodka with a Chaser":
Comedy as Civic Power in the Participatory Media Age   1

1. "Desperate Cheeto": How Comedy Functions as Deviant
   Creative Resistance   27

2. "It's All about Who You Know": Pitching and Producing
   Comedy in the Transforming Entertainment Industry   47

3. "Hollywood Won't Change Unless It's Forced to Change":
   How Activism and Entertainment Collide and Collaborate   75

4. "You Learn to Be Racist from People You Love":
   Co-creating Comedy for Antiracism Public Engagement   97

5. "Invisibility Is Not a Superpower": Asserting Native
   American Identity through Humor   126

6. "Maybe They Think Beauty Can't Come from Here":
   Resilience and Power in the Climate Crisis   152

7. "I've Always Been a Syringe-Half-Full Kinda Guy":
   Changing the Entertainment Comedy Pipeline   182

Conclusion: Taking Comedy Seriously   205

Acknowledgments   215

Appendix: List of Interviewees   219

Notes   221

Index   247

About the Author   261

FIGURES

Figure I.1: Screenshot: "Even Supervillains Think Our Sexual
Assault Laws Are Insane"   15

Figure I.2: *Stand Up Planet*, starring Hasan Minhaj, Mpho Popps,
and Aditi Mittal   20

Figure 1.1: Screenshot: "Desperate Cheeto"   29

Figure 2.1: Screenshot: "How to Medical"   51

Figure 3.1: Screenshot: Opening graphic for the "Welcome to
America" episode of *Alternatino* on Comedy Central   94

Figure 4.1: Screenshot: "Comedian Corey Ryan 'Buttercream
Dream' Forrester Has a Message for Racism"   121

Figure 4.2: Screenshot: "Plea to White Women: Comedian
Jay Jurden"   122

Figure 4.3: Screenshot: "The Hammer: Comedian
Corey Forrester"   123

Figure 5.1: Filming *You're Welcome, America!* in New York City 149

Figure 5.2: Cohosts of *You're Welcome, America!*, Adrianne
Chalepah and Joyelle Nicole Johnson, on set   150

Figure 6.1: Community gardens at the Vivian C. Mason Art &
Technology Center for Teens in Norfolk, Virginia   154

Figure 6.2: Comedian Clark Jones prepares to go on stage to
perform at the *Ain't Your Mama's Heat Wave* live comedy
show in Norfolk, Virginia   177

Figure 6.3: Movie poster for *Ain't Your Mama's Heat Wave*   181

Figure 7.1: Comedian Murf Meyer stands in front of a hometown
(Luzerne County, Pennsylvania) billboard for his comedy
podcast, *Murf Meyer Is Self-Medicated*   187

Figure 7.2: Marcos González and Gabe González pitch their
comedy project, *Los Blancos*, at the launch of the Yes,
And . . . Laughter Lab at Caveat in New York City, 2019   196

Figure 7.3: Poster for the 2021 Yes, And . . . Laughter Lab NYC
Pitch Showcase   198

Figure 7.4: Yes, And . . . Laughter Lab on the marquee at
Dynasty Typewriter, host of the 2021 Los Angeles
Pitch Showcase   199

Figure C.1: Laureano Márquez performs comedy in
New York City in December 2021   207

PREFACE

I have a few things to say about comedy people. The first is: you know if you are one of them.

Years ago, if you had asked a small handful of folks in my life—parents, relatives, childhood friends, or maybe even the high school teacher who told me that joking around in class was not a solid career path—whether my writing about comedy was a wild future proposition, I am pretty sure the answer would have been a solid "no." (Well, to be clear, the topic of silliness would not be surprising, but maybe the book-author part would be.) When I look back and put the various pieces together, this book feels predestined. I was, after all, what some southerners would call "a spirited child," a euphemistic way of saying I was too silly for my own good—just deviant enough to not entirely blend in. There are a few stand-out moments. I distinctly remember making my mom and aunts fall over laughing at my character impersonations of relatives (it sounds mean, but I promise it was motivated by affection). I insisted on the red ballet shoes instead of regulation pinks while I wiggled my way through a solo comedic dance instead of the rehearsed serious one at the recital. Then there were the requisite exasperated parent-teacher meetings—kindergarten through twelfth grade—because nothing (and I mean *nothing*) could stop me from talking and telling jokes to the kids around me.

And so, some years later, it felt like a small wink from the universe when I landed in legendary comedy TV producer Norman Lear's office for an unplanned half-hour meeting that became a three-hour one, followed by a job offer and a nearly decade-long stint working for and with one of Hollywood's greatest comedic minds (so, as it turns out, disrupting class with a steady stream of jokes *is* a decent professional route, thank you very much). Norman, however, is so much more than the words he penned for countless sitcom episodes—he is a very funny, kindhearted, everyday human. A comedy person. In the office, I was able to watch and learn on a daily basis as his deviance and bright spirit—his regular funny, not the fancy kind on TV—motivated all kinds of people to be better, to be authentic, to make impossible things happen, to embrace their vulnerability on the way to deep human truths, all of which, of course, pave the way to pathbreaking creativity and innovation (as you shall hopefully learn from this book). He also appreciated fellow deviants, so he was the first successful adult person in my life (not related to me, that is) to make me feel as though it was okay to proudly fly my silliness flag.

Jump a decade ahead to my inaugural adventures as a somewhat accidental professor. I was three classes into the gig when I realized how much air needed to be let out of seminar rooms that felt bloated with anxiety: first-year students in fresh college classes, me nervously teaching them for the first time, and the general potential for pomposity within the Ivory Tower. Humor was immediately part of my toolbox as an educator, and to this day, comedy changes the space every time I invite it in—for me and the students. We connect more, we learn from each other, we talk and listen differently. And dare I say it? We have fun. (And despite being shamed for my chattiness in high school, I am still the person to avoid during a serious work meeting that drags on a little too long—especially faculty meetings, always ripe for humor. The impulse to make someone laugh is too strong. Find a different seat, or risk trouble by association.)

To be clear, I am not a professional humorist. I am, however, a comedy *person*. I understand comedians (or I like to think so, anyway), including everyday ones. They do not exactly blend in, and hallelujah for that. Around 2013, despite (because of?) my proclivity for the daily silly, I began a serious route to researching and making comedy for social change, partially inspired and informed by prior professional experience and an abiding commitment to social justice, but also based on instinct. I marvel at the many avenues and adventures that have opened up since then. Working with comedy people has enriched my life in ways that far surpass mere professional ambitions and interests.

So, here, finally, is what I want to say about comedy people. For many different reasons, they seem authentically free in what they choose to display and how they connect, in how they use confession and acceptance to deal with things that are hard or confusing or just ridiculous.

There is pain and resilience and absurdity, but their willingness to say it out loud, and to play with others in order to "yes, and" their own ideas is powerful, and, yes, courageous. They are kind and generous in their support for one another. They are radically open and in touch with human vulnerabilities and failures; they use this clay to mold and create, rather than discarding taboos to sweep under the rug. Culturally, we need comedy people more than we might recognize or care to admit, beyond the ways we encounter them through the formal entertainment marketplace. We need the release valve of humor to regularly let the proverbial air out of rooms that are divided and hostile and self-important. We need to laugh in order to heal, find resilience, and arrive at revelations about topics we had failed to consider beyond our own calcified opinions or tunnel-visioned life experiences.

I have learned a great deal simply from being in the room with comedians, watching how they play and improvise together, how they deeply listen, how they accept terrible ideas and build on them, and how they call out egregious wrongs that deserve lampooning. These are tiny acts of radical kindness and resistance. And so, in the spirit of comedy people, this book begins here, with my own authentic offering of "aha!" understanding about whatever destiny led me from naughty little girl to the pages that follow. It was inevitable.

Introduction

"It's like Taking Your Vodka with a Chaser":
Comedy as Civic Power in the Participatory Media Age

The list of props is ridiculous: a hamster, a supersized bucket of fried chicken, a toaster and some bread, a workout ball, a snake, video game controllers, wax cream for lady mustaches, and a pedicurist named Helga. It is early 2004, and comedy virtuoso Norman Lear and I are on a sound stage in Los Angeles, prepping to produce what will become a fairly serious young-voter empowerment campaign through the vehicle of comedy—one that would prove consequential, we like to think, not in spite of this odd assortment of humans and creatures and fried food and household products but because of it. Comedy, after all, requires open creative space to ignite attention-grabbing moments of cultural recognition, and we are in search of the sparks.[1]

There is a back story, of course. What led to this moment was a fresh climate of comedic civic engagement, the dawning possibilities of the digital media age, a serious research project, and a remarkable assemblage of comedic talents ready to goof off with a purpose. A few years prior, Lear, the groundbreaking writer and producer who generated the mold for socially conscious TV comedy—also a fervent devotee of the promises of the Declaration of Independence ("America's birth certificate," as he was fond of saying)—launched a new nonprofit, nonpartisan organization and campaign, Declare Yourself, dedicated to inspiring young people to register and vote. At Norman's invitation, I was among the first to join the small leadership team. While I was hardly an expert at any particular skill at the time, I was certainly a member of the early millennium's young voter generation and a firm believer in the power of entertainment media to motivate my cohort of passive (or simply confused) would-be civic participants. My own predisposition matched Norman's—an ever-present belief in the energizing power of hope and optimism that can happen when a group of people can imagine and laugh together. So, when we shaped our campaign to joyfully exploit the engines of creativity and popular culture, I was all in.

The 2004 presidential election between Senator John Kerry and incumbent president George W. Bush might have been easily written off in the annals of political history as generally boring and uninspiring but for its location within the early 2000s convergence of digital media platforms and a crop of pop-culture-centered grassroots efforts that sprang up to push young-voter participation after more than a decade of lackluster turnout. Youth-motivating voting organizations launched in force that year, alongside others that found renewed energy: Sean "P. Diddy" Combs's 2004 Citizen Change campaign plastered music events and pop culture with its "Vote or Die" slogan,[2] Def Jam co-founder Russell Simmons held the Hip Hop Action Summit to rally young Black voters, and Rock the Vote blasted its messages through community events and media, alongside MTV's Choose or Lose, the World Wrestling Foundation's Smackdown Your Vote, and a handful of others.[3] Our Declare Yourself campaign resided among these ranks, working with young Hollywood talent as civic megaphones. Informally united under an umbrella of "20 Million Strong," the new pop-culture grassroots civic-engagement groups spoke to the urgency of young people's participation as the country continued to brush itself off from the tragedy of 9/11 and contend with an unexpected new war. It was also a moment, notably, in which hilarious journo-comedian Jon Stewart and his hit satirical news program, *The Daily Show*, were inspiring Gen-Xers and Millennials to learn about politics and develop media-literacy skills by demanding "an active viewer to sift through the distinctions between fact and fantasy"[4]—while also prompting hand wringing among traditional political scholars who feared such foolishness would push democracy and serious civic engagement off a cliff.[5]

The entertainment motivations of the young-voter empowerment initiatives converged with supportive public policy and technological possibility, as the 2004 presidential election was also the first federal contest to bear the fruits of the 2002 Help America Vote Act, which helped would-be voters complete voter-registration forms online for the first time.[6] Our own national public opinion research at Declare Yourself, facilitated under my direction, had revealed that young people generally failed to vote due to the murky and complicated registration process, not because they were apathetic. Simply offering online registration forms on the Declare Yourself website as a cornerstone of our campaign—ours was one of the first grassroots organizations in the country to do so—could be transformative,[7] but not sufficient to reach and motivate young voters. In the heyday of the Jon Stewart era, we knew we needed comedy.

Back to the sound stage:

And so it is that we find ourselves on bare sets in Los Angeles and New York during the early months of 2004, equipped with a furry rodent and lady-mustache cream and a cadre of the most talented comedy voices in the country, producing the Declare Yourself youth-voter- registration campaign in partnership with Comedy Central, home to *The Daily Show* and its pathbreaking civic-engagement language. The potential for humor is high in the hands of Norman Lear and director Kevin Smith, alongside talented writers and executives at Comedy Central. But we are stumped about how to script a unifying concept that will work with a boring—though research-based—registration message, performed by comedy pros who are up for the challenge: Wanda Sykes, Sarah Silverman, Molly Shannon, Amy Poehler, David Cross, Larry David, Ben Affleck (not a comedian but a funny person, as it turns out), and a few others. We land on a simple premise that honors the creative ingenuity of professional funny people and gives them the open space to find the silliness: for two days, the comedians select a prop from the bizarre collection and perform sixty seconds of improv with whatever food or animal or human or product inspires them, ending with a simple tag straight to camera: "In the time it took you to watch me [insert inane improv activity here], you could have registered to vote," followed on screen by the Declare Yourself online registration form link. The results are predictably weird, creative, and giggle inducing: Amy Poehler plays with "Mr. Chubbs," a furry hamster who shows off some serious method acting chops; Sarah Silverman waxes her lady 'stache; Ben Affleck pumices the heels of pedicurist Helga, who admonishes him to "rub harder"; David Cross manages some fake barf (also an available prop) while attempting a sit-up on an exercise ball; and Wanda Sykes, wielding a game controller next to a little boy on a dingy basement couch, reminds would-be voters that "in the time that it takes this little nine-year-old bastard to kick my ass at this video game, you could be online getting registered to vote."[8]

Comedy Central aired the funny campaign spots in prime-time TV slots repeatedly throughout 2004, and we watched the number of completed online voter-registration forms on the Declare Yourself website tick up—from hundreds to thousands to more thousands to more than a million.[9] No single organization can responsibly take credit for a remarkable election where young voters were concerned, but there is no question that pop culture—and for our part, comedy—was instrumental in reaching young people that year, alongside the newly available online registration processes. It was historic. In the 2004 election, 49 percent of voters aged eighteen to twenty-nine, and 47 percent between eighteen and twenty-four, turned out to vote, up from 40 and 36 percent, respectively, in 2000—marking the highest level of young voter turnout since 1992, after a decline every presidential election year since 1972.[10] All racial and ethnic groups were part of the dramatic expansion of young voters.

Looking back, I see the moment as a bit of a harbinger of the seismic media evolution to follow. I will not recount the full digital media revolution here, as others have done it in a whole series of books, so let's jump ahead two decades—where we sit in the midst of the remarkable media transformation embodied in Facebook and YouTube and Twitter and Amazon Prime and Netflix and other media revolutionaries. So much has changed, incubated in those early days of the 2000s. At the time, the political and activism landscape for digital public engagement was fresh and experimental and exciting. Postmillennial advocacy organizations were becoming sophisticated self-distributing media publishers while simultaneously working with the entertainment industry, a trend we can see clearly in the rear-view mirror of the 2004 election's new grassroots groups. And comedy's headline-making cultural influence was omnipresent—the backdrop of The Daily Show's years of peak influence served as fertile ground that unquestionably shaped the impulses of young activists and comedians who would become today's leaders and mentors to the next cohort.

In the rear-view mirror, 2004 feels like ancient history, but the juncture was prescient and meaningful. Several years after that first internet-powered election, a new generation of pathbreaking social-justice organizations—the subjects of this book, in part—opened their doors, led by innovative, entrepreneurial visionaries motivated by injustice. They were emboldened by their ability to leverage pop culture for social change in the changing media environment. In the same time frame, diverse new comedians began flexing their muscles and developing fan bases on YouTube, eventually landing with big entertainment brands like HBO (Issa Rae), Comedy Central and Netflix (Hasan Minhaj), MTV (Franchesca Ramsey), and NBC (Lilly Singh), among others.

As for the Declare Yourself comedy campaign itself, its imprint was not lost on me, the young producer and activist learning at the feet of Norman Lear, a person who had clearly put in his ten thousand expert hours at this weird business of comedy and social justice. I have carried the lessons of that lived experience—that is, the open creativity and deviant thinking required for comedy to interrogate complex ideas in provocative, memorable ways—into the years that came next, through several media projects, creative incubation models that bring together comedy and social justice, and research initiatives that examine the social-change influence of comedy.[11] Some sixteen years after our first internet-powered comedic voter-empowerment initiative, because everything old becomes new again, in 2020, I was part of a group of comedians and activists who revived the original 2004 campaign concept for a contemporary voter-empowerment social-media campaign, #InTheTimeItTakes, where comedians repeated the "watch me do this inane silly thing for one minute" concept (that is, the time it takes to register to vote) and spread the word.[12] This time, they used the infrastructure of participatory media that was barely coming into its own in the original Declare Yourself/Comedy Central effort. Thousands of Twitter and Instagram views later, the idea took firm root and others joined—comedians jumping in to make things happen for American democracy once again.

And thus, here we are—in this book and the stories that follow.

Today, the participatory traits of the postmillennial media era—a mashed-up composite of news, entertainment, ideas, memes, influencers, stories, and perspectives—are helping to build the cultural and political muscle of social-justice organizations and activist movements in the United States. By any media necessary, groups that have been historically alienated or disenfranchised by democratic institutions—people of color, women, undocumented immigrants, ethnic and religious minorities, gay and transgender people, the economically disadvantaged, the disability community, to name a few—are commanding our attention, shining spotlights on injustice, demanding equity, and inspiring us to reimagine the status quo. They are asserting their visibility to shape the realities of the moment, but also to mold the future, transforming public activism into constituencies and communities capable of long-term influence as the ideals and practices of democracy evolve and reconstitute. They are building civic power.[13]

They are also entertaining us. For contemporary grassroots advocacy groups and activist networks that represent the interests of traditionally marginalized people, capturing the public imagination is not a luxury but a fundamental strategic premise. They recognize that social justice is shaped by public opinion and policy, in turn cultivated by entertainment stories and pop culture, amplified by streaming networks and social media channels with no off buttons. Many of today's grassroots organizations understand, in other words, that building *cultural power* is a requirement for civic power, and they are forging new ways to get the job done. They are launching teams and departments labeled "cultural strategy," "narrative strategy," and "creative storytelling initiatives," producing and self-distributing their own entertainment stories, working with Hollywood to diversify TV writers' rooms, capturing attention and inviting their communities to participate—through YouTube and Vimeo and Instagram and Twitter and TikTok, and surely also future platforms—but also through formal entertainment-industry projects. Their efforts coincide with the shifting realities of Hollywood, where trend-shaping streaming networks and social-media entertainment players understand that the economics of their business require diverse stories and storytellers—and legacy TV networks are beginning to follow.

Against this backdrop, leading postmillennial social-justice organizations are embracing comedy to build their cultural power, directed by leaders who grew up in the humorous civic-engagement age of *The Daily Show* and who enthusiastically supported the rise of its socially conscious spin-offs—from *Last Week Tonight with John Oliver* and *Full Frontal with Samantha Bee* to episodic scripted comedy programs such as *Black-ish*, *Insecure*, *Fresh Off the Boat*, and *Reservation Dogs*, narratives that place diverse stories and perspectives hilariously front and center, told from the lived experiences of their makers. Social justice and the entertainment industry converge in this juncture, where civic power and pop-culture power collide, with comedy at the core. The immigrant-rights group Define American, for instance, an advocacy organization represented by a major Hollywood talent agency, works with the entertainment industry to create new comedy and infiltrate existing TV shows with humorous storylines that humanize immigrants; the racial-justice organization Color of Change, launched from the tragedy of Hurricane Katrina, coproduced a socially conscious comedy web series; and racial-justice group Hip Hop Caucus produced a live comedy stand-up show and docu-comedy TV special to mobilize young Black and Brown voters around climate justice.

These creative collaborations are not accidental. Leading digital-native advocacy groups and their leaders strategically choose comedy as a mainstream, movement-essential genre. They recognize the perils of a darkly polarized political climate, and they see comedy's power and potential influence—as a mechanism to attract attention, persuade, critique the status quo, open taboo cultural conversations, disrupt harmful dominant narratives, humanize those who are othered, and invite desperately needed hope and optimism into somber, complex issues that are often reduced to ideological sides, like racial injustice, climate justice, and Islamophobia.[14] And through the open-minded experience of co-creating with comedy professionals, social-justice organizations are embracing the deviant thinking and creativity that comedy can provide—an empowering by-product of a process that expands pathways to innovation through creativity.

While participatory culture and the activities of contemporary social-justice activists are occasionally documented in a broad or anecdotal sense, the process by which grassroots organizations build cultural and civic power through comedy—and the invaluable function of creativity and the comedic creative process—is a dynamic untold story. *The Revolution Will Be Hilarious: Comedy for Social Change and Civic Power* reveals how and why comedy fuels social change in the participatory media age, how postmillennial social-justice organizations collaborate with comedians and the evolving entertainment industry, and why creativity and cultural power matter for social justice. The book reveals transforming entertainment-industry and activism practices, and it explains why deviant creativity expressed through comedy builds civic power—and can help change the world. It provides an intimate portal into the functions of creativity in participatory politics, the artistic process involved in shaping diverse comedy with social justice at the core, the collective intelligence of entertainment and social-justice professionals working together to make people laugh while saying something important, and an insider look within the transforming entertainment-media industry.

The Revolution Will Be Hilarious argues that strengthening *creative power* is crucial for marginalized groups to build civic power. The ideas and stories in these pages position contemporary social-justice comedy as disruptive storytelling that hilariously invites us to agitate the status quo and reimagine social realities to inspire social change and come closer to the promise of equity and justice in America.

Civic Power and Participatory Culture

If you ask Eric Liu, former assistant domestic policy advisor to President Bill Clinton, America's civic malaise is a problem—but one that can be remedied. His 2013 TED Talk, viewed more than two million times, conveys a central thesis: "We need to make civics sexy again . . . as sexy as it was during the American Revolution or the civil rights movement."[15] In 2012, Liu and Jená Cane cofounded Citizen University, a nonprofit organization dedicated to helping ordinary Americans find and flex their civic muscles. Collective consternation arising from years of growing inequality has fueled inevitable public skepticism, as Liu said in a media interview: "I don't think people are wrong to feel that the game has been rigged. . . . But we're in a period where across the political spectrum—from the libertarian Tea Party right to the Occupy and Black Lives Matter left—people are pushing back and recognizing that the only remedy is to convert this feeling of 'not having a say' into 'demanding a say.'"[16] His ideas have obvious appeal: his Civic Saturday program—a kind of secular faith-based experience in which people come together to discuss issues, read inspiring passages, and form participation networks—is spreading in popularity since it launched four days after the 2016 Trump election.[17] After all, as he says, "Democracy's on us . . . It's possible to make change in civic life."[18]

Liu is tapping into collective pain steeped in frustration by people who feel sidestepped by the status quo. After all, the universal concept of "citizenship"—the idea of full access to meaningful participation and the benefits of the American democratic system—requires serious asterisks and clarifying footnotes when it comes to inequality. As scholars Stuart Hall and David Held wrote, "Rights can be mere paper claims unless they can be practically enacted and realized, through actual participation in the community. These then are citizenship's three leading notions: membership; rights and duties in reciprocity; real participation in practice."[19] These are not new ideas, and they are certainly not lost on historically marginalized people—or anyone who has felt as though, as Eric Liu says, we are playing in a democratic game that is rigged for those elites with power. As inequality continues to expand, other scholars—sociologist Gianpaolo Baiocchi and his colleagues—have phrased things a little more bluntly: "Americans hate politics. They are skeptical of elected officials, and they suspect that special, elite interests trump the needs of the average Joe. The political system is broken, unfair, and corrupt—on that, everyone agrees, even America's leaders . . . In short, *Americans have come to distrust their democracy*."[20]

As a basic primer, if we accept the fantasy of full equality within our structural systems and institutions—and thus, the myths perpetuated by the status quo—we ignore the inequity built into them and calcified over time. Instead, progress toward equity "needs to distinguish the formal level of theoretical universality from the substantive level of exclusionary and marginalizing practices,"[21] and further, "One must consider categories that are visibly inscribed on the body, such as gender and race, and their consequences for full participation. The moment a woman or a person of color enters the public square both difference and inequality come to the surface. It is difficult to conceal differences of gender and race, and given the prejudiced norms under which we still live, inequities will come to the surface," wrote scholars William Flores and Rina Benmayor.[22] We ignore inequity at our peril while we go about the cyclical, generational business of reinvigorating a fully alive, functional democratic system. The stakes of brushing past an unequal playing field are high—where rising inequality is plainly evident, trust in formal democratic institutions declines.[23]

This feels like a gloomy starting place. Where do we go from here? Well, the first step is to recognize, of course, that things are not equal and marginalized groups have to find creative ways to seek and secure equity—to confront American democracy's "deep, persistent problems of structural exclusion along lines of race and gender . . . a chronic legacy of antidemocratic exclusion," as scholars K. Sabeel Rahman and Hollie Russon Gilman wrote.[24] Active engagement and visibility are musts. Civic expression and participation are far more expansive ideas and activities than voting alone; they include building community and networks, shaping values and morals and perspectives at least in part through seeking and absorbing information from media.[25] In this context, I am talking about building civic power—and enhancing people's beliefs that their mobilized, collective voices are meaningful for social progress.

"Civic power," according to Rahman and Gilman in their book of the same name, must be centered in efforts to reimagine American democratic systems and participation in times of turmoil—that is, making social change and building power must originate from the ground up. In their perspective, strengthening civil society and marginalized voices is key for civic power that centers equity in social change. Bolstering the network-building and organizing capabilities of these groups is a pathway to "open up democratic politics to constituencies that are systematically disempowered and unprivileged . . . to expand the ability of citizens themselves to mobilize, to organize, and to advocate for their views" in order to shape social and political progress over time.[26]

Civic power originates, to a great degree, from social movements, due to the media amplification from noisy public critique alongside the cultural attention conferred—at least temporarily—on groups that are often left out. Our time is characterized by organized and organic demands for equity and justice, from the focus on racial justice of the Movement for Black Lives to the plea against gun violence from March for Our Lives,[27] with dissent arising from a mixture of hashtag activism that fosters networks for marginalized voices and concerns,[28] brick-and-mortar organizations, and the converged configurations of both. Following the logic of civic power, organic activist movements and like-minded grassroots advocacy organizations increasingly echo one another's shared messages, motivating new public participants and curating empowered voices to speak collectively.

#BlackLivesMatter's originating hashtag of 2013, for instance, advanced a set of narratives and values echoed by supporting groups like the ACLU and Color of Change, evolving over time to include an expansive network of participating organizations and policy agendas. But for long-term political power, wrote Rahman and Gilman, movements "must, at some point, embed their members and values within larger organizations that can exercise political power even more effectively than the movements themselves."[29] In this way, civic power locates "the central importance of organizing and civic organizations in driving social and political change" with a long view of social progress in mind: "The goal here is not to generate a momentary flash of public outrage or outcry; rather, it is to channel public activism into organizations that are durable, capable of strategic decision-making, and able to exercise long-term influence on policymaking."[30] In turn, public participation is invited and enabled by grassroots organizations, whose power and "strategic capacity" for influence with decision makers includes not only financial and human resources but the ability to shape and transmit supportive public messages and values.[31]

Enter participatory culture. An expanding cohort of activists is exploiting the possibilities of the postmillennial media age to publicly transmit the stories and identities and humanity and heroes and villains of their lived experiences. To build civic power, they are creating and disseminating narratives that work in favor of the social issues and communities they represent. These grassroots organizations are the engines and exemplars of participatory politics, a concept that scholar Henry Jenkins described as "what happens when a generation of young people who have grown up with more opportunities to meaningfully participate in culture turns its voice to struggles for social justice and political change. Participatory politics may include engagement with electoral and institutional politics, but it may also be directed towards shaping the world through informing public opinion or directing pressure against corporate interests."[32] The need to ignite new ideas and enthusiasm for civic action is acute, as Jenkins and his colleagues found in interviews with more than one hundred young activists from various social movements: "One of the things that kept surfacing in those exchanges was the idea that the civic needed to be rebuilt, that the language of mainstream politics did not address the concerns or awaken the imaginations of the emerging generation of citizens," he wrote.[33]

The effective contemporary visionaries of participatory politics— many profiled in the chapters to follow—take culture work seriously. The social-justice leader Ai-jen Poo, for instance, who founded the effective advocacy organizations Domestic Workers Alliance and Caring Across Generations, is declarative about building "narrative power" for people who lack the influential political tools of wealth and ownership: "I think of it in terms of different forms of power to create social change. There is political power, organizing and voter engagement are part of it. There is also narrative power—the ability to tell the story of why things are the way they are and shape the public narrative," which sparks a kind of collective public imagination about "a new way of being that we want to move forward."[34] Narrative power, in this sense, means the ability for marginalized groups "to influence and disrupt the big underlying stories and themes that perpetuate and reinforce prejudice, inequality, racism, injustice, and that reflect and are reflected by the perspectives of the decisionmakers and arbiters of popular culture and media," as philanthropist David Morse reflected about the work of Poo and her activist contemporary, Rashad Robinson, who directs the powerful Color of Change organization.[35] In this perspective, structural policy change cannot happen—or be maintained—without narrative change, a fundamental shift in a culture's feelings and beliefs about people and their fundamental humanity. Narrative power, in this context, is a means to a broader structural objective, as Robinson reminded attendees of the 2020 Sundance Film Festival: "Let's not mistake presence for power. Presence is visibility; power is the ability to change the rules."[36]

Ai-jen Poo and Rashad Robinson are not alone in locating cultural power at the heart of grassroots public-engagement and social-change strategy. A cadre of social-justice leaders and activists is embracing culture initiatives, wielding stories and entertainment as active tools of empowerment for marginalized groups. This way of thinking insists that civic imagination—envisioning the world we want to create and believing in our ability to shape it, not only focusing on its problems[37]—is a vital ingredient of every effort for social change. It is a lens that invites entertainment storytelling and creativity to play starring roles in the business of encouraging solidarity and human connection. But we are wise to remember that these ideas are not synonymous with clinical public-relations messages or predictably tidy tactics or mere constellations of facts to be hopefully delivered by news media or other "serious" vehicles of information.

The creative impulses of innovative postmillennial social-justice leaders, who well understand the role of culture in bolstering policy change, have converged with a transforming entertainment industry. In the not-distant analog past, where tactics and outputs of "artivism" were often seen as radical art existing in fringes outside the mainstream, the tools of high-production-value media storytelling are now fully available to creatively inclined activists. At the same time, the production and distribution appetite of the streaming entertainment business is voracious—and in need of diverse storytellers who can speak to audiences that demand to see themselves reflected. To be clear, the entertainment industries are light years away from a fully diverse system of cultural gatekeepers, but the upheaval of the business points in favor of hearing from storytellers previously deemed by Hollywood marketing machines as too "risky" to reliably sell to whitewashed (and heteronormative and patriarchal) mass audiences.

Take, for instance, a few notable trends: the power streaming networks—Netflix, Amazon, Apple, Hulu—are creating homes for diverse storytellers talking about social-justice topics, influencing legacy networks that are forced to compete.[38] In the convergence era of Silicon Valley and Hollywood, within the many channels that comprise YouTube-hosted "social media entertainment," new voices are breaking through and capturing millions of audience eyeballs.[39] And marginalized creators are forming their own systems of independent media production and distribution via innovations like Open TV.[40] Across the industry, many of the hottest TV showrunners and creators are talking overtly about social-justice topics and equity—weaving these topics through their stories and finding deeply committed audiences—wielding enormous influence over the marketplace. The list includes Shonda Rhimes (*Gray's Anatomy*), Jill Soloway (*Transparent*), Ava DuVernay (*When They See Us*), Gloria Calderón Kellett (*One Day at a Time*), Kenya Barris (*Black-ish*), Steven Canals (*Pose*), and others.

The transition of the entertainment industry and the burgeoning cultural prowess of contemporary social-justice groups converge here. Two developments are simultaneously unfolding: on the one hand, social-justice groups and marginalized communities are able to participate more fully in shaping culture to build their civic power. At the same time, creative artists (performers, writers, comedians, directors, producers) from marginalized communities are increasingly invited into the evolving entertainment industry to share their realities and truths. These sectors share some mutual interests but vastly different ways of doing business, so how and why might they collaborate? And lingering questions—the heart of this book—remain: How can a kind of disruptive creativity shaped with comedy—with social justice baked into the core—be fostered and created to help build civic power? And why does it matter?

Fueling Civic Power with Comedy

"It's like taking your vodka with a chaser. . . . It is my personal belief that social movements cannot be sustained on anger. Anger will burn out," said twenty-six-year-old Amanda Nguyen, a 2018 Nobel Peace Prize nominee who successfully advocated for the first federal Sexual Assault Survivors Bill of Rights law in 2016 through Rise, the organization she founded four years prior.[41] She was describing the painstaking organizing work of rectifying loopholes in the US criminal justice system that impeded sexual assault survivors, including Nguyen herself, in their efforts to access and use their own medical evidence to seek justice. Specifically, she was talking about comedy as the "chaser" to the painful sting of a traumatic issue. Nguyen's pathbreaking work can hardly be attributed to comedy alone, but she credits her creative partnership with Hollywood-based comedy producers Funny or Die—which produced and distributed short-form online comedy videos (including titles like "Even Supervillains Think Our Sexual Assault Laws Are Insane")—with helping to unlock stalled legislation and capture the imaginations and attention of policymakers, the public, and media.[42] For her, combining the forces of serious social-justice activism with comedy was an easy decision—a strategic no-brainer for a campaign she intended to win: "Humor, undoubtedly in the Millennial peer group and also Gen Z, really resonates with us. . . . Humor definitely helps make the medicine go down more easily, and what we're trying to do is get them to be engaged. Comedy is one of the easiest and most powerful ways to do that—to combat activism fatigue, to reach beyond the low-hanging fruit of the people who already care, and to get politicians to care too."[43]

FUNNY⅏DIE

PARTNER

EVEN SUPERVILLAINS THINK
OUR SEXUAL ASSAULT LAWS
ARE INSANE

Figure I.1: Screenshot: "Even Supervillains Think Our Sexual Assault Laws Are Insane"
(YouTube/Funny or Die)

Nguyen's is a story about an advocacy leader and innovator engaging "by any media necessary,"[44] but it is also a revealing anecdote about collective intelligence, co-creation, and comedy's creativity. If we agree with the premise that strengthening civil society and disenfranchised voices is key to fueling social change and equity—and that building cultural power is needed to enhance the visibility (messages, values, identities, lived experiences) of historically marginalized groups—then we can imagine how creative power is crucial for contemporary social-justice organizations. Comedy propels creative power because its very foundation is assembled from deviant thinking that offers new or unexpected entry into contemplating realities and problems and injustice. This is an argument in favor of the collective intelligence that can emerge from comedy people and social-justice people and communities working together in a creative process that disrupts usual ways of doing business—building paths to innovation.

And here is where we arrive closer to the central journey of these pages. We are entering the realm of art and amusement that converges with justice, where creative minds and change makers invite us to dream and laugh and feel and see a new way of being. For advocacy organizations daring into the messy waters of culture and entertainment as a mechanism to capture the public imagination and build community—that is, to build civic power—creating safe, predictable messages to reach carefully manicured lists of people is the opposite thinking. The idea of art in social justice is affectionately contemplated by enthusiastic thinkers across some scholarly and public-interest arenas, but *fully* embedding and honoring art in the public-engagement work itself—particularly when it is framed as fluffy and diffuse compared to the somber vocation of professional civil society—is yet another matter. Creativity and culture are still too often relegated to the theoretical sidelines of serious advocacy work, while many groups still "favor instead the prosaic tools of letters, press releases, and petitions," in scholar Suzanne Nossel's words.[45] As "artivism" scholar Stephen Duncombe wrote, "Activism moves the material world, while art moves a person's heart, body, and soul. The scope of the former is social, while the latter is individual. In fact, however, they are complimentary [*sic*]. The social is not some mere abstraction; society is composed of people, and change does not just happen. It happens because people make change. As such, the individual and the social are intertwined."[46]

This book focuses on a specific genre—comedy—but the dual undercurrent is creativity and why it should matter in social-change work. We cannot take creativity and the creative production process for granted and assume that it just happens. Incorporating the creativity of comedy (or any form of deviant art) in mission-driven justice efforts requires organizational commitment. As Nossel implored, "If art can be viewed as a valid tool for change, the question then becomes: What is preventing practitioners from engaging it earlier and more often? Human rights and political activists' reticence toward art could be attributed to their lack of familiarity with the utility of art. It may also derive from a world in which social change is to be rigorously monitored, evaluated, measured, and reported upon."[47] Nossel, in my experience working at the intersection of social change and media, is on the right track. The functions of creativity and culture and comedy need to be made explicit, perhaps, to incite a mass humanitarian-sector rethink about why these are hard tools (not silly side projects) that should live alongside the traditional tactics of progressive social change—the stuff of policy briefs and press conferences and fact sheets and news articles. How, then, can social-justice advocates go about the challenging work of newly engaging publics in dire social challenges—breaking through with ideas that can disrupt a kind of numbing hum of information or what Amanda Nguyen calls "activism fatigue"? They need creativity, the main ingredient that lives in the soul of comedy.

When activists choose to collaborate explicitly with comedians, they do so because they recognize that comedy's creative deviance can cut through cultural clutter, but also because it can entertain and invite feelings of play. This kind of light, they say, is desperately needed in issues that can be ideologically divisive or too complicated and difficult to engage publics beyond a painful stream of fatiguing outrage or wonky statistics. But perhaps most importantly—as intimately illustrated in the chapters that follow—social-justice advocates with creative power understand that humanizing issues and inviting connection and solidarity with their fellow humans is imperative to reaching beyond a like-minded choir or falling into the narrative trap of evoking pity. For them, comedy matters a great deal.

The Journey of the Book

The Revolution Will Be Hilarious invites readers into an expanding, enterprising arena of participatory culture and politics through in-depth interviews with comedy writers, performers, and producers; social-justice leaders; and Hollywood executives—alongside my ethnographic case studies crafted from within the creative, collaborative processes of contemporary comedy that interrogates and spotlights social-justice issues and lived experiences that have been, and are, neglected on the big cultural stage. The book also provides a journey into the radically evolving entertainment industry in the digital, streaming age of media, as seen through the experiences of its inside players. It unpackages the following questions: What role does comedy's creative process play in fueling the ability of grassroots organizations and communities to engage publics with challenging social-justice issues? How do social-justice organizations and comedians co-create entertaining comedy designed to build the cultural power of marginalized groups? And how are contemporary entertainment-industry leaders and gatekeepers working with social-justice-activism organizations as creative collaborators?

I come to this book with a particular back story and vantage point within specific professional communities, both of which hopefully enrich the intimacy of the stories and depth of the analysis. By 2006, when scholar Henry Jenkins published his groundbreaking book, *Convergence Culture: Where Old and New Media Collide*, I was several years into doing the kind of "participatory culture" work he wrote about. During my formative years as a producer, researcher, and strategist in Los Angeles and Washington, DC, I was socialized by peer media producers and creators, all of us hustling across digital media platforms popping up in rapid fire—ideating and armed with the efficacy of popular culture and spreadable media and the exciting power of digital grassroots engagement. Among other examples, Jenkins's book discussed our 2004 youth-voter empowerment campaign and my documentary and grassroots organizing endeavors with pathbreaking Brave New Films. To be clear, he did not write about me individually, but he presciently captured the moment and forecasted where it might lead.

Since that time, my creative, strategy, and scholarly efforts have developed in lock step with the professional ecologies that have evolved participatory media work centered in social justice. These communities of practice—cultural activists and storytellers—include the documentary and public-engagement people,[48] the groups and individuals who lead narrative and culture change inside social-justice organizations, and leaders within the transforming entertainment industry who are embracing the power of new creators and audiences. These networks—where I locate myself, too—are motivated by the values and possibilities Jenkins and his colleagues eloquently articulated later in *Spreadable Media*: "If we see participatory culture, though, as a vital step toward the realization of a century-long struggle for grassroots communities to gain greater control over the means of cultural production and circulation—if we see participation as the work of publics and not simply of markets and audiences—then opportunities to expand participation are struggles we must actively embrace through our work, whether through efforts to lower economic or technical obstacles or to expand access to media literacies."[49]

To be sure, there are existing constraints in these undertakings. Several years after scholar Manuel Castells' beautiful 2012 book about justice movements powered by social media, *Networks of Outrage and*

Hope: Social Movements in the Internet Age,[50] we are reckoning also with the reality of real democratic destruction at the hands of corporate-owned social-media platforms.[51] Facebook and its ilk, it turns out, are motivated by their profit margins at virtually any cost, despite our earlier utopian hopes. Surveillance and privacy concerns and the malicious spread of misinformation are as characteristic of the postmillennial media age as the possibilities of participatory culture that can amplify marginalized voices.

Similarly, it would be breathtakingly naïve to imply that the whole of the entertainment industry has embraced the market potential (or democratic value) of media content that portrays diverse characters and stories, told by makers from a full array of communities. Without question, it is exponentially harder for women; people of color; queer and transgender people; creators from the disability community; and similarly culturally sidelined folks to fully access and achieve success in the entertainment marketplace, despite exciting outliers.[52] We have a long, long way to go. These challenges are all true and devastatingly important, and I do not take them lightly even while this volume does not dwell on pessimism. This book, instead, relentlessly focuses on the possibility of play and entertainment and the efficacy of individuals and groups that have so doggedly figured out how to leverage culture for real social influence and progress. These organizations and advocates continue to believe, despite the barriers, that change is possible, and that social equity is a necessary pursuit, regardless of where we find ourselves technologically and culturally and politically. As a media producer and engaged scholar dedicated to participatory research—that is, I collaborate within professional and creative communities of practice and co-create new mechanisms to advance social change through creativity and culture[53]—my lens matches theirs.

Evolving from this origin story and perspective, in 2013—after producing the documentary *Stand Up Planet* starring Hasan Minhaj, which interrogates global poverty through stand-up comedians from different countries—I launched the beginning of a multifaceted research and creative exploration to understand how contemporary comedy works as audience persuasion and force for mobilization in social justice, and similarly, to investigate why comedic art is not leveraged more often in formal efforts for social change. I spoke at film festivals and social-change

Figure I.2: *Stand Up Planet,* starring Hasan Minhaj, Mpho Popps, and Aditi Mittal

convenings, wrote articles and conducted research, coauthored a book, and gradually found like-minded thinkers and creative people along the way. With new collaborators, we developed a research-based perspective about how to co-create comedy for social justice in ways that would honor the full creative deviance of comedians, and I certainly honed my (evidence-based) opinion about how *not* to create comedy for social change—that is, as sort of watered-down, mildly amusing "key messages" cooked up in a clinical strategic-communications kind of environment. To further advance these ideas, I secured funding to create the first-ever comedian-in-residence position (now creative director of comedy initiatives) at our innovation lab and research center, indelibly filled by Bethany Hall, whose comedy chops include the cult-classic *Chris Gethard Show* and *30 Rock* and other writing and performing gigs.

It became clear, through these efforts, that these ideas are ripe and ready to take root—not just to contemplate through research but to build into real creative practice and entertainment. Through many conversations and convenings, we learned that an expanding cohort of leading social-justice organizations—the postmillennial groups socialized in the participatory-culture era and early civic influence of

The Daily Show—was ready to work with comedy (and some were already doing it), but they wanted to know precisely why it was influential and how to collaborate. At the same time, the entertainment marketplace was beginning to make a little more room for diverse, funny creators and comedians talking about their lived experiences. And yet, so many other voices are not yet heard. And finally, through our expanding network of comedy professionals, thanks in great measure to working with Bethany, an actual comedian (and a very well respected one in the artistic community of comedy people), we determined that comedy writers and performers were excited about making new work that could lift up injustice in novel and attention-grabbing ways. We had a hunch that modeling new sector co-creations between comedy and social justice would be a breakthrough whose time had come.

Out of this exploration and an enthusiastic, open-minded network of collaborative relationships, we launched several comedy and social-justice participatory development and production initiatives: the Yes, And . . . Laughter Lab (YALL)—co-created and codirected with cultural strategy agency Moore + Associates, in partnership with Comedy Central—and the Comedy ThinkTanks collaborative comedy incubation program, under the deft creative architecture and direction of professional comedian and social-justice warrior Bethany Hall. These research-based programs work differently, as detailed in later chapters, but they are fully embraced by powerful social-justice groups and entertainment-industry partners who are newly working together to amplify diverse voices and generate new comedy for public action and the entertainment marketplace. The unusual bedfellows range from writers and performers on *The Daily Show* to talent managers to executives at Comedy Central and TruTV and MTV to philanthropies like Open Society Foundations to powerhouse production companies like the Reform Media Group to social-justice leaders like Define American, Color of Change, National Domestic Workers Alliance, Hip Hop Caucus, IllumiNative, and more. Together, we are fueling the collective intelligence of comedians and social-justice organizations and entertainment decision makers, asserting civic power through culture and creativity alongside community organizing. It is now the work of many.

The "me" in the "we" here is also useful to highlight. It is important to note and name, of course, that I come to this body of work—and this book—with a particular identity, role, and point of view. As a heterosexual White woman engaged in social-justice creative media production, strategy, and research, throughout my career I have always centered deep collaborations with people who have been historically marginalized by virtue of race, ethnicity, religious beliefs, gender identification, and sexual orientation. In contemporary terms, then, I work as an ally and I center allyship in everything I do, even as I understand the structural dynamics of this country's history and contemporary systems. In her excellent article, "White Folks' Work," Dr. Meredith D. Clark defines allyship as "the processes of affirming and taking informed action on behalf of the subjugated group,"[54] and I take seriously the role and ideals of collaborative allyship while I honor traditions of multicultural, multiracial, multigenerational organizing both here in the United States and around the world. Indeed, Kristen Marston from The League (at Color of Change during the early writing phase of this book) puts it simply and bluntly: "Either you are doing the work or you're not. If you are, trust that people know. That's being an ally." In that spirit, in this book, I reflect, cite, and quote women and BIPOC (Black, Indigenous, People of Color) writers, scholars, and interviewees as much as possible—and with as much of their uninterrupted quotations as publishing word limits allow. Similarly, the ethnographic stories here recount ally collaborations between myself, members of our team at the Center for Media & Social Impact, and the Yes, And . . . Laughter Lab and beyond, working alongside diverse comedians and social-justice leaders. While I am the one who crafted the pages that follow, the creative works described within them should be contemplated and appreciated for the creativity, leadership, and hard work of many diverse artists and leaders.

In *The Revolution Will Be Hilarious*, I invite readers—activists, community organizers, researchers, communication strategists, entertainment executives, students, comedians, and comedy fans—to explore how strengthening *creative power* is crucial for traditionally marginalized voices to build civic power. *The Revolution Will Be Hilarious: Comedy for Social Change and Civic Power* positions contemporary social-justice comedy as creative, disruptive storytelling that hilariously invites us to agitate the status quo and reimagine social realities to inspire social change and come closer to the promise of equity and justice in America.

We leave this introduction and enter chapter 1, "'Desperate Cheeto': How Comedy Functions as Deviant Creative Resistance," which provides historical and theoretical foundations for appreciating the importance of subversive comedy. Opening with the silly naughtiness of Randy Rainbow and his scathingly hilarious—and rabidly shared—musical parody indictments of President Donald Trump as an authoritarian threat, the chapter begins by situating creative deviance historically used by democratic movements in the United States and abroad, from the Yippies in the United States and humor within Soviet and East European samizdat to the Bread and Puppets and guerrilla theater in Latin America. As its primary focus, chapter 1 argues for and explains comedy's societal influences and its functions in creating social change—that is, the role of comedy as creative deviance that builds civic power.

Chapter 2, "'It's All about Who You Know': Pitching and Producing Comedy in the Transforming Entertainment Industry," begins with the story of comedian Sarah Cooper's rise to quick stardom through her hilarious lip syncs of Donald Trump's press conference remarks during the COVID-19 pandemic. With a deep dive "under the hood" of a transforming Hollywood, this chapter takes readers into the process of developing, pitching, producing, and distributing comedy in the revolutionary streaming-entertainment industry in the United States. Social capital, power dynamics, and norms for producing (and discovering) comedy are shifting in the participatory media age even as constraints for traditionally underrepresented creatives (women, people of color, LGBTQ+ persons) remain entrenched, as this chapter reveals through interviews with Hollywood showrunners, managers, comedy writers, and entertainment industry executives.

Chapter 3, "'Hollywood Won't Change Unless It's Forced to Change': How Activism and Entertainment Collide and Collaborate," opens with the racial-justice uprisings of 2020. The reckoning started years prior by Black Lives Matter—itself a continuation of centuries-long human rights struggle in the United States—continues to push for urgent change in the entertainment industry. Activists pressuring Hollywood in matters of racial, ethnic, gender, and sexual-orientation identity are not new, as this chapter highlights, but collaborative and creative postmillennial social-justice organizations are creating new norms and practices in their work with the entertainment industry—newly including comedy. Crafted from in-depth interviews with entertainment-industry executives and social-justice leaders, this chapter introduces the community of practice and evolving norms of "narrative and cultural strategy" strategists who work inside social-justice organizations, endeavoring to shift Hollywood portrayals of traditionally marginalized groups through creative collaboration, launching new pipelines into the industry, and often mobilizing public pressure.

Chapter 4, "'You Learn to Be Racist from People You Love': Co-creating Comedy for Antiracism Public Engagement," delves into the development, production, and distribution process of a comedic public-engagement campaign on TikTok, Instagram, and Twitter in collaboration with E Pluribus Unum, the racial-equity organization founded by New Orleans's mayor, Mitch Landrieu. A network of cultural leaders, organizers, and antiracism organizations came together to find new ways to reach passive White people in the Deep South, leveraging comedy for the first time. This chapter introduces the Comedy ThinkTanks initiative that brings comedians and social-justice-activism leaders together as co-creators through a modified variation of the original writers' room model that shapes comedy for the entertainment marketplace, including sitcoms, late-night public affairs shows, and sketch programming. Grounded in theoretical underpinnings that explicate creativity, creative process, and play to foster innovation, creating original comedy focused on social issues involves wild and open creative process, in turn inviting social-justice groups to see their efforts in new ways, opening themselves up to new ways for publics to engage through optimism and play. In telling the story of the #RacismIsNoJoke antiracism comedy campaign, the chapter explores the value of contemporary comedy in painful and entrenched justice challenges, produced with a multiracial allyship approach.

Native American bias and invisibility is the core exploration of chapter 5, "'Invisibility Is Not a Superpower': Asserting Native American Identity through Humor." For IllumiNative, the social-justice organization leading the contemporary charge against the cultural and structural erasure of Native peoples, the stakes of remaining silent in the face of discrimination are too high. On the basis of our comedy co-creation writers' room hosted on a Native reservation in Oklahoma—an unprecedented gathering of comedians and strategists across four tribes along with non-Native comedy writers—we evolved into producing a short-form comedy talk show, *You're Welcome, America*, centering the joy and resilience of Native and Black communities in the United States, shared from the perspective of Native and Black women comedians as cohosts.

Chapter 6, "'Maybe They Think Beauty Can't Come from Here': Resilience and Power in the Climate Crisis," travels to coastal Norfolk, Virginia—the site of a looming environmental disaster on the order of 2005's Hurricane Katrina—a sister city that matches New Orleans in its below-sea-level location and disproportionate number of people of color who are uniquely vulnerable to the toxic combination of poverty, climate change, and public health challenges in a rapidly gentrifying area. There, we created a live comedy show in collaboration with Hip Hop Caucus, the grassroots racial-justice group, to bring together young Black comedians to interrogate climate change as it affects vulnerable communities of color. Hip Hop Caucus produced the show *Ain't Your Mama's Heat Wave* as a live stand-up special and docu-comedy that centers the group's grassroots community-organizing strategy to mobilize young Black people around environmental justice—and to vote.

Chapter 7, "'I've Always Been a Syringe-Half-Full Kind of Guy': Changing the Entertainment Comedy Pipeline," tells the story of the development, launch, and influence of the Yes, And . . . Laughter Lab (YALL). YALL is creating a new entertainment pipeline and philanthropic sector to support social-justice-infused comedy, and it has expanded during a time of heightened attention to cultural representation and equity on screen. At twice-yearly events hosted in New York and Los Angeles, YALL competitively invites the funniest diverse comedians to pitch their comedy ideas to a cross-section of Hollywood decision makers and representatives of social-justice and philanthropic organizations, training them to work in participatory media across two sectors—entertainment and social-justice activism. This chapter interrogates the entertainment industry's continued diversity challenges—including comedy—while it explores new comedy voices, projects, and collaborations that are breaking down barriers between entertainment and philanthropy.

Finally, the conclusion, "Taking Comedy Seriously," closes the book with reflections on and analysis of comedy's use by and for oppressed people to fuel creative and civic power, and future opportunities and barriers to overcome in this expanding area of participatory-culture—and indeed, political—work. Setting forth paths for evolution takes us out of the book and into the future.

At its core, *The Revolution Will Be Hilarious* implores us to take the role of contemporary comedy seriously as we imagine building a more equitable playing field and dealing with challenges together. There is no time to waste, after all.

1

"Desperate Cheeto"

How Comedy Functions as Deviant Creative Resistance

It is safe to say that Randy Rainbow—he of the silky-voiced Broadway vibrato and sparkling Colgate smile—did not fancy himself as a scathing political satirist when he made YouTube his playground in 2009. But farcical short videos about his toxic "new boyfriend" Mel Gibson, serving Chick-fil-A tenders to controversial politician Rick Santorum, having "guy talk" with Kanye West, and dating disgraced politician Anthony Weiner?[1] Check, check, check, and check. Creatively mining celebrity sound bites to splice hilarious faux conversations, Rainbow cheekily danced around scandals, famous people, and public affairs as he built a fledgling career under his marquee-ready name. He dipped more frequently, as years passed, into the unique musical parody style that would become his creative trademark, playing with the jaunty cadence and apple-cheeked schtick of the Great American Musical as he distorted lyrics and sang his way closer to the edges of naughtiness.

Charming, silly, giggle-inducing, and earworm-generating? Yes. But politics? Not so much. And then along came Donald Trump—the shapeshifting serial business failure, con man, and reality-TV-character-turned-presidential-candidate—and Randy Rainbow could not resist. Or, rather, resistance became his art, and his art was resistance.

Randy Rainbow trained his comedic lens in the direction of the Trump pulpit—and various bit-playing Republican Party characters—in early 2016. The US presidential primaries were heating up, and the absurd shock value of hyperbolic, hate-filled fear appeals was ripe for lampooning.[2] After several years of distributing funny, nonpolitical YouTube videos to middling views, although occasionally breaking more than one hundred thousand, Rainbow entered the Trump chaos with a video titled "Randy Rainbow Performs at a Donald Trump Rally."[3] Wearing a "YAAAAAS Trump" t-shirt and oversized red-flowered headband of the toddler-princess variety, he edits himself as a sweetly gleeful Nazi-saluting "USA! USA!" performer alongside flag-costumed little girls singing and dancing in homage to Trump. Together, they enthusiastically salute his blustery brand of xenophobic retrograde patriarchy to the cheers of a MAGA-hat-wearing crowd in lockstep. The horrifying satirical juxtaposition is funny and outrageous, and the social critique lands perfectly. It was a hit—one of his first videos to break five hundred thousand views.

Under his new spotlight, Rainbow meticulously tracked the 2016 primary season with "GOP Dropout," a series of musical parody videos that escorted each Republican candidate off the political stage—Carly Fiorina, Jeb Bush, Ben Carson, Ted Cruz, Marco Rubio, John Kasich— with catchy personalized jingles he performs as a pompadour-wearing 1950s dreamboat to the tune of "Beauty School Dropout" from the film and musical *Grease*.[4] As reporters breathlessly covered every blip of Trump's minutiae regardless of its news value, Randy Rainbow created his first viral video in September 2016. In "BRAGGADOCIOUS! Randy Rainbow Moderates Debate #1," a mashup of his spliced-interview and musical-parody comedy, Rainbow inserts himself as both debate moderator and comically observational chanteuse who zips brightly along to the tune of "Supercalifragilisticexpialidocious" from the musical film *Mary Poppins*, replacing the chorus to describe Trump as "supercallous fragile ego."[5] More than a million people watched and shared.

A star, years in the making, was born.

The gaudy, narcissistic, malaprop-ridden silly buffoonery of Trump and his new White House briskly gave way to clear signals of a dangerous aspiring autocrat in his infancy. Randy Rainbow responded. He increased his artistic pace and production, taking on nearly every moment of the Trump years with satirical critique that skewered absurdities and shocking behavior with hilarious flair. Viral video shares ticked up, and media coverage followed. *The Randy Rainbow Show* became an essential, unrelenting satirical thorn and creative doomsday chronicle as Trump revealed himself to be increasingly unpredictable and unsafe— and did so too late to be controlled or neutered through the usual norms of long-standing democratic institutions. In 2017, in the wake of the

RANDY RAINBOW EXCLUSIVE

DESPERATE CHEETO

Figure 1.1: Screenshot: "Desperate Cheeto" (YouTube/Randy Rainbow)

administration's disastrous response to Hurricane Maria in Puerto Rico, Rainbow's "Desperate Cheeto," a parody of the hit song "Despacito," punctuates the increasing chaos inside the White House and gnawing sense of public dread about Trump's desire for power. Wearing a blonde Trumpian comb-over wig and orange bottle tan, Rainbow croons, "Will our country still be here at the end of your four years? . . . How can we have chosen such a mental case? Every day you devastate the human race. America, good luck, so long and sayonara . . . and what is all the orange stuff that's on your face?"[6]

In 2017, Randy Rainbow launched a live touring show that entertained sold-out crowds in ninety cities around the United States over the next several years, cut short by the 2020 COVID-19 pandemic.[7] In 2019 and 2020, *The Randy Rainbow Show* was nominated for a Primetime Emmy Award for Best Short Form Variety Series. And one week before the 2020 US presidential election—following more than ninety episodes of satirizing Trump and his authoritarian ambitions through every hiccup of an increasingly frightening regime—Rainbow's comedy culminated in an explicit act of creatively, comedically deviant activism: "If Donald Trump Got Fired," a hilarious sing-along with Broadway legend Patti LuPone, benefiting the ACLU.[8] A decade after YouTube beckoned, Rainbow is a stage and screen persona shaped against the backdrop of a volatile moment in American history, a musical comedy performer who developed his indelible satirical style and voice in public and in real time. He sees purpose beyond his silliness: "I use my platform every day to speak truth to power and shine a light on inequities and injustices of the world."[9]

Whether or not it was his plan, Randy Rainbow became one of the country's most potent satirical critics and watchdogs, pointedly spotlighting and ridiculing looming dangers even as the early smugness of elite pundits and journalists prevented their ability or willingness to call out Trump's brazen lies and grotesque norm violations, which evolved into his outright attempt to thwart the 2020 election and permanently disfigure American democracy.[10] We needed—and need—comedy as deviant creative resistance. As political scientists and international scholars with firsthand experience have repeatedly warned, today's authoritarian leader is not our grandmother's fascist. The guideposts that lead to democracy's destruction do not look like they used to; gone are the days of 1970s military tanks and violent overthrows as the primary theater of unlawful power grabs.[11] The danger can be as real from elected officials as it is from the traditional imagery of military leaders. Present-day authoritarianism can be so subtle and gradual as to nearly escape detection—and likely would, were it not for the vigilance of activists, civil society, and other societal watchdogs and observers, including journalists and comedians. As Steven Levitsky and Daniel Ziblatt wrote in their 2018 book, *How Democracies Die,*

> The electoral road to breakdown is dangerously deceptive. . . . Constitutions and other nominally democratic institutions remain in place. People still vote. Elected autocrats maintain a veneer of democracy while eviscerating its substance. . . . Newspapers will publish but are bought off or bullied into self-censorship. Citizens continue to criticize the government but often find themselves facing tax or other legal troubles. . . . People do not immediately realize what is happening. Many countries continue to believe they are living under a democracy. . . . Democracy's erosion is, for many, almost imperceptible.[12]

The United States is vulnerable to this precise flavor of democratic demise. The danger was plainly visible in Trump's attempts to discredit a lawful presidential election, which led to a bona fide coup attempt—but also in his party's willingness to follow him blindly without any evidence of system irregularities,[13] following years of attacks on science, journalism, comedy, social media, and anyone in his own administration or political party who dared to defy him. (And who attacks the mail?[14] That, too.) Lingering menaces to American democracy are omnipresent. Authoritarianism is, at its simplest level, a mindset and belief system that sets in "when followers submit too much to the authorities in their lives."[15] The ideals that undergird fascism are dangerous not only in the hands of would-be strongmen but also in ordinary people acting in lockstep. Trump bequeaths a legacy embodied in his most ardent followers, who show "shockingly high levels of anti-democratic beliefs and prejudicial attitudes" and willingness to support authoritarian ideals over democratic functioning in the future, according to sweeping research.[16] A jittery culture of anger and fear simmers.

So, where did and does comedy come in? How does it play an important part here? In the shadowy specter of authoritarian peril and associated threats to equity and justice, the conditions are ripe for sparking the rise of humorous deviance to offer needed critique, but also to ridicule and defuse fear bombs, the life force of autocracy. Comedy gives us an entry point and something to work with, even for people who consider politics an abstract, elitist machine that feels confusing or remote from their daily lives. After all, what is scarier: a "Desperate Cheeto" or a Darth Vader–like character whose fear tactics seem impenetrable? To be sure, the comedy does not negate the potential of the latter, but it does encourage people to engage, learn, share, and stay alert.[17]

Authoritarianism operates entirely from positions and tactics of fear, including threats of intimidation and oppression to enforce absolute compliance, with little regard for rules of law or norms of decency. The potential for violence, in turn, exacerbates feelings of alarm.[18] In the face of fear, ridicule can often be the most potent force for diffusion and resistance. Humor can mock and render frightening bluster ridiculous, to great effect, as pro-democracy Serbian humanitarian leader Srdja Popovic and journalist Mladen Joksic wrote in *Foreign Policy*: "By using humor, activists confront autocrats with a dilemma: the government can either crack down on those who ridicule it (making itself look even more ridiculous in the process) or ignore the acts of satire aimed against it (and risk opening the flood gates of dissent). Indeed, when faced with an act of brazen mockery, oppressive regimes have no good choices. Whatever they do, they lose."[19]

Journalist Nicholas Kristof agrees about comedy's utility in resisting authoritarianism and fueling public engagement: "Denouncing dictators has its place, but sly wit sometimes deflates them more effectively. Shaking one's fist at a leader doesn't win people over as much as making that leader a laughingstock. . . . Dictators fear mockery."[20] Similarly, said scholar Andrew Little, "One lesson from opposition to autocracies is that humor is a powerful tool. A major part of how dictators stay in power is by making individuals scared of opposing them, and it's easier (and more fun!) to protest against a ridiculous leader than a scary one."[21] Not many of us, it seems, are truly unsusceptible to the pull of something funny.

Donald Trump, as perhaps the first real presidential threat to democracy in the modern history of the United States, follows the playbook of his fellow global authoritarian contemporaries, operating with a craven disregard for basic decency. He maneuvers with an entertainer's hypnotic power, winning the worshipful adulation of millions who admire his brand of fear-stoking patriarchal autocracy. In so doing, Trumpism established the conditions that gave rise to a vibrant renaissance of comedic public resistance through the likes of fresh voices like Randy Rainbow on YouTube, alongside TV stalwarts like *Saturday Night Live* and *The Daily Show*. Comedy, in this context, is creative deviance that fosters social change, builds civic power, and interrogates injustice and oppression. As imagined and unpackaged here, comedy acts as a form of artistic resistance to show what is grotesque and unjust—performing a function as a societal corrective—but also to provide play and silliness. And, as it turns out, we need comedy as creative deviance more than we might care to admit—or dare to take seriously.

Creative Deviance as Resistance: Historical Global Highlights

Comedy resides within a great tradition of artistic activism as a mechanism to push for social change. The relationship between art and activism is potent and codependent.[22] In this context, artists working in resistance to oppression (or activists working creatively through art as resistance) are motivated by a variety of possible outcomes: to foster dialogue, build community, make a place, invite participation, transform environment and experience, reveal reality, alter perception, create disruption, inspire dreaming, provide utility, facilitate political expression, encourage experimentation, but also potentially to "maintain hegemony," or even "make nothing happen."[23] The goals may be immediate change or a gradual cultural shift,[24] but the creative expression is meant to capture attention and disrupt—to jolt past polite sensibilities, awaken people to injustice, or provide an expansive new vision. Comedy fits beautifully here.

The idea of ordinary people, artists, and organizations using comedy and playful mockery as creative deviance and resistance to power has many historical precedents, dating back at least to ancient Rome when citizens drew penises on the walls of the city to mock Caesar's infidelities.[25] But a few examples from the twentieth century also illustrate how and why comedy and satire can be employed in a variety of ways as creative forms of political resistance—from Yippies in the United States "levitating" the Pentagon as anti–Vietnam War action to underground samizdat jokes in the Soviet Union and communist Eastern Europe to the public performances of Bread and Puppet Theater for over five decades in the United States and across the globe.[26] In each instance, humor provides a "safe haven" for critique in authoritarian and democratic regimes alike, where overt criticism of state power in repressive societies can lead to arrest, prison, forced labor, torture, or death. Comedic critiques are a much safer route to travel. But why is comedy perceived as less dangerous?

First, humor can often be anonymous, with no identifiable author or "originator" of the resistance, seemingly arising organically from the people. This was often the case with Soviet-era humor, when Soviet and East European citizens had a rich culture of jokes and humor that citizens told each other as a form of personal resistance.[27] Such shared narratives were needed precisely because the reality created by state media was often opposite of what people knew to be true but could not openly discuss. Humor allowed for counternarratives and recognition of a shared alternate reality from that which the state would exclaim as the glorious achievements of communist society. One joke, for instance, goes like this: "What is colder in a Romanian winter than cold water? Hot water!"[28] This leads to the second point: comedic critiques are easily spreadable but not easily traceable. Who doesn't want to share a laugh about the institutional forces that control our lives? Such clandestine sharing creates not just levity but also community. It is a form of shared communal rebuke of authority.[29] But the joke teller did not necessarily create the critique—the jokester just shares it—and is thus somewhat immune from prosecution.[30]

But the opposite can also be true, in that through overt public performance, the "play" is indeed the thing. In the 1960s in the United States, the Yippies—a band of youthful antiwar activists led by Abbie Hoffman and Jerry Rubin—mastered what scholar Todd Gitlin calls "the politics of dis*play*" (italics in the original).[31] They engaged in an array of media-attention-seeking stunts, guerilla theater, and public performance art (such as an army recruiting booth in Times Square that brandished the banner, "See Canada Now"). Gitlin reports the logic of play at work in perhaps their most famous stunt and antiwar media event—levitating the Pentagon:

> The movement's twice-yearly body count [demonstration], for the sake of impressing a dubious "public opinion," had the worst possible attribute in the eyes of a subculture devoted to killing conventional time: it was boring. New tactics were called upon to infuse the movement with countercultural spunk. Since five-sided shapes were evil, why not apply for a permit to levitate the Pentagon, then invite witches and incantations to do the deed? . . . When Washington police announced they were ready to use a new stinging, temporarily blinding spray called Mace, Abbie sprang into symbolic counteraction, announcing a new drug, "Lace," ostensibly "LSD combined with DMSO, a skin penetrating agent. When squirted on the skin or clothes, it penetrates quickly to the bloodstream, causing the subject to disrobe and get sexually aroused."[32]

Play, spectacle, and public performance are also central to Peter Schumann's Bread and Puppet Theater, which began in New York City in 1963. Utilizing the spectacle of twelve- to fifteen-foot-tall paper mache puppets and stilt walkers—often employing effigies representing political actors and themes for commentary and critique—Puppet Theater has been conducting numerous street performances in the United States and across the world for over half a century. These include critiques of the International Monetary Fund and World Bank for their policies in the impoverished global south, a Japanese production criticizing Richard Nixon and the general responsible for the My Lai massacre, and, perhaps most famously, *The Nativity, Crucifixion, and Resurrection of Archbishop Oscar Romero of El Salvador*, performed in front of the cathedral in Leon, Nicaragua, in 1987.[33] The participatory nature of street parades and festival performances that link artists and audiences is entirely the point, where the grotesque figures and overwrought performances are the means for bringing political critique to life through an involved, community-centric spectacle and performance.[34]

Flash forward to the twenty-first century, where comedy as creative resistance has been, and is, alive and well in recent movements and efforts for social change around the world. In contrast with the analog media era, however, comedic agitation is now aided, amplified, and consumed by millions through social media and streaming networks. Beginning in late 2010, the democratic Arab Spring uprisings took hold through widespread protests throughout the Middle East and "spawned an active sphere of dissenting cultural production" that included art, graffiti, cartoons, and other satire and comedy.[35] The public sphere in the Arab Spring was definitively creative and funny, an evolution in activist communication. Opposition protestors and movements intentionally used political comedy and satire—puppets, cartoons, street art, YouTube—to ridicule elected leaders and to skewer the absurdities of blatant injustice. They positioned humor as a centerpiece of the resistance, inviting participation from ordinary people both physically and through Twitter and Facebook.[36]

The silliness was not without risk, however. Perhaps the most famous casualty of the region's authoritarian intolerance of humor was Bassem Youssef, the so-called Jon Stewart of Egypt, a heart surgeon who turned to YouTube at the height of the uprisings to hilariously criticize government propaganda. His eventual TV show, *Al-Bernameg* (The Show), styled after *The Daily Show*, sparked fury from both the current Islamic leader and the military government. As the BBC reported, "Youssef's brand of comedy was groundbreaking. Egypt has a rich history when it comes to social satire—this comedic tradition is essentially that people just make fun of themselves. His comedy marked the first time that satire had been publicly directed at government authority."[37] Threats to his life followed. In 2014, he was forced to leave Egypt, perhaps forever.

In the same time frame, a new wave of political satire emerged in Bahrain in response to the government's inhumane treatment of its citizens, the "gap between brutal reality and the whitewashed PR image . . . paving the way for a chasm of absurdity that was best resolved with satire and parody."[38] In Bahrain, this particular brand of humor and creative resistance—including cartoons, balloons, slogans, and signs, aided and amplified by social media—was seen as new for a country with little tolerance for criticizing power.[39] Similarly, in 2019, the BBC reported that "satire has never been as popular in Iraq as it is now, even though it's an extremely dangerous game to play."[40] The satire is pointedly targeted directly at power—both Iraqi government leaders and religious fundamentalists. Comedy programming that criticizes the government is wildly popular on YouTube, particularly for young people, with comedic styles that range from puppets to animation to public affairs programming in the style of *The Daily Show*, influenced by US-style comedy that criticizes power and injustice. It is an explicit creative mechanism to counter fear, says Ahmed Wahid, a popular Iraqi comedian.[41] The impulse to use comedy as resistance was in display as early as 2014 as Iraqis dealt with the rise of the extremist Islamic State,[42] but comedians using YouTube and social media to produce, distribute, and promote their work is the centerpiece of the recent comedy explosion. Millions are watching and participating.

Elsewhere, humor is credited with helping nonviolent movements to bring down two African dictators, Algeria's Abdelaziz Bouteflika and Sudan's Omar al-Bashir, in 2019.[43] In places like Finland, Sweden, and Scotland, when dealing with far-right extremist groups that take to the streets to intimidate and stir chaos, peace protestors have literally sent in the clowns. In contrast with other tactics, like pushing back with retaliatory fear and violence from the other side, clowning has been employed as one of the most viable mechanisms to counter fear. As longtime activism scholar George Lakey writes, "Their [right-wing extremists'] victory comes when their opponents respond in a like manner and try to out-intimidate the intimidators."[44] But humor (and in some cases, actual clowns) is a diffuser.

In response to the evolving, social-media-era global phenomenon of comedians speaking truth to power and injustice, a consortium of comedy TV showrunners, producers, and writers around the world created the global Comedy for Change network in 2014 (I am a member). In 2020, Comedy for Change launched the Finger Awards, a hilarious and serious effort to award international comedy efforts—ranging from TV programs to coordinated campaigns, stunts, and viral social media activities—that successfully extend a big metaphorical middle finger to status quos of oppression and injustice. Among the awards: a musical-parody anthem created by top political satirists across sixteen European Union countries to influence the European Parliament election of 2019; a reproductive health program in Germany called the Tampon Book; and *Taboo*, a Belgium TV show that centers people with disabilities, who are often dehumanized elsewhere in media portrayals.[45]

Back in the United States, the focus of this book, a rich tradition of dissenting, playful, mediated comedy is blossoming across genres and methods of distribution. The creeping authoritarianism and indecency of the Trump years, while not nearly the sole jumping-off point for contemporary comedy as deviant resistance, helped to provide generative fuel for a whole new crop of boundary-pushing TikTok/Twitter/Instagram-famous comedians like Blaire Erskine, Brent Terhune, Sarah Cooper, Eva Victor, and Niccole Thurman,[46] who raised their creative voices alongside powerful activist groups. Stalwarts like *Saturday Night Live*, *The Daily Show*, *Full Frontal with Samantha Bee*, and *The Late Show with Stephen Colbert* kept their sights relentlessly focused on public affairs of the moment, from politics and injustice to the historic COVID-19 pandemic. There was a lot to be angry about, and comedy provided catharsis and ways for publics to stay alert and informed, build resilience, and participate.

To be sure, this book does not presume that clowns and comedians are the magical panacea to our ailments of oppression and injustice. But the book does take seriously the special ability of comedy to fiercely (and hilariously) interrogate injustice and contribute to shaping societal norms and public opinion. A more precise understanding of how comedy works for social change—why we laugh and how it matters for social progress—is where we turn next.

How Comedy Fuels Social Change and Builds Civic Power

Social change—endeavoring to shift societal conditions and public opinion to prevent or dismantle injustice—requires civic power, helping to strengthen constituencies and communities that can garner attention and exert long-term influence. A society's shared norms of equity and oppression shift and reconstitute, and thus, advancing social progress is a constant cycle and pursuit, never a precise and tidy destination. We take steps forward and backward. Social change flows and takes root in a culture not only through (and actually, sometimes not very much through) a rational deliberation of information and facts but through the stories we tell and the emotional stirrings they evoke, the ways they inspire us to look and imagine beyond our own limited visions. We must attend to this process actively, from one generation to the next. Embodied in entertainment and media, creative culture is omnipresent and crucial. Culture is the backdrop and sculptor that molds what we feel and believe and value—the underlying infrastructure of democracy, policy, and institutional power. What we see and experience in mediated artistic reflections of ourselves is vital to social change. There are no "facts" to check here in these cultural waters, but instead, we swim in the narratives we see reflected around us. They become the stories we tell ourselves and others—the stories we come to believe, sometimes (often?) in spite of factual information to the contrary. Like it or not, this is the power of culture. As Stephen Duncombe writes,

> There are no immutable laws of gravity determining the outcome of an election, nor empirically verifiable tests of what constitutes a good society. As such, it is largely the power of public opinion that determines their form and value. . . . The truth does not reveal itself by virtue of being the truth: it must be told, and we need to learn how to tell the truth more effectively. It must have stories woven around it, works of art made about it; it must be communicated in new ways and marketed so that it sells.[47]

As a form of creative culture that can reach far beyond the erudite boundaries of finer arts, comedy across media platforms—from TV and streaming networks to social media—is a beguiling way to draw us into understanding, deconstructing, laughing at, criticizing, and imagining the world, beckoning us to pay attention because play and entertainment are magnetic forces. Most humans, after all, are not immune to fun, and comedy is a bit of a sneak attack when it skewers injustice. The arc of justice is aided by comedians acting as sharp-tongued cultural watchdogs, but also as deviant artists who can imagine and gently invite us to see what a just society looks and feels like, disarming us through their humor and silliness.

In this regard, comedy and social justice are symbiotic.[48] As cultural forces, they both observe the status quo in ways that move beyond the usual or expected, and they demand that we employ a new way of looking—for comedians, this distorted view is a requirement for getting the laugh, and for social change agents, it is the sole mission. This way of thinking is deviant in the best possible way: taking a known reality, turning it around and finding a new way in, and presenting it in such a way that other humans will recognize both the status quo and the comedically deviant new portal by which to see it—and maybe even correct it. Comedy is valuable for social justice not only due to its emotional and cognitive effects on audiences, or its cultural functions, but because its very essence comprises unexpected, creative, playful, incongruent ideas: deviance.

Early and enduring definitions of comedy hinted at this symbiosis with social justice, even if they did not use twenty-first-century semantics. They spoke of functions, not a rigidity of form—wisely, since what is funny shifts from culture to culture, and from one generation to the next, along with genres and approaches to comedy. Ancient Greek philosopher Aristotle, perhaps the earliest known pontificator on the subject, wrote about comedy as a form of "buffoonery" that offers a mechanism for reflection and social critique, helping a society participate in pushing back against a reality that is so absurd as to be worthy of ridicule.[49] Comedy is thus capable of acting as a societal corrective. Psychologist Sigmund Freud, in his pathbreaking 1905 book, *Jokes and Their Relation to the Unconscious*, focused on comedy's ability to act as both social critique and catharsis, but also to bring taboo topics into the culture for dialogue.[50] In Freud's point of view, a society needs to acknowledge and discuss its ignored, complex, intimate, even painful topics—and comedy offers a way in. Comedy offers a needed form of societal release.

But definitions alone can only take us so far. To move deeper into contemplating precisely how comedy helps build civic power, we must engage in two levels of understanding about "how comedy works" for social change. The first level fixates on the *audience*—why we laugh when we experience comedy, including the cognitive and emotional experiences at play, and how we process, interpret, and behave together when we see and hear mediated comedy about social topics and realities.[51] The second level—and a primary through line of this book—focuses on how comedy serves powerful social-change functions broadly within *culture*. Either level alone is insufficient in shaping our holistic understanding about how and why comedy can be such a potent force for building a more just, equitable society. But by considering them together, we can imagine the cumulative cultural impact of comedy that interrogates social-justice topics and shines a light on neglected voices and their lived experiences.

First, as audiences, why we laugh at comedy is meaningful in the context of social change—that is, the individual process of understanding and interpreting a joke with enough depth to find it funny. Our brains *and* our emotional selves are called to attention when we experience comedy, and this matters. Comedy gets the laugh because it alters reality, embodied in a funny person's creative ability to use rhetorical devices like intimate confessions or quirky perspectives or absurd metaphors or visuals or voices or characters or body language and storytelling—the list goes on. The laugh comes precisely because of this distinction, or incongruence, between the expected and usual way things are (the status quo) and the bent or new reality depicted in the context of a joke or humor.[52] In other words, as Lauren Feldman and I wrote in earlier work, "To feel amused enough to laugh, the audience must be able to recognize both the status quo and the incongruent, unexpected reinterpretation of the status quo that comedy offers. Comedy is a sophisticated form of cultural expression, then, that requires both a comedian's and an audience's understanding of a state of affairs in order to process—and find funny—the humorous contortion of reality."[53]

We work cognitively to "resolve" the distortion in our minds,[54] which requires a shared cultural recognition of a reality—"salience"—and thus appreciation for the comedic lens on it, to help us arrive at the laugh.[55] But comedy is hardly only about our thinking selves. We are also motivated to laugh at comedy because it provides emotional and physical pleasure,[56] and it evokes a distinctly positive emotional response.[57] Being amused by and liking the comedian are also key to our affection for comedy. So, we laugh because we are playing and we are thinking, contemplating the status quo and the way a comedian has distorted it and helped us to see things in a fresh light—and because it makes us feel good. That is no small thing when we think about attracting people to contemplate social injustice or realities that can be complex, sad, stressful, scary, dire, and depressing—or to see, with fresh vision, people who are ignored, pathologized, negatively stereotyped, or dehumanized in media reflections. Imagine an audience, for example, watching the funny and mundane daily trials and tribulations of Mitch and Cam, a loving same-sex couple on the hit sitcom *Modern Family*; to be sure, they are not making soap-box speeches about their legal rights and hopes as gay men who have created a family together, but there is certainly a clear message about gay marriage within their domestic squabbles and sweetness: "This is normal."

Also at the audience level, according to my earlier work with Lauren Feldman, which synthesizes years of research and thinking across disciplines, comedy exerts four main "social change influences" or effects: "to increase message and issue attention; to disarm audiences and lower resistance to persuasion; to break down social barriers; and to stimulate sharing and discussion."[58] In other words, when it comes to civic, social, and political issues and topics, comedy is often better able to attract public attention than other serious-message delivery mechanisms, and the route to persuasion through comedy comes as we are being entertained and experiencing emotions like hope and optimism, which can activate us to action.[59] Comedy cuts through social barriers, helping us move past discomfort when we think and talk about taboo or hard topics, or those we don't understand. And because we are more likely to share comedy with our peers and friends than other genres of media, we amplify the reach of comedic messages. When it comes to social change, all of this is meaningful. We need messages that spark feelings of play, hope, and optimism to engage people who might not otherwise tune in to certain forms of news or information—or would actively argue against them.

At the broader cultural level, comedy serves several core functions that foster social change and build civic power, particularly for traditionally marginalized groups and challenging or neglected topics. We come to know this, notably, through the motivations and machinations of comedians themselves. Comedy provides creative space for traditionally marginalized people to assert and reflect their *cultural citizenship and identity* in ways that are funny and humanizing, acts as *social critique* in a watchdog role, supplies expansive thinking through *civic imagination*, and helps to fuel *coping and resilience* in conditions of oppression. These are not mutually exclusive; the same comedic work can serve all of these functions at once, or one or two.

First, when comedians assert and celebrate their unique cultural identities and lived experiences, media representation combines with the disarming virtue of comedy. This is central to social change with an eye toward justice and equity. Stemming from the theory of cultural citizenship, whereby traditionally marginalized people are generally less visible or negatively stereotyped in cultural reflections,[60] comedy can help act as a corrective cultural force through empowering representation.[61] In asserting one's cultural citizenship, William Flores and Rina Benmayor argue, "Culture provides . . . a sense of belonging to a community, a feeling of entitlement, the energy to face everyday adversaries, and a rationale for resistance to a larger world in which members of minority groups feel like aliens in spite of being citizens."[62] As a composite idea, comedy and social justice center voices and people who have been oppressed and often dehumanized—women; BIPOC (Black, Indigenous, People of Color); LGBTQ+ people; members of the disability community; undocumented immigrants—along with social problems seen as taboo. And, with humor as the centerpiece, comedians can take a lighthearted or pointed approach that moves beyond (or challenges) oppressive tropes. In so doing, comedy can help audiences to see and experience people in non-othering ways.[63] Comedy is unique among media genres in this ability to disarm, and comedians themselves— those with often-marginalized identities—are clear-eyed about their own motivations to make comedy that honors and celebrates their lived experiences. TV writer and showrunner Mindy Kaling, for instance, centers this idea in her Netflix comedy show, *Never Have I Ever*, about the life of a first-generation Indian American girl like her: "For all of us in the writers' room, particularly those of us who were the children of immigrants, which comprised most of my staff, it was about sharing those stories of feeling 'other.' . . . One of the best parts about being in that room was realizing that they felt so many of the same things I did, and it was such a relief. It made me feel like, 'OK, I'm, like, normal.'"[64] Shows like *Transparent, Ramy, Insecure, One Day at a Time,* and *Fresh Off the Boat* all feature comedians claiming and affirming their cultural citizenship. As powerhouse comedy showrunner Gloria Calderón Kellett (*One Day at a Time*) puts it,

> In the Latinx experience, we're mostly seen in media through our trauma. That's dangerous because I think it only shows one part of a community. Is there trauma? Sure. I mean, all of those things are well-documented, but what is not documented is the joy and the pride and the beauty. When you're only showing a myopic point of view of a community, it clouds how people see that community, if that's all they get, and this is true with so many underrepresented communities. . . . I don't get to see Latinos in a comedic light nearly enough. That is sort of my contribution.[65]

Beyond representation, comedy as social critique is well documented and understood—a basic foundational function of humor that tracks to ancient days. Social critique is clearly the primary machination of satirical news programs like *The Daily Show* and *Full Frontal with Samantha Bee*, but we see this function on display also across comedic media genres beyond entertaining public affairs programming, à la Randy Rainbow. Observing a social-critique function allows comedians to point out what is grotesque and wrong, or to spotlight uncomfortable truths and topics, often sparking public dialogue. In the 2020 Netflix comedy special *Nate*, for example, comedian Natalie Palamides plays the titular male character, "Nate," while she provokes her audience to interact with topics of toxic masculinity and consent—hilarious while devastatingly on point.[66] Michelle Wolf, in her famously provocative monologue at the 2017 White House Correspondents' Dinner, clearly struck a nerve with uncomfortable journalists when she pointed out their own complicity in Trumpism: "You guys are obsessed with Trump. Did you used to date him? Because you pretend like you hate him, but I think you love him. I think what no one in this room wants to admit is that Trump has helped all of you. He couldn't sell steaks or vodka or water or college or ties or Eric, but he has helped you. He's helped you sell your papers and your books and your TV. You helped create this monster, and now you're profiting off of him."[67]

Comedians, in this way, often say what journalists—in theory, bedrock guardians of democracy—can't or won't, particularly when it comes to a necessary critique of news media as institutions of power.

Criticism alone, however, is not sufficient for social progress. It is not enough to talk only about what is wrong, which is also an inherently negative process that can be draining (albeit arguably less exhausting when packaged with humor). As a parallel goal, painting the portrait of what *can* be—through the civic imagination—reveals and normalizes a world in greater harmony, through play and vision, hope and optimism. Civic imagination, which scholar Henry Jenkins defines as "the capacity to imagine alternatives to current social, political, or economic institutions or problems," helps one to "imagine oneself as an active political agent."[68] Comedy can help provide the fuel of civic imagination by humorously inviting people to see and imagine a better world, but also to participate in that vision through their own attitudes and behaviors and values.[69] On the Emmy Award–winning hit dramedy *Schitt's Creek*, as one of many exemplars, showrunner Dan Levy chose to depict gay couple Patrick and David (played by Levy, who is a gay man) in a loving, accepting small town devoid of homophobia; it was an explicit creative choice, not delusional thinking on the part of Levy, who explained his position in a media interview: "I have no patience for homophobia. . . . As a result, it's been amazing to take that into the show. We show love and tolerance. If you put something like that out of the equation, you're saying that doesn't exist and shouldn't exist."[70] In response, fan letters to Levy "specifically mentioned how the lack of prejudice against the couple made them do some self-reflection."[71] In comedy as civic imagination, lives that are too often pathologized are normalized and treated with equity and respect. As comedian Jeff Hiller, who identifies as gay and nonbinary, expresses, "I can tell you, I rented literally every movie that had even the whiffs of gayness at Blockbuster between 1990 and 1994. I was desperately in search of that, to be a part of the cultural conversation. . . . And a comedy show like *Designing Women*, that was all I had, and it wasn't much, but somehow I felt part of the conversation and culture."[72] By permitting us to conjure a world that is equitable and just, aspirational comedic civic imagination can expand our vision for what can and should be.

Finally, for both comedians and their audiences, comedy is a coping mechanism for dealing with oppression, fear, and anger. This is not to say that comedy helps us settle for injustice, but instead, that we need strength to move forward. Comedy is not only cathartic, but it helps build resilience, a vitally important skill in building civic power, boosting strength and fortitude. In this context, comedy has been historically leveraged by disempowered groups and individuals to resist oppression and marshal the mental resources necessary to continue the struggle.[73] Indeed, in the case of politically targeted anti-authoritarian activist humor profiled earlier in this chapter, morale boosting, internal resilience, and the chance to relieve tension are perhaps more important than any outward-facing effect.[74] This idea endures. Comedy, as writer and showrunner Calderón Kellett says, "can help make light of a situation that is sometimes more serious. . . . Seeing the bright side of things and trying to find the humor in the situation is a coping mechanism as much as just a way of life."[75] Comedy is, as comedian Molly Gaebe puts it, "a survival tactic."[76]

And yet, these functions of comedy, while inspiring, are not the whole story about how humor can manifest in a society. It is also true that comedy has a dark, destructive side. Comedians can entertain audiences with their own pernicious views about "targeted others," thus perpetuating injustice. There is a distinction between "positive, empowering comedy that encourages group connection and solidarity and 'negative' or 'hostile humor' that separates and excludes. Not only can humor be morally objectionable when it treats something that should be taken seriously as a subject for play; it can also keep sexist and racist stereotypes in circulation, thereby supporting prejudice, aggression and unjust power formations. . . . 'Negative' forms of humor can cause harm and suffering by humiliating its victims."[77] We must always consider power dynamics at play between comedians in dominant positions or identities in a culture and those in less powerful standing when we contemplate comedy that either punches up or punches down, to use comedy parlance—that is, lifting up and providing an expanded perspective or necessary social critique, or instead victimizing those with less entrenched power.

Similarly, not all topics lend themselves to comedy, and not all comedians from dominant gender and racial groups seek to punch down, just as every comedian from a traditionally marginalized group does not categorically create empowering humor (see, for example, Dave Chapelle's stand-up comedy jokes about the trans community).[78] Binaries in the messy arena of comedy are not especially productive. Still, this book focuses relentlessly (and with unabashed optimism) on comedy's positive functions in the context of social change, particularly given the context of a transforming media system (the focus of chapter 2).

As a force for social justice, comedy is complex and valuable—it breaks down social barriers and opens space to discuss taboo topics; persuades because it is entertaining and makes us feel activating emotions of hope and optimism; serves as a mechanism for traditionally marginalized people to assert and celebrate cultural citizenship through media representation; acts as both social critique and civic imagination to envision a better world; and builds resilience to help power continued struggle against oppression. When we consider the ebb and flow of social progress, we rightfully speak of social movements, voting and civic engagement, laws and corporate policies. These processes and outcomes, however, are human systems, shaped by collective public and private values and affections, demands, and hopes. They need the underlying connective tissue of artistic expressions that advocate for, and reflect, a more equitable world. If we are thinking expansively, embracing the myriad ways in which entertainment culture serves as the cultural nucleus of a society's heart and soul, we would explicitly center comedy alongside more somber ways of engaging publics toward goals of social change.

. . . . .

The disruptive, deviant, playful creativity of comedy can cut through cultural noise and clutter—and the passive, numbing, disempowering inertia of status quos and dominant media narratives—to shake us into a new way of seeing. Sometimes we don't necessarily even realize comedy's subversive nourishment of social justice and civic power because we are too busy being entertained and amused. Comedy is, in this context, a cultural intervention empowered by the participatory networked media age, explicitly a tool for marginalized storytellers and stories, and also for social-justice activists who embrace it. To be sure, this is a hopeful vision, and it relies on formal infrastructures that allow comedy people to share their work widely with audiences—the entertainment industry and social media platforms. There is good reason to be optimistic. In a wildly transforming media revolution, new voices are breaking through and building power. We travel there next in chapter 2.

2

"It's All about Who You Know"

*Pitching and Producing Comedy in the Transforming
Entertainment Industry*

Sarah Cooper had a serious day job, as most comedians do, long before
she was paid to make people laugh. A career path in comedy is generally
weird and unpredictable—less "path" than insistent artistic calling—and
hers wound its way through the corporate world well before she stepped
out into the great unknown of full-time funny business. The cultural
brochure for the American dream, after all, does not include the beer-
covered floor of a basement comedy club. For an ambitious New Yorker
making her way in the world, tech behemoth Google was a pretty good
place to land.[1] But comedy called for Sarah Cooper, and in 2014, she
answered. Goodbye, user-experience designer job, paid vacation days,
and annual performance reviews. Helloooooooo, comedy.

There is no handbook for an actual-money-paying comedy career. Effort and entrepreneurial spirit are requisites alongside talent, of course.
Experimenting with comedic voice, playing with genres, bombing in
front of audiences, building networks and relationships, landing talent agents, honing the craft of being funny enough to get the laugh: all
necessary. Sarah Cooper did it all—she performed open-mic stand-up
around New York, took improv classes, started a blog, and played with
her humor writing. Outrageous bits from her experience in the business
world, as it turns out, were endless fodder for satirical material (perhaps
surprising no one who has worked in it, present company included). Her
hilarious faux self-help books, viciously funny takedowns of corporate
culture—*100 Tricks to Appear Smart in Meetings* and *How to Be Successful without Hurting Men's Feelings*—attracted some attention.[2] When she

landed a gig as a writer and correspondent on Stephen Colbert's pilot for CBS All Access, *Old News*, things looked promising.[3]

While Cooper was honing her comedy craft, a different hustle heated up on the other side of the globe. A few years earlier, among thousands of new smartphone toys, Chinese developers released two apps that seemed destined for aficionados of armchair karaoke, lip syncing, air guitar, and living-room dance routines. This is not, despite conventional conjecture, a niche group. Musical.ly, which allowed users to create and distribute fifteen-second lip-sync videos, was an immediate entertainment hit with quick-adopter teens, who were already using their phones to amuse themselves well beyond social media platforms like Facebook and Twitter. In 2015, a year after its release, Musical.ly easily took the number-one App Store spot. Around the same time, China's short-form video app, Douyin, came to market in 2016, taking the place of recently departed Vine, a progenitor of the short-short-form media craze for consumers well versed in making user-generated content more than a decade after the launch of YouTube. By 2017, Douyin's one hundred million users were averaging one billion views each day. One year later, Musical.ly and Douyin—by then under a new name, TikTok—merged. In 2018, new and improved TikTok took off in the United States and around the world.[4]

TikTok's star rose faster than legacy social media platforms, and the sheer number of uploaded videos and usage rates stunned tech watchers. Hollywood, still figuring out streaming entertainment and the possibilities for short-form video and storytelling (Snapchat? Instagram?), did not quite know what to make of it. But the Hollywood-meets-Silicon-Valley era of "social media entertainment" was firmly on the ascent by then, a force by which, as scholars Stuart Cunningham and David Craig wrote, "players, platforms, norms, principles, and practices [are] ceding significant power and influence to powerful digital streaming and social networking platforms. . . . Creators have harnessed these platforms to generate significantly different content, separate from the century long model of intellectual property control and exploitation in the legacy content industries."[5] Whether or not the entertainment industry was ready for TikTok, millions of people clearly were.

Flash forward to early 2020. As Sarah Cooper was figuring out her next comedy move, a once-in-a-generation pandemic converged with a perfect storm of absurd politics. What happened next would change the trajectory of her career, nearly instantaneously.

The first alarm bells of the looming COVID-19 crisis went off in January 2020 when China fully locked down the city of Wuhan, ordering eleven million residents to stay home while government officials tried to stem the outbreak of a mysterious, deadly coronavirus. In March 2020, with cases on the rise across the globe, the World Health Organization officially declared COVID-19 a pandemic.[6] Governments around the world, including the United States, took the unprecedented step of shutting down daily life. Restaurants and businesses closed. Online video platform Zoom became the portal to school- and office-based labor of the information economy. Essential workers kept food and health systems up and running, risking their lives in the doing.[7] By April, with diagnoses and deaths climbing and no coordinated intervention in sight, New York City had become the pandemic's epicenter. Temporary refrigerated "mobile morgues" popped up around the city to supplement overflowing hospitals and funeral homes, unable to accept more dead bodies.[8] It was, by all interpretations, a disaster—and perhaps one that could have been averted, or at least minimized.

Sarah Cooper, like many people, was stuck at home honing her skills at America's new pandemic pastime: social media doom-scrolling through a flurry of scary statistics and news articles. TV and film production halted, and live entertainment events—including comedy—were canceled. And then, along came Donald Trump's press conferences. The daily White House Coronavirus Task Force press briefings, under normal circumstances in a crisis, should have been a necessary mechanism for the president of the United States to share vital public health information with the American people. But in Donald Trump's hands, they were farcical theatrics littered with partisan jabs, "fake news" taunts to journalists, and rambling self-proclaimed heroism against a backdrop of weary, muzzled medical professionals and scientists. As Cooper reflected, "I was watching the daily [White House] Coronavirus Task Force briefings and being bombarded with images of him spouting nonsense and being backed up by people who were supposed to be keeping him accountable—and they weren't. . . . I thought it would be interesting to see what it was like to be this person who has absolutely no substance, but still gets respect and is seen as credible."[9] Standing before an incredulous press corps at the White House podium in April 2020, Trump pontificated about the scientific merits of, among other stream-of-consciousness utterances, pumping toxic antiseptic bleach and UV light into human lungs and other organs, attacking the coronavirus like a Lysol disinfection of a dirty bathroom.[10] The background tableau of assembled scientists said nothing to refute him. It was entirely too much for Sarah Cooper: "Being a black woman, I could never get away with talking like that in a meeting, let alone as president of the United States."[11]

Cooper got to work. Watching the most bizarre of the Trump coronavirus press conferences, she knew how to mine it for comedy gold, spotlighting the absurdity and danger of his words—and the complicity of his assembled medical experts—through a lip sync, props, and animated facial expressions. TikTok was the right platform, but it was still an experiment: "I'd done a lot of stuff on the internet before. I'd made videos. I have a website. I have blogs. . . . But I'd never really played around with TikTok. TikTok was the new kid on the block."[12]

On April 23, 2020, hours after the infamous disinfectant White House Coronavirus Task Force press conference, Sarah Cooper launched her comedy lip sync, "How to Medical," on TikTok, redistributing it also on Twitter and YouTube.[13] For forty-nine seconds, timed perfectly with the sounds of Trump's own words, Cooper hilariously animates—through gestures, props, exaggerated facial expressions, and gesticulations—the absurdity of a leader who would tell Americans to consider ingesting poison as a serious virus remedy: "When I saw the part about 'ultraviolet light hitting the body, through the skin . . . or some other way,' it was just so visual to me. I thought, *How would the light enter your body . . . up your butt*? When he talked about injecting disinfectants, I was like, *What*?"[14] Her interpretation was a hit, with twenty-four million combined views across TikTok and Twitter.[15] Well after Trump abruptly ended his COVID-19 press conferences, calling them "not worth the time"[16] even as death rates climbed and the virus spread, Cooper continued. She followed her TikTok debut with a steady series of Trump lip syncs with titles like "How to Bible,"[17] "How to Water,"[18] "How to Mask,"[19] and "How to Bunker."[20] Media coverage followed, celebrity fans shared her clips, and Cooper found herself with millions of followers

Figure 2.1: Screenshot: "How to Medical" (YouTube/Sarah Cooper)

virtually overnight. "How Sarah Cooper Trumped Donald Trump—without Saying a Word," blared a *Vanity Fair* headline.[21]

In lightning-quick real time, Cooper prominently entered public consciousness and a long tradition of political satire. So, too, did TikTok. By recontextualizing Trump through a seemingly silly social media platform preferred by high schoolers, Cooper played with a participatory new entertainment medium to create and distribute scathing, hilarious poetic mimicry that spoke truth to power by lampooning grotesque foolishness. Cooper's use of TikTok helped establish a new humor subgenre and demonstrated the power of the newest social media network as a cultural and political weapon of the oppressed, allowing her to push back against, as she put it, "someone with power taking advantage of people who don't have power."[22]

In June, only two months after "How to Medical" placed her on the public radar, with media outlets breathlessly covering her every move, Cooper landed the holy grail for would-be comedy and entertainment star writers and performers: representation from William Morris Endeavor, the powerhouse Hollywood talent agency.[23] She was everywhere: guesting on *The Ellen DeGeneres Show*, hosting *Jimmy Kimmel Live*, and appearing at the online Democratic National Convention in August, using her trademark style to "perform" and ridicule Trump's remarks about mail-in voting as fraud.[24]

Enter Hollywood disruptor Netflix, which knows a rule-breaking entertainment opportunity when it sees one.[25] An October surprise, unforeseen even six months earlier, manifested as Sarah Cooper's one-hour Netflix comedy special, *Everything's Fine*, a variety show directed by Natasha Lyonne and executive produced by Maya Rudolph of *Saturday Night Live* fame. Cooper understood the stakes: "I've gone from basically making TikToks at home to talking to Natasha Lyonne and Maya Rudolph every day."[26] One week before the 2020 US presidential election, six months after Cooper's first TikTok, and four months after she landed a major entertainment-industry agent, viewers tuned in to her heavily marketed comedy debut.

While Sarah Cooper's talent is the centerpiece of her ascent, it is clear that TikTok helped make her—and itself—an entertainment comedy star. Its creative possibilities and potential for wide distribution are obvious, but that is not the only notable observation here. A fascinating confluence of forces is at work in the changing dynamics of a contemporary entertainment industry that is not only compelled to constantly reinvent and experiment but is also opening the playing field, bit by bit, to rule-breaking comedians who have historically had a tougher time making it past the legacy gatekeepers of a traditionally closed system dominated by straight white men. Cooper's renown and emergent stardom did not stay within the confines of one particular platform, as is the case with many young "influencers" who capture fans within the bounds of Tik-Tok or Instagram. Her unique, timely, activist brand of humor exploded immediately into the mainstay of the entertainment industry, a business reeling with the changes in the streaming and social-media revolution, now forced by a historic pandemic to try out even newer rules. Cooper's rise from obscurity in less than one year—from teen-loving social media app TikTok to full-blown comedy TV special distributed by the most powerful outlet in the contemporary entertainment business—was hyper–light speed. The calcified old gates of Hollywood are cracking open, just a little, inch by inch, year after year.

In the midst of metamorphosis, Hollywood is increasingly embracing comedy crafted through the lens of (and perhaps because of the lens of) activism and cultural resistance, from artists playing across a full spectrum of platforms and new pathways. Comedic talents are pushing their way into the exploding possibilities of the competitive TV landscape, building new roads along the way, like Issa Rae's rise from YouTube series *Tales of an Awkward Black Girl* to powerhouse TV producer, writer, and star of Peabody Award–winning *Insecure*; or Abby Jacobsen and Ilana Glazer's journey from web series to award-winning hit Comedy Central series *Broad City*; or Lilly Singh's path from YouTuber to host of NBC's *A Little Late* with Lilly Singh. For comedy professionals who have traditionally been less visible on screen but have plenty of fodder for comedic material—women; people of color; LGBTQ+ persons—"this past decade has been completely revolutionary," says powerhouse comedy producer Ryan Cunningham (*Inside Amy Schumer, Broad City*), and it is only the beginning.[27] A cultural revolution is happening daily, pushing new norms and power into Hollywood systems, a transformation enabled by competitive platforms and the voices of creative people sharing unique stories and lifting up others on their journey.

Entertainment in Transition in a Multiplatform Universe

Apoplectic tweeters aimed a collective blowtorch at the Hollywood Foreign Press Association on the day of the 2021 Golden Globe Awards nominee announcements. Snubs, of course, are to be expected, but one in particular—omitting creator and star Michaela Coel's HBO drama-comedy series *I May Destroy You*—ignited next-level outrage from Hollywood insiders and fans.[28] For a show called "astonishing" and "genre-defying" by critics—a darling of creative artists, TV writers, fans, and TV critics[29]—the fury was unified. Squeezing dark humor out of a soul-baring personal journey through sexual assault trauma and survival, Coel "touches all the tentacles of what it means to be a human being," said comedian and TV creator Natasha Lyonne.[30] Story after snub-gate trade story published scathing quotations from executives, actors, directors, writers. Deborah Copaken, a writer for the Netflix series *Emily in Paris*, astonished to learn that her own show was nominated for Best Comedy Series over Coel's, wrote in an op-ed for the *Guardian*, "'I May Destroy You' was not only my favorite show of 2020. It's my favorite show ever. It takes the complicated issue of a rape—I'm a sexual assault survivor myself—and infuses it with heart, humor, pathos and a story constructed so well, I had to watch it twice, just to understand how Coel did it."[31]

Something certainly went wrong here. (Or did it, given the structural realities of Hollywood's inner workings?) How could a popular, dark comedy-drama TV program, and one so uniformly regarded as groundbreaking, be ignored? Writer-director-actor Sarah Polley had a theory: nominating a show about a White woman's sexual assault experience (*Promising Young Woman*) and erasing another—Coel's experience as a Black woman—had an obvious motivation. "It's a clear statement about which stories we are ready to hear and which ones we continue to ignore."[32] "Racism," wrote trade reporter Zach Sharf for *IndieWire*, "is the only explanation."[33]

A Sarah Cooper story this is not. But Hollywood is, after all, nothing if not riddled with paradox, equal parts creative dream factory and ruthless commercial business molded from the same undercurrent of structural racism and patriarchy that courses through all other institutions of American life. The entertainment industry in the United States, "a set of corporations commonly referred to as Hollywood,"[34] stripped to its barest essentials, is an enterprise based on individual artists selling their best creative ideas to business executives who are beholden to gargantuan profit-centric commercial media conglomerates, devoted to anticipating, finding, and building bigger audiences better than their competitors. But not just any audiences. Long ago, Hollywood established its systems to appeal to the so-called mass audience, otherwise known as White, heteronormative people and places rendered through a dominant male gaze. As the reality of a diverse American populace begins to dawn on the industry, though, the new game is about appealing to a wide cross-section of disparate audiences. And even so, the players have not yet fully figured out how the new rules should work, exactly. It is a weird time for a business that happily built and supported structures of power that determine whose stories are told and lauded.

And so, we might regard the paradox of *diverse* storytelling—and the story of the *I May Destroy You* snub—as especially vexing in the present day. On the one hand, it turns out that precisely zero members of the Hollywood Foreign Press Association were Black at the time,[35] but on the other hand, diversity is a clear virtue and money maker in contemporary entertainment. Altruism and matters of representation are not (and have never been) the currency of the entertainment industry, but money most assuredly is. (A CBS vice president of research once said, "I'm not interested in culture. I'm not interested in pro-social values. I have only one interest. That's whether people watch the program. That's my definition of good, that's my definition of bad.")[36] These days, in the spirit of money, TV programming created by, and depicting the nuanced lived experiences of, women, BIPOC, and LGBTQ+ people—scant though it may still be relative to the full landscape of entertainment material—is lucrative and in greater demand than at previous junctures. In fact, excluding those diverse voices and on-screen representation is actually a money-losing proposition.[37]

If market value were not incentive enough, diverse audiences, armed with the power of the viral tweet, are refusing to silently accept homogenous entertainment material.[38] So there is pressure, too.

Industry executives are starting to pay attention: entertainment TV programming is dramatically more likely to showcase a broad array of lives and stories than in years past; in 2019, 92 percent of the three hundred most-watched shows featured prominent women, people of color, and LGBTQ+ characters and subjects.[39] And yet, the paradox again: TV screen time is still not reflective of the US population; Nielsen's recent study of the top three hundred shows across broadcast, cable, and streaming TV showed that women, Native Americans, and Latinx people were the most underrepresented compared to their shares of the population.[40] In general, as NPR reported, "Many groups who are marginalized in the real world remain underrepresented in media depictions—especially on cable TV, where white characters got 88 percent of screen time."[41]

A similar pattern shows up in creative decision-making jobs behind the scenes: in the 2018–19 season, only 22 percent of episodes across broadcast, cable, and streaming TV were directed by members of underrepresented racial and ethnic minority groups, and women were also marginalized in notable proportion as directors.[42] As show creators—the all-powerful creative "showrunner" lead-writer creative visionary TV role—people of color and members of ethnic minority groups were in charge of only 15 percent of scripted cable programs, 11 percent of network shows, and 10 percent on streamers; women fared slightly better, but still dramatically less than their share of the population, as show creators of 29 percent of streaming programs, 28 percent of broadcast, and 22 percent on cable.[43] And yet, pause to consider that this state of Hollywood affairs is *dramatically* better than it was a decade ago, not to mention twenty, thirty, or forty years in the past, when women and people of color were virtually nowhere to be found in decision-making executive and creative roles. This book holds onto that scrap of change and builds upon it.

So, it would seem that Hollywood decision makers are increasingly showing *some* diverse lives on screen, but not enough to reflect the many lived realities that populate the real world. And yet, slowly but somewhat surely, they are making and distributing the shows created by those voices. The questions, as the evolving entertainment world order continues to unfold: Will more than one diverse program be set up to succeed? How and why does this racial, ethnic, and gender power imbalance remain in place, despite clear economic reasons to ensure its demise? We should be reminded that entertainment TV's entire economic model has flipped in the competitive digital era with its dozens and dozens of scrappy outlets primed for niche-casting rather than mass audiences—"from maximizing all eyeballs to eyeballs with particular characteristics"[44]—and this is our clue. It is hard to imagine narrow-casting prowess when senior decision-making TV executives are still overwhelmingly White (84 percent) and male (60 percent),[45] an artifact of a set of marketing myths shaped from a bygone so-called mass-audience day in US entertainment. The challenges, in other words, are deeply structural.

Regarding the changes wrought by internet-powered TV—businesses still based in large part on the persistent founding structures of the original entertainment business—helps us see the obstacles and the hope for creating more pluralistic cultural reflections. Entertainment television, "the ground zero of life and imagination,"[46] has shifted from predictable fare to rebellious upheaval many times over since its birth in the middle of the twentieth century, jumping from one evolutionary phase to the next. What was true in the beginning is true today: new content and technology and trends are neither all positive nor uniformly terrible. The era of "legacy TV," a system of "linear or traditional television network distribution,"[47] has evolved into a competitive niche system with more outlets and programs than ever before since internet-streaming entertainment arrived on the scene in the 2010s.[48] As one indicator of the streamers' powerful insurgency—astonishing to those who might remember watching the same fifteen shows together during the broadcast era before cable became a real contender around 1996[49]—in 2017, "about 500 original scripted television series [were] produced for the U.S. market, more programs than at any time in the history of the medium, and a number that has more than tripled in the past two decades."[50] Internet distribution has changed and "markedly improved how we watch," involving a "collision of new technologies, changing business strategies, and unprecedented storytelling."[51] American audiences are positively swimming in entertainment content, and it is available anywhere and everywhere: on the original broadcast networks of NBC, CBS, and ABC, later joined by PBS, Fox, the WB and UPN; cable channels such as Discovery and A&E; premium subscription cable like HBO and Showtime; and streaming networks like Netflix, Hulu, Amazon, and Apple. User-created and -distributed social media entertainment on YouTube, Facebook, TikTok, Instagram, Twitter, Snapchat, and Vimeo is surround-sound content; as of 2017, "The top five thousand YouTube channels have received over 250 billion video views in aggregate."[52] More entertainment streaming services are available than ever before as individual legacy TV networks and film studios continue to launch their own services.[53]

In the midst of such a radical media reimagining, what does this revolution in content and pipelines—and underlying frenzy by profit-seeking executives to launch the new idea, and to find and hold audience affection—mean for diverse creatives, including comedians? Where and how can we feel optimistic about an entertainment industry that is changing, little by little, beginning to embrace traditionally marginalized storytellers and comedians? Building new norms and habits inside contemporary Hollywood in transition is an early-stage process.[54] Even so, plenty of fundamentals remain entrenched. What are the rules to make it in the industry, and what are diverse new executives, comedy writers and performers, and showrunners doing to change them, shift the entertainment pipeline, and create space for themselves?

Social Capital and Gatekeepers in Comedy Production

Poking around under the hood of the present-day entertainment TV industry—the practices and norms built on the foundation of a business that was never designed for a full spectrum of diverse artistic people in the first place—reveals a great deal about the reality *and* the momentum for change. And as the industry goes, so goes comedy, a consistent centerpiece of lucrative entertainment subgenres: episodic sitcoms, sketch comedy, comedic public affairs and satirical news programs, late-night shows, drama-comedy serials, and stand-up comedy specials. Comedy on screen, as a microcosm of a larger business, is our focus, even as it sits among a broader set of cultural practices in the business of manufacturing and distributing amusement.

Understanding a community and way of life, as any anthropologist or sociologist will tell us, requires some degree of immersive expertise. Hollywood is its own culture—a morass of professional practices, habits, folkways. Show biz players know full well that their industry functions as much by its unspoken cultural norms of engagement and its passed-down stories as by formal rules. It can be a game of Twister for people trying to break (and stay) in, except for those who arrive via old-fashioned nepotism. The "rules" are opaque and inconsistent, not readily available or equitably doled out. Making entertainment, after all, is a largely unregulated system of people and relationships—hardly based solely on talent.[55] To be sure, unique skill and a specific creative vision *are* required. But to know and succeed in Hollywood is also to be able to discern where the power resides at any given moment, to understand that nearly every conversation can be roughly broken down into a simple equation: "Are you buying, or are you selling?" It is hard to know, particularly the first time, how to "take a meeting," how to navigate the various unspoken rules inherent in pitching creative vision or navigating unwritten power dynamics. Or how a successful career trajectory requires mastery at "giving good meeting,"[56] not just talent or craft. Or that the meaning of "yes" in that meeting can range from "probably not" to "yes, we will buy your idea" to "I do not plan to return your calls." For a business that requires executive dedication to "a Darwinian imperative to survive by gaining advantage over competitors in a given market sector,"[57] finding and developing the sure-fire new idea is based in large part on social capital and networks of relationships. And here, we find challenges and opportunities for change.

"So much of this industry is who you know—networking and pulling people up,"[58] says prolific comedy TV producer Ryan Cunningham (Comedy Central's *Inside Amy Schumer* and *Broad City*). This basic gospel is not diminished by shifting platforms and newer pathways into the system. Making it in entertainment and comedy requires cultural capital—accumulated knowledge, behaviors, and skills that confer status and build power[59]—and the ability to access and build networks of peers and decision makers. Social capital, those crucial and painstakingly constructed relationships and the insider knowledge that comes with them, is the fuel of the entertainment business, then and now.[60] "It's true what they say in Hollywood about how it's all about who you know," says Kathy Le Backes, entertainment industry executive and producer. "So much of success is having a network and having connections, and having that hustle to network as well, and put yourself and your work out there, and build a rapport with people, build relationships with network executives, producers, solo writers, assistants, all of it. The success really is about having connections and staying on people's radars."[61]

Building social capital and networks requires its would-be players to know which spaces matter and how to work them—festivals, screenings and summits, breakfast meetings and happy hours, industry convenings and conventions.[62] "To make it as a comedy writer or producer," according to Kesila Chambers, producer with comedian Paul Feig's digital production company, Powderkeg Media, which champions comedy projects created by women, LGBTQ+ people, and people of color, "you have to be able to understand that opportunities can come from anywhere."[63] True. And yet easier said than done, says Deniese Davis, comedy power-house Issa Rae's longtime producing partner, who now runs the Reform Media Group:

> Success in this industry is so personable and relationship-oriented. So many things get done by simply way of referrals and recommendations. But also, reputation is key. The best way to build reputation is to have worked with or know as many people as you can who can speak on your behalf. So if you are breaking in, you're not just only breaking in on your own merits, you have someone in your corner who is able to speak on your behalf and really lobby for you. It's a catch-22. How do you bring someone in if they don't have the experience and you're giving them the experience for the first time? Social capital is important in that sense of being able to have some sort of network or relationships that really do support and back you when you're breaking in.[64]

It is not a one-size-fits-all situation. Access to building and mobilizing social capital in the entertainment business is not the same experience for everyone, and it never has been.[65] Historically, marginalized groups and individuals—women, people of color, members of the disability community, LGBTQ+ people, immigrants—have had a harder time, and the long-standing structures of comedy production and its gatekeepers tell us why. A project that reaches audiences on screen, or a writer who gets hired into a comedy writers' room, requires "yes" across a gauntlet of decision-making people. Development executives (the people who read scripts and initial creative ideas), distributors (i.e., broadcast, cable, and streaming network executives), producers and production companies (the people and companies that make the work), managers and agents, showrunners, and lead writers all have the power to make or break opportunities for comedy writers, fledgling show creators, and performers, to recommend, vouch, and fight for them. Erika Soto Lamb, vice president of Social Impact at Comedy Central and Paramount Global, puts it like this: "Development executives of the comedy world recognize that it's a network of people who know each other. How do you break into that when you may be a brilliant, hilarious, comedic storyteller, but aren't already positioned with that network?"[66] In this precise way, diversity challenges are explicitly built into the foundation of the business, says Mahyad Tousi, executive producer of the CBS sitcom *United States of Al*:

> If you're a "minority" or if you're an "other" of any kind, like an immigrant, this affects you in a couple of different ways. It affects you first of all from a legacy perspective. It's a legacy business and it's run on nepotism and relationships. And the legacy of it is white and male. Another component is whether you come from a disenfranchised background economically. There's an economic component that we can very easily say is proportionate in terms of how it applies to people from different backgrounds. . . . If you again are not in the majority zeitgeist narrative framework, what you know is not familiar to those people. And they don't understand the comedy necessarily. Because they don't understand it, because they're not familiar with it or they don't know anybody else that's familiar with it, and therefore you are considered niche, not mainstream.[67]

This matters in the daily doings of how comedy is greenlit for production and how comedy writers get jobs; both processes require access and cultural fit. In this context, deep in the day-to-day business of creating, producing, and distributing comedy, challenges are glaringly visible in the structure of two all-important gatekeeper activities for comedy writers and producers: the pitch and the writing packet.

The pitch is the holy grail that props up the engine of the entertainment business—a kind of performance art that requires its performer to skillfully navigate relationships while persuasively unpackaging the brilliance and future market success of an idea.[68] In a pitch meeting, a comedy writer/producer walks a team of decision-making distribution executives through the idea and the "world" of a new show, its characters and its storyline, spotlighting where and how it is funny and unique, often but not always using a carefully designed "pitch deck" to bring ideas to life visually. Pitching also takes place in a general meeting, where a comedy writer/creator is invited to meet and greet a creative or executive decision maker (showrunner, production company, network executive), or a would-be writer has a chance to be hired into a comedy writers' room. Make no mistake—a "general," to use industry parlance, is about pitching oneself. And the stakes are high: Who does the gatekeeper want to admit to the exclusive club of the business? Who will be hired and nurtured in the industry?

Comedy creators need to appeal to a dual level of decision makers in the pitch process: gatekeepers at the *executive level* inside a network or production company (who decide whose ideas move into development and production, thus anointing some as all-powerful showrunners), and gatekeepers at the *creative level* (the showrunner who decides which writers can uphold visions of a show while also bringing something fresh and funny). Comedy's gatekeepers determine who gets a comedy writer's job, whose idea is heard, how a pitch meeting comes together, which show gets a greenlight with a production deal—ultimately, who gets ahead. And as scholar Todd Gitlin once wrote of Hollywood norms, "More layers in the hierarchy means more executives with the power to say no."[69] Who these decision makers are matters. Josh Church, development executive at Judd Apatow's Apatow Productions, sees this clearly:

> If there aren't enough people in gatekeeping positions including mine that are women and people of color—producers, executives, studio executives—then we just see what's happened over the years where there's a lack of multidiverse, multicultural programming in television and movies because there's just a lack of those people in these positions.
>
> It's been a lot harder for creators of color and Black creators and women creators, LGBTQ+ creators who haven't seen people who look like them in those seats. They are always pitching to a white executive. They'll go to producers and executive rooms and be the only person like them in the room.[70]

Dig deeper and we arrive at a core question: Does the gatekeeper—network executive or lead writer or showrunner—understand or even recognize the cultural experience that makes someone's work funny? Comedy material and comedic voice are, after all, reflections of lived experiences. "There almost becomes a need to translate what you're doing for the people you're working for. I think about this all the time," says Jose Acevedo, comedy producer and development executive at Tiny Reparations, comedian Phoebe Robinson's production company:

We go into a pitch meeting to sell a show that is about very specifically the Latinx experience or the Black experience or the queer experience. Everyone in that room might be straight and White. So, you're having to perform this extra function of not just what does this mean to me, but why is it relatable to an audience that looks and has a different life experience than the person creating it. I think that's why there's so many media outlets that only have one or two shows about the queer experience or about people of color. They feel like they have that entire sector of the human experience covered because they're making these one or two shows.[71]

As comedian and writer Mamoudou N'Diaye (*Space Force* on Netflix) puts it, "The lens is still very White, cis-hetero, patriarchal. A lot of the places that you end up pitching to or talking to are full of White people who, no matter how well meaning, still have a subconscious bias like, 'If I don't really understand this as a White executive, I don't think America's going to understand this.'"[72] Producer Deniese Davis (*Insecure* on HBO) agrees:

When you are a filmmaker or a writer of color, it's really hard to guarantee or to know that someone is fully understanding the culture of the story or the authenticity of that story that you intend to tell. . . . A pitch that is written and directed by a person of color has protagonists that are of color or the stories around a very specific culture. You're pitching to rooms of all-White executives and you're hoping that they understand the importance. Sometimes they just don't get it. Or they do, but they don't see the value in it, right? Because in their mind, niche storytelling doesn't lend itself to a huge success or a large audience. Quite frankly, we've seen that is not true.[73]

Challenges persist also for comedy women in a business dominated by men. Ryan Cunningham tells a story about working on an early edit of comedian Amy Schumer's sketch show: "I fell off the couch laughing" at an episode about watching porn from a woman's perspective, while the male editor—"a lovely guy but a very White man"—didn't really get it. He did not fully grasp the hilarity of a scene created from a woman's lens, she reflects. Her view was completely different because, as she says, "Oh, yeah, because 50 percent of the writing style is for women, and the writing is from women's point of view."[74]

Regardless of their possible affection for the ideas or the creative people behind them, decision-making executives and showrunners determine where they will take so-called risks. The stakes are high; their jobs depend on audiences and their ability to forecast them. As a built-in safety mechanism, betting on a sure thing that has worked in the past is the routine default move, says Josh Church, which has historically meant White, male, heteronormative—the backdrop of the so-called mainstream of Hollywood's origins as far back as the original broadcast TV era.[75] In the pitch process, choosing the unexpected or neglected voice or story must be an explicit act by decision makers with power.

The comedy writing packet can be a similarly essential route to steady employment as a comedy TV writer, deepening the relationships and social capital that lead to future gigs. For the writing packet, the creative vision of a TV program's showrunner—the lead writer in charge of the storytelling, and ultimately its success—is key. The show is guided by the showrunner's creative point of view, executed from one episode to the next through a room of writers who work together to uphold that original vision.[76] When showrunners hire new writers, aside from calling people they already know, they may put out calls for speculative ("spec") scripts, sketches, and jokes written in the voice and tone of the show. This is the comedy-writing packet, an unpaid and time-consuming task. "Mysterious" is the right descriptor. Comedy writers know it can be the golden ticket to some TV writing gigs, but that is about all they know for sure. "It's a bit of a dark art that doesn't get discussed publicly much," writes comedy writer Matt Ruby in his blog, "so I think there's pent-up demand for more conversations about packet advice and how the whole submission process works."[77]

Like the pitch, packets and spec scripts can make or break careers, as comedy TV writer Chelsea Devantez tweeted: "My first job in TV came when Jon [Stewart] read my blind submission to his HBO show and hired me. I had no recommendations or connections. He just liked my packet. And that opportunity changed my life."[78] As a strategy to increase diversity and equity in the writers' room on Stewart's new Apple+ TV show (which Devantez went on to helm), she notes, "We wanted to make sure this packet was accessible to everyone—by making it self-submit (no manager or agent necessary), available to applicants from all backgrounds, doable while working another job, and short enough so that we would be able to make it through every single one of the 2400 blind submissions that came in."[79]

Few comedy TV writers would claim full mastery of this opaque ritual. Sasha Stewart, however, is a veritable expert on the writing packet, having written her way into a successful TV career (*The Nightly Show with Larry Wilmore* and other shows). The experiences of women, people of color, and LGBTQ+ writers, as she says, are inherently distinct as they strive to match the voice and sensibilities of a White, male showrunner decision maker. Writing talent is writing talent, and funny is funny, but the point is that many diverse lived experiences have a harder time making it to screen. Comedy writer and performer Niles Abston tells it this way:

> I was talking to this comedy writer who's written for a few shows and is making money. He's had consistent work—White guy, written for a bunch of shows. He was asking me, what examples do you have? I had written a couple spec scripts as episodes of the show *Atlanta*, and an episode of *The Boondocks*. So he goes, "Are the only examples you have for Black shows?" And I was just like, "Well, aren't your samples all for White shows?" And he just kind of looked at me because he had never thought about it like that, but every TV show you submit for is White. Every script or late-night packet that you write for is White. So, the two, three Black shows that I like watching, I write samples for those shows. And it still shows I'm funny regardless of what I'm writing for or who the characters I'm writing for. But I think that guy had such a long career in the industry and probably had never even sat down and thought of the fact that, "Oh, every show and every showrunner I had to submit to is a White person just like me."[80]

The result? As Sasha Stewart puts it, "Comedy is missing this whole awesome range of experiences that we could all be empathizing with, we could all be learning about each other from, and that we could all be laughing with."[81] Calls for writing packets and spec scripts do not follow precise anticipated rules or timing—they can happen anytime, they can be "invitation only," meaning only certain writers are invited to apply through their agents or managers, or they can be "open packet," allowing anyone to send material directly. But they are show dependent, focused on the voice and tone of the show and showrunner. Cultural and structural challenges abound. Underlying social capital is essential for access, and shared recognition of comedic sensibility—what makes something funny to an audience—is crucial. Stewart explains,

> If you [showrunner taking a pitch or writing packet] hear a joke that you've never heard before, you might not fully understand it and therefore not laugh with it, and therefore not think that that writer is as talented. But really, it's just that you just haven't had the experience of hearing that joke before. To put it bluntly, if you've never heard a period joke before, if you don't understand what really goes on in a woman's period, then if you're reading a writing packet about a woman who's writing a period joke, you're not going to get that joke and therefore you might not hire that woman. Because you'll say, "Oh, well, she's not very funny." But it's not really that she's not funny, it's just that you haven't heard that kind of joke before.[82]

On the other hand, flipping the scenario reveals an opening. Stewart reflects on the story of comedy breakout star Amber Ruffin, who got her start as a writer on Seth Myers's late-night show. Today, she headlines *The Amber Ruffin Show* on NBC, the first Black woman to headline a network television late-night comedy show.[83] In Amber Ruffin's rise to success, we see a possibility for change, additive over time. Stewart explains,

> If Seth Meyers was asking for packets and he didn't have Amber Ruffin's various segments on his show, then somebody who's writing a packet for Seth Meyers who is a person of color would just be writing for Seth, they wouldn't be writing for Amber. So they wouldn't necessarily know that they could create this whole other universe of funny sketches and funny monologue jokes and ideas for a person of color who's actually going to be on TV sharing them. But when Seth Meyers hired Amber, he didn't know that

that's what he was going to be doing. And then he hired her and then suddenly he was like, "Oh, wow. She's really funny. Let's put her on the show."[84]

Success and diversity in existing entertainment programming matter for organic shifts in the comedy audiences will see on screen, in other words. Amber Ruffin's show now opens space for writers to submit packets that appeal to her comedic voice and cultural experiences, not a White male lead. New writers will have a shot on her show, leading to the next and the next, on the way to selling their own comedy shows. And voilà: change, or at least the structural possibility for it.

What are we to make of all of this, then? Poking behind the scenes of Hollywood norms and gatekeeping within the world of comedy is revealing. Building and leveraging social capital is a constant task. The pitch and writing packet are hardly the only ways for comedy voices to be invited in,[85] but they are dominant—and they are surrogates for any number of smaller, less formalized processes by which comedy talents are either excluded or granted admission to a full career. Comedy writers and creatives cannot avoid these gatekeeping activities. Barriers still block the way of hilarious comedy from the lived experiences of storytellers who are not fully invited on stage.

And yet, change is happening.

Shifting Power in the Comedy Revolution

"If it's not new, no one is going to watch it," says Joel Church-Cooper, comedy showrunner and writer (*Brockmire*). "There is only one place to go for the truly new stories, which is underrepresented people based on gender, race, sexual orientation. There are creative people in the industry, but the industry is mainly about money. By very nature, that content has to be diverse. We are now thin-slicing media in a way we never did before."[86]

The paradox continues. Despite deeply entrenched obstacles and impediments, unique voices and viewpoints are a requirement for cutting through the clutter, and distributors across platforms are desperate for them. They also need people in the inner ranks who know how to find them. In a gloriously ironic twist, the comedic voices of women, people of color, and LGBTQ+ creative people now seem fresh and unique to a marketplace that has virtually excluded them for decades. Comedy producer

Ryan Cunningham agrees with Church-Cooper: "This past decade has been completely revolutionary for comedy," particularly for traditionally marginalized voices precisely because audiences are demanding unique cultural specificity to match a niche-oriented multiplatform entertainment universe: "Over the last six or seven years, the [comedy shows] that have been really successful are superspecific. Comedy used to be much broader and more general. Networks and studios are specifically looking for unique voices to lead them . . . because there's been so many more places to share your story, so many more platforms that work, and that has really democratized the whole industry in so many ways."[87]

Finding and developing fresh, highly specific comedy has become a core pursuit for powerhouse comedy producers and executives, a change from the "broad comedy" of the past. While building Issa Rae's production and management group, for instance, Deniese Davis and her team prioritized comedy creatives with unique vision and stories: "The priority and focus is underrepresented writers, looking at kind of all marginalized voices and stories, and saying, 'Who are the people that we feel like are just continually being overlooked in this industry?' We're always focused on looking for people who have very distinct and original kind of voices."[88] Jandiz Cardoso, a former NBC Universal executive (who now works for the Sundance Institute) tasked with finding and developing comedy talent across the company's many entertainment brands, is on the same track. She tells the story of Franqi French, winner of the 2020 competitive *Stand Up NBC* show who landed on the influential *Variety* "Top 20 New Faces" list:

> She is a dark-skinned, Black, Muslim bisexual mother who lives in the DC area, and she was never convinced that this could have been a full-time career path for her. She ignored her ambitions for so long. Because she didn't perhaps believe the industry wanted it, had any desire for it, that she had a contribution to make that would be welcome. I want to dispel that for people so they realize that now is the time. People still don't believe it because they don't see it enough, perhaps. A lot of people try to bend and remold their voice to what they think the industry wants and in actuality, we don't want what already exists. We want what we haven't heard yet, what will surprise us and what we want to offer to audiences that they don't already have.[89]

Where does Hollywood find these unique voices, now that it is trying to find more of them? At least in part, the comedy revolution is unquestionably aided by social media as a gate opener, particularly for comedic voices that are traditionally unseen or relegated to tokenism. YouTube, Twitter, Instagram, Facebook, and TikTok have allowed user-generated and creator-distributed comedy to emerge in their own pipelines, yes, but they have also provided platforms for powerful new comedy players who are crossing over into legacy, established entertainment brands. To be clear, this is no technocratic argument; social media has not *caused* talented new voices to create their work and hone their craft. But the fertile creative territory afforded by social media creative comedy expression—and its wide distribution—is a boon to comedic voices that were locked out in the past. As a destination for creatives, wrote scholars Stuart Cunningham and David Craig, "Social media entertainment is a far more diverse and open cultural space than traditional media."[90] Social media platforms are simultaneously comedy playgrounds and scouts and curators of hot new voices who arrive with dedicated fan bases and audience appeal. Talented diverse comedy writers and performers are migrating from the social media world to big-entertainment distribution, increasingly dissolving any old boundaries that might have existed even a decade ago between the two.

"Oh my gosh, it has changed everything," says Makiah Green, former Netflix comedy executive, reflecting on the transformative power of YouTube, Twitter, TikTok, and Instagram for showcasing diverse comedy voices. "I think that internet has provided an opportunity to level the playing field. The lines between TV and film and web series are completely gone now. . . . The reality is there's people on TikTok who are more recognizable than people on more traditional television."[91] Prashanth Venkataramanujam, who was the head writer and showrunner for the Peabody Award–winning breakout hit comedy public-affairs show on Netflix, *Patriot Act with Hasan Minhaj*, sees a flipped model for gatekeepers' relationships with comedy talent:

Back in the day, within the structures of legacy Hollywood, at least in TV and with theatrical distribution, there was an infrastructure in place to scout, source, and develop talent, develop writers, develop performers, improvers, stand-ups, actors, comedic actors. If you were very, very talented in exactly the way that these people were looking for, or felt comfortable signing off on you, you could rise very quickly in the comedy world or in the pilot world or the acting world. You needed to match. It's kind of like a plug and an outlet. What's happening with streaming and the disruption with social media and TikTok . . . the market and the new ecosystem rewards enterprising people more. And the beauty is, you don't need to make sure your craft and your talent match what a casting director or someone watching a diversity showcase is specifically looking for.[92]

Deniese Davis agrees: "The rise of social media and online has really challenged the old model. Look at Issa's career, look at Franchesca Ramsey, look at so many other people who've been able to truly build their brand and sometimes an audience that allows them to have a little bit more influence when they come over to working with these studios and networks. You have a lot more power in the room when you're able to come in and have built something without them, right?"[93]

Social media affordances are not just disrupting Hollywood structures that have generally excluded diverse and women's voices. They also help diverse comedy power players to change the game from the inside by diversifying comedy writers' rooms and bringing in new talent. Showrunner Gloria Calderón Kellett uses her Twitter platform to recruit women, LGBTQ+ people, and BIPOC writers and performers as a regular activity: "Through Twitter, am I meeting new writers that I might not have had access to? Yes. Am I reading [diverse comedy] writers that I might not have gotten to meet or whose material may not have been sent to me? Yes. And so that is really thrilling. And then more often than not, I recommend them to other people."[94]

But here again, the paradoxical truths of Hollywood and its transformation: social media is hardly a route to unequivocal, guaranteed success for every comedy writer or performer who gives it a try. In some ways, as comedians Niles Abston and Chaz Carter reflected in an interview, it can feel more difficult to shape funny material while also mastering the kind of comedy and video editing needed for DIY social media content. Original Hollywood structures are still in place when it comes to seeing, hearing, and developing comedy voices and stories from traditionally marginalized creative voices—and believing in them enough to invest real capital for production, distribution, and marketing.[95] The hustle is compounded in the social media reality even though it is possible for more outlets to embrace all flavors of comedy. The business still needs an overhaul to embrace diverse voices surfaced through social media (or other paths, for that matter). As comedy producer and development executive Jose Acevedo observes,

> Emerging platforms with a low barrier of entry for creators are always going to be a good thing [for underrepresented creatives]. There's a sort of drawback double-edged sword. The drawback to it can be gatekeepers seeing someone doing something really well on social media on YouTube, TikTok, giving them a shot to do it in the sort of system that they work in. If they try to put it on TV and it doesn't work that one time, that becomes their sort of case study and why this—"capital T"—doesn't work. . . . That's not the fault of that original creator necessarily. I don't think we've built proper pipelines to figure out how to bring them to television in a way that's thoughtful and servicing those individual projects.[96]

Broadly stated, "Social media removed all the barriers that kept suppressed [creative] voices down," says Jandiz Cardoso. Sarah Cooper, Issa Rae, Franchesca Ramsey, Hasan Minhaj, Lilly Singh, and Blaire Erskine are only a few of the comedy stars who shaped and shared their voices on YouTube and Twitter before migrating to power places in mainstream entertainment. Social media has not transformed Hollywood and comedy wholesale, and hard work remains. Once the comedic voices and lived experiences of women, LGBTQ+ people, and people of color are more visible through social platforms, will they be invited fully in as successful comedy storytellers? This is where to focus the efforts for disruption, according to Cardoso: "Social engagement and trends are this free and immediate mass-scale test market that filters and elevates what are essentially talent pitches and concept IP for buyers and developers— essentially, where we can watch the culture and industry shift."[97]

Necessity, as the trite idiom goes, is the mother of invention, and oppressed people are experts at creating their own opportunities—after all, who is going to hand them over? The ultimate change comes with shifting social capital itself, creating new pathways to success. So, it matters that an expanding nucleus of power in entertainment and comedy is forged by new creatives who are creating structures and practices that work for them. Progress and a dogged pursuit of and need for change are both true, as the Hollywood paradox continues.

Mentorship and building networks have always been essential in the business of "who gets in and who moves up" in the entertainment industry.[98] Three levels of change are centrally important, says producer Jose Acevedo: first-time comedy writers who are queer or people of color are starting to get more TV writing jobs, but diverse showrunners are still lacking, and so are diverse network and distribution executives who decide whose shows get made in the first place—and how they are marketed for success. Executive Makiah Green agrees: "I want to see more actual autonomy being granted to people of color as creatives. Period, period, period. And when shows [made by people of color], when these shows do get bought, what's the budget? How much marketing dollars are they getting? You can't greenlight a show and then give us the lowest possible budget, put out two tweets, and then wonder why it's not performing."[99] The pressure needs to continue. Social capital and power dynamics are slowly changing with every successful comedy show and every independent production and management group dedicated to unseen comedy voices.

Issa Rae's Hoorae Productions, for example, includes her production company and Color Creative, a management operation dedicated to finding and nurturing talent like her. Their masterclass series, networks, and resources for creatives of color are meant to change the game for underrepresented writers and performers, says Deniese Davis:

> We are looking to emulate Issa's own brand and what she's been able to build for herself, and have us be that infrastructure support to take these young creators or these young filmmakers and build them into that. It's really, really hard to change these archaic institutions that have always existed in the way that our business is run. . . . One of the fastest ways to change that is more investments and more entrepreneurial startups and companies and studios that are independent. The best way to do it is to create your own. We're starting to see these smaller studios and companies like Array really be proactive and being the go-to place that could understand these type of stories and support them financially or in other ways. The more creators have a plethora of options and are not just beholden to the powers that be or that have been forever, that is going to

really change the game and kind of change the dynamic. The balance will shift and the more opportunities will arise out of that.[100]

At her production company, Glo Nation, following her cult-classic sitcom *One Day at a Time*, Gloria Calderón Kellett is leveraging her network deal to produce Latinx comedy, staffed by writers across the spectrum of race, ethnicity, physical ability, gender identity, and sexual orientation. "*One Day at a Time* changed the game for me," says Calderón Kellett. "As a result, I got this Amazon deal where I'm encouraged to share my point of view. It has been great for me. I want it to also be great for other people. I'm hoping to make many shows and employ many people and continue to try to lift up various members of disenfranchised communities as a result."[101] Native American comedy showrunners like Sierra Teller Orenelas and Sterlin Harjo are breaking new ground with unprecedented comedy TV about Indigenous people and culture, staffed by Native writers—shows like *Rutherford Falls* and *Reservation Dogs*.[102] For Bobby Wilson, an Indigenous comedian, both were profound: "Sierra, like a goddamn Navajo guardian angel, floated down from the Hollywood Hills and took me into her little wings. And I got [my first TV writing] job. It was truly incredible. And it got me into this Hollywood space that became very strange and now very normal."[103]

Boomgen Studios, run by Iranian American scholar Reza Aslan and his producing partner, Mahyad Tousi, tells hilarious and dramatic stories from the perspective of creatives from the Middle Eastern diaspora, including their CBS sitcom, *The United States of Al*, a buddy comedy about a Marine combat veteran and his Afghan interpreter who arrives in the United States.[104] "The real change [in Hollywood and comedy]," Tousi says, "comes with who's telling the story."[105] As another example, mega-producer/director Ava DuVernay sits at the heart of the Hollywood revolution through her entertainment successes and her company, Array, which champions stories by and for Black, Indigenous, and people of color, building new pipelines for lucrative production and distribution deals.[106] Powderkeg, Irony Point, Runningwoman, Tiny Reparations, Day Zero, Hoorae, Reform Media Group, Array, and more: all new production companies, and all building power for comedians with stories we have yet to hear consistently. Through their successes, they are reshaping the dynamics of social capital and power to fully include voices that have been oppressed for decades—no longer side players or tokens, but full participants in the business of reflecting their own funny stories. They are seizing the moment and bringing others along. Change lurks here.

A wholesale cultural shift means space and investment in show-runners, comedy performers, writers, and producers who are women; BIPOC; LGBTQ+; and members of the disability community—more Amber Ruffin and Amy Schumer and Sarah Cooper and Sierra Teller Ornelas and Gloria Calderón Kellett and Lilly Singh and Hasan Minhaj—not because it is obligatory but because it is good business for diverse audiences watching across an unprecedented spectrum of outlets and platforms. And here is the optimistic news: it is happening. Slowly but visibly. The multi-outlet entertainment industry cannot survive without learning how to appeal to a wide cross-section of disparate audiences; it must wean itself from hypnotic worship at the archaic altar of bland "mass market appeal." Change is happening as successful women and people of color are leading successful comedy shows and building powerhouse enterprises to build up and mentor underrepresented storytellers.

At the same time, changes in the decision-making structures of Hollywood are imperative. Shifting power among the ranks of executives and changing processes for greenlighting and keeping in the cultural mainstream diverse entertainment and comedy from creators who are sharing lived experiences and interrogating social-justice topics are constant pursuits. From the efforts of years of cultural organizing and a historic social-justice uprising, there is fresh urgency that extends well beyond the business stakes of the multiplatform universe and diverse audiences. Change is also happening on-screen because social-justice activism demands it. The business of entertainment, the enthusiasm and critique of audiences, and social-justice activism are converging, shifting the business of entertainment—and activism practices. Chapter 3 tells this story.

3

"Hollywood Won't Change Unless It's Forced to Change"

How Activism and Entertainment Collide and Collaborate

On a quiet evening in Minneapolis, George Floyd, a forty-six-year-old unarmed Black man, begged for mercy outside a corner grocery store while a White police officer kneeled on his neck for more than nine minutes, choking the breath from his body. In clear view of bystanders and other police, Officer Derrick Chauvin murdered Floyd on May 25, 2020.[1] The world watched, too, as eyewitness video spread quickly through social media, evolving into news headlines over the hours and days that followed.

Images of Floyd's last moments joined a grotesque visual trove of racial violence and terrorism that spans photographic centuries of lynching, brutality, and torture inflicted on Black bodies. As with the images that came before—the photos of fourteen-year-old Emmett Till's mutilated face in 1955, film footage of police dogs attacking peaceful civil rights protestors in the 1960s, and numerous contemporary images— seeing the trauma of Floyd's death pulsing through daily life sparked rage and deep pain. Millions of people joined their voices in dissent, sparking a racial-justice uprising that dominated the pandemic summer of 2020 and well beyond.[2]

Exactly why this moment, this murder, and this video were so uniquely explosive is a matter of speculation. Was it the nature of the COVID-19 shutdown, with more people glued to their phone screens? Did the clear violent display stir something new in collective moral consciousness? Whatever it was, the reckoning was immediate. Outrage rippled quickly and ferociously across Twitter and other social media platforms. Protestors marched in streets across the country for months. Universities and major corporations published statements of solidarity:

Black Lives Matter.[3] They pledged to address structural racism, not only in matters of policing but in their own ranks. Was it authentic or just lip-service public relations in a heated moment? Regardless of the real answer—which is, if history is a truthful guide, a bit of both—movement and change were clearly afoot just a few months later: "Police accountability bills have been introduced in Congress. Americans are discussing what defunding law enforcement actually means. Corporations are recognizing Juneteenth. Mississippi is changing its flag. Tributes to Confederates and others who espoused hate are falling. Athletes kneeling during the National Anthem aren't seen as so un-American anymore."[4]

Notwithstanding the acute fury and action, the 2020 summer of racial reckoning was an inevitable breaking point powered for years by the protest infrastructure of the digital century's Black liberation leaders. #BlackLivesMatter, which launched in 2013, gained fresh traction sparked by the 2014 police murder of Michael Brown, another unarmed Black man, as scholar Keeanga-Yahamatta Taylor writes:

> What began as a local struggle of ordinary Black people in Ferguson, who for more than one hundred days "slammed the door shut on deadening passivity" in the pursuit of justice for Brown, has grown into a national movement against police brutality and daily police killings of unarmed African Americans. It is no exaggeration to say that the men and women in blue patrolling the streets of the United States have been given a license to kill—and have demonstrated a consistent propensity to use it. More often than not, police violence, including murder and attempted murder, is directed at African Americans.[5]

The struggle, of course, is centuries old. It is a grotesque understatement to say that Black communities in the United States are well versed in inflicted trauma passed down across generations. In the 1960s civil rights era, "For the vast majority of African Americans, unemployment, under employment, substandard housing, and police brutality constituted what Malcolm X once described as an 'American nightmare.'"[6] Differential experiences for Black people in the United States, as legal scholar Michelle Alexander asserts, are the outcome of a "new racial caste system" that serves to disenfranchise, dehumanize, and exclude.[7]

As a system of social control, the power of a racialized caste system is its far-reaching tentacles and deep historical roots planted within institutions of contemporary life in the United States. Dismantling it—along with other forms of oppression—requires focus far beyond policing. It is a task that also demands the voices and intentional labor of non-Black allies working together with communities of color.[8]

In this context, Hollywood, as the chief cultural purveyor of our collective beliefs and values, was not immune to the pressure that erupted in the summer of 2020. A reckoning was past due, many decades in the making. Racist imagery in films and TV was hardly in short supply. The entertainment industry had already weathered the recent grassroots power of Twitter-fueled #OscarsSoWhite in 2015 and the 2017 #MeToo movement resurgence that agitated sexual assault and gender inequity in the business. For an industry long accustomed to placating social-justice activists behind closed doors, the visibility of networked public outrage added gasoline to new fires that were harder to snuff out or control. Hollywood was on notice, and its players got the memo.

Entertainment companies, TV networks, and film studios quickly rushed to publish public statements of solidarity.[9] Emancipation Day—Juneteenth—was suddenly in the entertainment-industry spotlight. For the first time, a handful of major media companies, including the *New York Times*, Vox, and behemoth ViacomCBS (now Paramount Global), observed paid time off for employees on June 19, 2020.[10] Leading entertainment networks—HBO, CBS, BET, MTV, National Geographic, Vice, OWN, NBCUniversal, Tru TV, TBS, and Starz—dropped their regular schedules and ran all-day "programming roadblocks" and lineups featuring Juneteenth-themed films and TV material.[11]

In perhaps the most immediate tangible move, A&E and Paramount networks finally pulled the plug on TV juggernauts *COPS* and *Live PD*.[12] It was a shocking turn of events in the Hollywood sense—the shows were reliably lucrative for decades, despite the harm they inflicted. More than twenty-five years of research unequivocally proves that negative, harmful images of Black and Hispanic people in reality-based crime shows are pervasive, and they shape what we believe and feel in real life.[13] Damage had been evident since the late 1980s, and yet, the shows remained on the air. Online racial-justice group Color of Change, relentless in its cultural activism to shift damaging representations of Black people, never wavered in its advocacy as it primed and pushed the network cancellations right over the edge. As a sign of how quickly things changed, in January 2020, when Color of Change released *Normalizing Injustice*, a major research report about damaging images of Black characters on scripted crime-procedural-drama TV programs, the response from the entertainment industry was tepid at best. But in June, as racial-justice protests swelled across the country, Hollywood executives wanted to talk.[14]

The 2020 uprisings agitated an ongoing dissection of injustice in the entertainment business and the images it projects to the world. It is too early to say where and how and which changes will stick, but it is a glaringly evident contemporary case study that reveals an important truth: "Hollywood won't change unless it's forced to change," says TV producer Ryan Cunningham—through economic success and cultural power, to be sure, but also through the pressure of activism.[15] Cautious optimism balanced with healthy realism is in order, as change is an incremental process. Entertainment companies are beginning to shift their hiring practices across executive and creative levels, announcing new diversity initiatives backed by millions of dollars, opening the potential to shake up social capital and power structures from the inside.

As one of a handful of examples, in February 2021, Netflix launched its Fund for Creative Equity, a $100 million enterprise that will invest in leading creative social-justice organizations with a track record of successfully training and mentoring underrepresented storytellers, including Ghetto Film School, Film Independent's Project Involve, Firelight Media, Black Public Media, and the Los Angeles Latino International Film Festival's Latinx Inclusion Fellowship Series.[16] At the same time, Netflix said it will create new hiring and training procedures within its own ranks. Similarly, the organization Diverse Representation—which works to increase Black agents, managers, attorneys, and publicists in the industry—launched the Black Entertainment Executives Pipeline program in collaboration with Color of Change and entertainment-industry production companies, studios, and TV networks.[17]

In December 2020, the MTV Entertainment Group announced a $250 million initiative designed "to fuel the creation of more content from production companies owned and operated by BIPOC and women" by focusing on production, including directors and writers but also crew.[18] On the network side, CBS announced a new plan to ensure diverse TV writers' rooms, including women and people of color;[19] and Disney Television is figuring out its new programs moving forward, says its leading talent-development executive, Tim McNeal, who cited the racial-justice activism as a spark: "There has definitely been a shift in consciousness that has allowed us to start leaning in to having difficult conversations about the inequity that exists and continues to exist in the entertainment business. Because of those difficult conversations, we have been able to move forward."[20]

Were the 2020 racial-justice uprisings distinct from pressure moments of years past? Will companies and organizations continue to progress with real action and change, well beyond simple statements of solidarity? Time will tell. Unequivocal proof and predictions will always be murky because culture is messy, but entertainment-industry executives and activists feel a stir of change. "The media and the trades are uplifting racial justice to top-of-mind conversations and making sure that they challenge us and ask us to do better constantly, as well as our audiences," says Jandiz Cardoso. "Audiences are flexing their muscle of influence. They're being very vocal, especially now, the young content creators and the young audiences are not afraid to say what they want, what they love, how to galvanize, and step out from the margins and demand it."[21] Makiah Green, former Netflix executive, sees it the same way: "Activism is changing the entertainment industry one thousand percent. I can literally pull email following the George Floyd and Breonna Taylor protests and all of the unrest in the streets to tell you there is a direct correlation to actions and initiatives that were put into place [in the entertainment industry] in the weeks that followed."[22] For the team at Color of Change, the protests of 2020 influenced their work in clear ways, according to its former culture and entertainment advocacy director, Kristen Marston, even though, as she says, "It's unfortunate that it took the racial uprising for a lot of the relationships we already had and have been nurturing to really flourish. I'm very grateful for that, but at the same time, it is unfortunate. But I think it was an eye-opener. . . . But now, even behind the scenes in Hollywood, people have been more open to having conversations like Black Lives Matter."[23] And yet, says Latinx showrunner Gloria Calderón Kellett, continued pressure matters:

> I think that this racial reckoning that we're experiencing is making sure that the conversation is more at the forefront, which is essential as a first step, but it's certainly not enough. We need real action. We need actionable things that studios and networks and human beings are doing on the regular in order to make change. *One Day at a Time* was the only Latinx family on network in 2020. We were it. That's not great. Not to mention an Asian American family, a Muslim American family, a disabled family. *Speechless*, the one show with a disabled lead, canceled. Where are Indigenous people on TV? It's not enough yet. So let's see how this plays out. I am cautiously optimistic.[24]

When injustice is a matter of life or death, freedom or oppression, why care about entertainment in the first place? Then and now, cultural activists and organizations who spend their time agitating and collaborating with Hollywood know that more than a century of harmful images has a direct connection to real-world violence, discrimination, persecution, maltreatment, or even just callous neglect—and the portrayals are difficult to correct when historically marginalized people are not the ones telling their own stories. And on the optimistic side of that equation, visible and aspirational entertainment portraits of people and places can supply hope, optimism, and power through representation. What we experience in entertainment media moves our hearts and sparks our imaginations; it inspires our ambitions, beliefs, dreams, heroes, villains, potential life storylines, and cautionary lessons, as much as we might be tempted to dismiss it as "just" entertainment. What entertainment activists always dance within, even in acts of protest and critique, is the power and potential of *civic imagination*, "the capacity to imagine alternatives to current cultural, social, political, or economic conditions; one cannot change the world without imagining what a better world might look like."[25] Entertainment culture is our hope, always, to show audiences—in human ways that evoke our emotions, that make us cry and laugh, that allow us to play, that bring to life characters and worlds we will never forget—how we might live differently.

Well before 2020, the social media and streaming entertainment age ripened a game-changing time of empowerment for social-justice activism and organizations that seek to change the entertainment-based cultural reflections of marginalized people—women; BIPOC; LGBTQ+ people; the disability community. They are seeding a rich cultural tapestry of voices, lives, experiences, and humanity that has yet to be seen at all, or not much beyond token reflections. It is a potent setup, as future chapters unpackage, for explicitly creative collaboration among comedy, entertainment, and social justice. Entertainment-targeted activism has come a long way from its analog media roots, and yet, it builds on decades of entrepreneurial labor and creative enterprise.

Pioneering Entertainment Activism in the Analog Media Age

In the 1970s, producer and writer Norman Lear was, by any reasonable measure, the new king of American entertainment television—and the comedy sitcom specifically. Until Lear arrived on the scene, fledgling TV sitcoms projected a Whitewashed romp of banalities, as he recalled: "*The Beverly Hillbillies, Petticoat Junction*—those were the shows on the air—the biggest problem anybody faced was the boss coming to dinner and the roast beef got burned, you know?"[26] Off-screen, American life crackled with pain and rage. The Vietnam War was in full swing with a climbing death count. Furious social movements for equity demanded justice for oppressed people tired of waiting. Antiwar and liberation protests were constant, ubiquitous, frenetic, and angry as the country tried to figure out its next chapter. Change was in visible, live pursuit on the streets, but not in the American entertainment TV diet.

Lear, by then a veteran TV comedy writer who took his creative inspiration from "the foolishness of the human condition,"[27] knew the unrest was ripe for humor as resilience and conversation starter. Comedy was vital, in his mind—not mere amusement—to encourage people to really talk to each other about their disagreements, fears, differences, worries. In 1971, CBS premiered what would become Lear's first network hit, *All in the Family*, which created comedy around the wince-inducing debates and adventures of a working-class family and its buffoonish patriarch, Archie Bunker—a real-time mirror that reflected discord in the country, split between social progress and bigotry, between acceptance and entrenched ignorance. Awards and critical adoration followed—and so did millions of viewers. Lear seized the moment by creating and launching three new network comedy shows that injected social issues and hard realities into humor: *Maude, Sanford and Son,* and *Good Times.* By 1974, Norman Lear dominated the TV schedule and the Hollywood awards circuit. He was on top, already one of the most successful writer-producers in TV history. But he was not immune to criticism, acclaim aside.

At work in his CBS office one day in 1974, Lear was not expecting unannounced visitors.[28] "We came to see the garbage man," said the three members of the Black Panthers when they arrived.[29] One of the most visible Black liberation activism groups born of the civil rights movement, the Panthers had set their sights on Lear and his show *Good Times,* which featured the story of a Black family living in a Chicago public housing project. The show was "garbage," they said in the meeting with Lear: "[The] show's nothing but a White man's version of a black family. . . . Every time you see a black man on the tube he is dirt poor, wears shit clothes, can't afford nothing. . . . That's bullshit, we got black men in America doing better than most Whites."[30] The Black Panthers were unhappy about many aspects of the show's images and characters, and as Lear recalled, upward mobility was the core criticism: "[They said] why does the [lead] guy have to hold down three jobs and occasionally—in an episode, it almost seems like he's looking for a fourth—he's so hungry to make some money to support his family and why can't there be an affluent black family on television? . . . They were pissed off that the only family that existed [on TV], the guy had to hold down three jobs."[31]

Lear, who was already contemplating an *All in the Family* spin-off sitcom featuring the Bunkers' Black neighbor, George Jefferson, reflected deeply on the Black Panthers' visit and their view of *Good Times.* Hours after the meeting, he knew that George Jefferson and his family would be an entirely different portrayal of a Black family than American audiences had ever seen on TV, much less in a comedy. George Jefferson was not going to live a working-class existence next to Archie Bunker in Queens. Instead, he would head to the high-rise opulence of New York City's Upper East Side. On January 18, 1975, *The Jeffersons* premiered to the tune of its indelibly positive and memorable theme song—"Movin' on Up"—welcoming millions of viewers into the wisecracking adventures of George, a successful Manhattan businessman, his wife Louise

("Weezy"), son Lionel, hilarious maid Florence Johnston, and their neighbors, Tom and Helen Willis, the first Black-White interracial married couple on American TV.[32] *The Jeffersons* ran for an astonishing eleven seasons, winning Emmy Awards and NAACP Image Awards, making history as the longest-running American television show featuring a Black family to date.[33]

And so it was that TV's first pathbreaking comedy program about an upwardly mobile Black American family came to be: partially pushed, sparked, and enabled by activists who were determined to change destructive cultural reflections that kept them down. But Lear himself, an unusual Hollywood mogul in many ways, was open to both dissent and fresh ideas, fiercely devoted to showing lives that were otherwise ignored in network television. By that point in his career, he had created a system in his production company to meet with activists who responded to his shows in ways that were both favorable and critical, providing him with valuable material and inspiration but also preparing him for public or network critique.[34] More than forty years into the future, Kenya Barris, creator and showrunner of the hit ABC sitcom *Blackish*, would credit Norman Lear's shows—particularly *The Jeffersons*—for his own approach to tackling racial-justice topics through comedy.[35] It is impossible, many decades later, to fully measure the far-reaching societal impact of the Black Panthers' activism, or that of any number of cultural-advocacy leaders who appeared in Lear's office to discuss and debate his bold portrayals—of women, people of color, LGBTQ characters. And it is equally absurd to dismiss the activism as trivial. It was embedded in the entertainment work.

The complex origin story of *The Jeffersons* took place nearly fifty years ago, but core ideals of entertainment-targeted cultural activism were already set in motion. For as long as screen-based popular culture has reflected a version of who we are and who we might aspire to be, activists have pushed for magnanimity and accuracy on behalf of marginalized people. Even in the hectic earliest days of screen-based entertainment—silent film of the 1920s—thinkers and activists understood the unparalleled power of entertainment storytelling and the culture industries to uphold or dismantle oppression, as antiracism scholar-historian Ibram X. Kendi writes: "Cultural advancement would prove key to that reevaluation of the Negro which must precede or accompany any considerable further betterment of race relationships, [Howard University philosopher Alaine Leroy Locke] prophesized in the era's definitive anthology, *The New Negro* (1925). He proposed media suasion by 'our talented groups' to persuade away racist ideas."[36]

Pressuring the entertainment industry to change patterns of cultural representation in matters of race, ethnicity, gender, sexual orientation, disability, and underrepresented social issues is not new, even as norms and formalities in the work have shifted dramatically in the participatory digital-media era. Activism directed at Hollywood has a rich historical legacy as a kind of political organizing focused on "protecting the rights of a minority group or marginalized interest against the entrenched powers of giant media corporations."[37] With early roots in the analog media age, a network of cultural advocates sought to correct damaging portrayals of social groups and identities within entertainment media reflections (TV and film), recognizing that tackling "defamation" in news alone was not nearly sufficient.[38]

Given its ever-present and episodic nature, TV was and has remained the primary site of activist intervention since the early days of entertainment media advocacy, heating up in the 1960s, '70s, and '80s. "The 1960s and 1970s gave birth to many quests for equality," wrote activist William Donohue, and they centered culture alongside policy as their targets.[39] Diversity challenges in the TV landscape—along lines of gender, race, ethnicity, sexual orientation, disability—were evident by then, and social movements aimed their fire at the culture shapers, given that "public concerns about the racial and gender exclusivity of labor markets in broadcast television, specifically, and in media industries, more generally, increased throughout the period. In the United States, social groups had long targeted media representations as indicative of social inequalities in the body politic."[40] Entertainment television, as pioneering scholar Kathryn Montgomery wrote in her pathbreaking 1989 book, *Target Prime Time*, had already failed many: "To minorities, women, gays, seniors, and the disabled, television is a cultural mirror which has failed to reflect their image accurately. To be absent from prime time [entertainment TV programming], to be marginally included in it, or to be treated badly in it are seen as serious threats to their rights as citizens."[41]

Cultural activism took shape in formative decades—the 1960s through the 1980s—in response to racist, homophobic, sexist, discriminatory images perpetuated over and over in entertainment TV. "Historically, advocacy groups have arisen in reaction to media depictions that offend a certain identity group or element thereof," wrote scholar Gabriel Rossman at the tail end of the analog media age. "The offensive media portrayals can take three forms: the stigmatizing, the diminishing, and the poor role model."[42] The Gay and Lesbian Alliance Against Defamation (GLAAD), for example, was founded in 1985 "by a small group of writers and academics who were angry with how the *New York Post* was covering the AIDS crisis."[43] GLAAD moved immediately into entertainment advocacy, reflected one of the group's former entertainment media directors, Bill Horn, because "you could probably count on one hand the positive lesbian and gay characters that had been on television, recurring or otherwise. And you had your occasional police drama with a gay character who was portrayed in an extremely negative light."[44] In parallel, the founder of the Media Action Network for Asian Americans (MANAA), Guy Aoki, after watching racist, dehumanizing entertainment TV images of Asian Americans for years, recalled that "it was more than I could take" watching TV on the fiftieth anniversary of the Pearl Harbor bombing: "Rather than shedding new light on the subject, all too often the stories just revised old fears and prejudices" that were "having an effect on the Japanese and Asian American communities."[45] As yet another example—even earlier than the 1960s—the National Association for the Advancement of Colored People (NAACP) targeted CBS and mobilized its members against the racist minstrel show *Amos 'n' Andy* when it premiered on TV in 1951 after years as an economically successful radio program.[46] The feminist trailblazer National Organization for Women (NOW), after its founding in 1966, developed a bona fide practice to organize against dehumanizing, sexist portrayals of women in entertainment and to develop cooperative strategies with the industry.[47] The National Council of La Raza (now UnidosUS), which launched in 1968 to represent US Latino communities, reflected in a 1994 report that "Hispanics are almost invisible in both the entertainment and news media. . . . When Hispanics do appear, they are consistently and uniformly portrayed more negatively than other race and ethnic groups."[48] Moments of pain and anger motivated these organizations' original collective impulse to change damaging, repetitive entertainment images that were causing real-world harm.

Pioneering cultural entertainment activists pushed for "mainstreaming" oppressed people—including and normalizing their lives and lived experiences in entertainment reflections.[49] And by media including a full range of social identities as "normal" and fully human, free of damaging negative stereotypes, as the thinking goes, marginalized social groups become "more central, more legitimate and powerful in capitalist society."[50] Writing about LGBTQ+ historical activism in particular, scholar Victor Doyle relates this cultural advocacy work to Bourdieu's concept of "cultural intermediaries," whereby media activist organizations make meaning and mediate among social movements, audiences, and media institutions that produce and disseminate powerful cultural images.[51]

During those formative years that gave birth to contemporary practices, entertainment activists—groups like NOW, NAACP, GLAAD, MANAA, the Black Panthers, to name a few of the prominent, visible original players—developed a full spectrum of tactics and experimented to find the most successful routes to make meaningful change within the incredibly powerful, multi-billion-dollar corporate business of creating and disseminating entertainment. Analog-era entertainment advocacy established a stick-and-carrot approach, from targeting networks for media regulation (during the three-broadcast-network era when the FCC held a great deal of power) to mobilizing public pressure against advertisers and calling for programming boycotts and creating awards programs. Their efforts generally fell into two camps: "hostile" strategy, as in a market-based approach to fuel public dissent, pressure, and boycotts;[52] or "cooperative" strategy, which sought to reward positive portrayals and build cooperative relationships within the industry, including awards, free consultation, promotion of programming, and open meetings.[53] Cooperative strategy "on the whole" was more historically effective, although hostile tactics were not unnecessary.[54] Together, the original groups successfully canceled offensive TV shows, developed consultancies to work collaboratively with the industry, created valuable relationships, and, as a lasting legacy, launched a range of awards programs that worked precisely within the sweet spot of Hollywood's adoration of adoration: the GLAAD Media Awards, NAACP Image Awards, ALMA Awards (formerly National Council of La Raza Bravo Award for Latinx representation), Environmental Media Awards (EMA), paving the way for newer programs born in the digital era of entertainment.

And thus, entertainment-targeted activism arrived on the scene and firmly established itself during the busy analog-media decades of dissent and struggles for equity and change. As the new millennium approached and took firm hold, as the mass entertainment media market gave way to niche viewers amid an explosion of new media outlets on cable and streaming, and as audiences were able to vocally share their affection or anger about TV representation directly via social media, the entertainment industry changed. And so, too, did the activism.

How Social-Justice Activists Collaborate with the Contemporary Entertainment Industry

The founders of the nonprofit Muslim Public Affairs Council (MPAC) did not consider Hollywood within its advocacy work until Lebanese American radio legend Casey Kasem, vocal about "the defaming of Arabs" in TV and film, suggested an entertainment-industry awards show.[55] Constantly pushing back against dehumanizing portraits of Muslim characters in entertainment, by then deeply entrenched over decades of American TV and film, seemed exhausting. But creative decision makers seemed to enjoy basking in the positive limelight of awards shows, as the thinking went, and maybe it would help. In 1991, the first MPAC Media Awards gala—which aimed to recognize "artists, actors, activists, and executives who use art and media to create authentic, nuanced portrayals of Islam and Muslims, promote inclusion and social justice, and inspire action"[56]—went off without a major hitch. Nominees were laughably hard to come by, given the entertainment industry's Whitewashing, but the decision was fortuitous, says MPAC's long-running Hollywood Bureau director, Suhad "Sue" Obeidi: "Ever since then, we've been working steadily in Hollywood, not as a focused department or a focused program, but just being available to the entertainment industry. We were available whenever the industry wanted to tap brains, get a consultation. . . . That's how MPAC consulted on *Three Kings* with George Clooney, for example, back in the day. So, time marched on and unpacked itself, and the industry was slowly, slowly calling on MPAC."[57]

And then tragedy intervened. On September 1, 2001, the World Trade Center and the Pentagon were hit by passenger commercial airplanes hijacked by extremist terrorists from the Middle East. Collective shock and mourning settled over the country. For millions of Muslims in the United States, the pain compounded as Islamophobic hate crimes ticked up.[58] TV writer Shawna Ayoub Ainslie reflected years later in an article titled "20 Ways 9/11 Changed My Life as an (American) Muslim," "I was afraid to go outside. If I stayed inside, I couldn't mess up, except maybe with my words, which I policed carefully. I couldn't speed, I couldn't frighten anyone, I couldn't break any law—no matter how tenuous—and therefore couldn't be thrown in Gitmo."[59] Relentlessly damaging images of Middle Eastern terrorists popped up in American TV and film, equating Islam and an entire region to violence and terrorism: "Media, especially Hollywood films, unabashedly and unfairly portrayed Muslims as nothing but extremists with no regard for human lives," concluded one study.[60]

Nearly overnight, MPAC's advocacy and policy efforts turned to the entertainment industry, as Obeidi recalls: "When 9/11 happened, the entertainment industry started slowly calling [MPAC]. Unfortunately, they were creating content that was so horrible, just so anti-Muslim, anti-Islam—just a lot of inaccurate information. They would cherry-pick the Quran and, suddenly, it was a scene in an episode, or a whole show. And definitely, it wasn't authentic."[61] MPAC's leaders knew, swimming in a sea of destructive images of South Asian, Black, and other Muslim communities in American entertainment, that casually and occasionally engaging Hollywood producers and creative decision makers would not be sufficient. An awards show was not enough. In 9/11's aftermath, Sue Obeidi and the MPAC team, including founders Salam Al-Marayati and Dr. Maher Hathout, began to expand the organization's intentional, ongoing collaboration with the entertainment business. In 2011, Obeidi was named the first director of the new MPAC Hollywood Bureau.

Out of a moment of pain and necessity, an organization that thought of itself primarily as a policy think tank is now one of the most powerful voices on behalf of Muslim writers and creatives in Hollywood. MPAC's Hollywood Bureau operates screenwriting pipeline programs and labs for Muslim TV writers, consults TV and film producers and writers about accurate and authentic portrayals of Muslim communities and characters, acts as a respected thought leader in influential Hollywood spaces like the Sundance Film Festival, hosts public panels and events featuring Muslim creatives and comedians, and helps place Muslim writers in TV writers' rooms. It is crucial work, says Obeidi, and it underscores even their wonkiest public policy efforts: "The entertainment industry impacts people's perceptions—how they feel, the way they think, their actions. Pop culture impacts emotions and values and action. Nothing comes second to pop culture. You can create a bill in Congress that says, 'Hate crime is illegal against Muslims.' You can reverse the Muslim ban, sure, but that does not impact how people feel about us. . . . The entertainment industry is the most impactful, most important industry there is, period."[62]

MPAC is part of an expanding and powerful network of social-justice-activism organizations that work in increasingly collaborative and creative ways with the entertainment industry to shift portraits of communities that have been marginalized and dehumanized in popular culture. The exemplars, beyond MPAC's Hollywood Bureau, include groups like Define American (immigrant representation), Caring Across Generations and National Domestic Workers Alliance (caregivers and marginalized women), Storyline Partners (a collective of narrative-change organizations), IllumiNative (Native American visibility), Color of Change (Black justice and representation), RespectAbility (disabled community advocacy), Coalition for Asian Pacifics in Entertainment (Asian American representation), Time's Up (equity for women), Pillars Fund (Muslim representation), and E Pluribus Unum (racial justice), joining original groups like GLAAD (queer and trans representation) and others. Their postmillennium origin stories are fresh, often sparked—like their predecessors—by painful moments of injustice, but also a recognition of their creative and activism power in the digital and social media environment in which they emerged. Online powerhouse Color of Change, for example, launched its Black liberation work in 2005 in the wake of Hurricane Katrina's devastation of Black communities in New Orleans, along with dehumanizing media images. Define American launched in 2011 with a dramatic story of its founder, Jose Antonio Vargas, "coming out" as undocumented. For these organizations, entertainment media is social-justice ground zero, as Kristen Marston reflects: "Entertainment narratives directly impact people. They move people into action. They affect the way that they vote, the way that our teachers treat us, the way that our doctors treat Black people. . . . Art imitates life and life imitates art, and it's very important that we're seeding stories and images in entertainment media that are reflective of the wide variety of things that the Black community represents, and also the issues in our community."[63]

The cultural backdrop is, as always, important—and in this case, key to understanding the evolving *creative* and fully collaborative efforts from present-day cultural activists. As the new millennium's early years progressed and the entertainment industry continued to shift in the multiplatform digital universe, game-changing outlets for generating and sharing self-produced media and networked dissent—Facebook in 2004, YouTube in 2005, Twitter in 2006—radically opened the playing field of creative expression outside the ranks of professional entertainment- and information-media gatekeepers, blurring the lines between amusement and information, and between self-produced and professionally made content. Cultural power lurks in these junctures, wrote Henry Jenkins and his coauthors, as "new hybrid systems of media-content circulation can bring unprecedented power to the voices of individuals and groups without access to mainstream forms of distribution."[64] Social-justice organizations are fully engaging in this networked entertainment environment, and in ways that are far more creative and entertaining than those of the original cultural advocates. They are both dogged activists and full artistic participants in the "creator culture" of the disrupted entertainment business.[65]

As a reminder, Jenkins's thoughtful presentation and analysis of "participatory culture" and "participatory politics" are meaningful here in the context of a radically changing entertainment-media business and contemporary social-justice activists who both target and work within it. As Jenkins writes, "Participatory culture refers to a culture in which large numbers of people from all walks of life have the capacity to produce and share media with each other, often responding critically to the products of mass media, and often circulating what they create fluidly across a range of different niche publics." Similarly, "Participatory politics refers to what happens when a generation of young people who have grown up with more opportunities to meaningfully participate in culture turns its voices to struggles for social justice and political change."[66] And with at least discursive power afforded to traditionally marginalized voices through the visibility of networked hashtag activism, individuals and organizations who advocate for representation in entertainment storytelling (and also create stories directly) leverage social media networks as distributors and message amplifiers, however flawed they may be. Sarah J. Jackson, Moya Bailey, and Brooke Foucault Welles write in *#HashtagActivism: Networks of Race and Gender Justice,* "Ordinary African Americans, women, transgender people, and others aligned with racial justice and feminist causes have long been excluded from elite media spaces yet have repurposed Twitter in particular to make identity-based cultural and political demands, and in doing so have forever changed national conversations. . . . Counterpublics, the alternative networks of debate created by marginalized members of the public, thus have always played the important role of highlighting and legitimizing the experiences of those on the margins even as they push for integration and change in mainstream spaces."[67]

The evolution in cultural activism follows the metamorphosis of the entertainment industry, which simply must work with and listen to a full spectrum of diverse niche audiences to survive; the mass market is over.[68] Against this backdrop—a convergence of participatory culture, participatory politics, hashtag activism, and the entertainment industry in transition—contemporary entertainment activism is a new and evolving practice, led by dynamic social-justice groups that matured in the age of self-generated entertainment and changing media gatekeepers. They have diligently honed their ability to shape mainstream entertainment-media stories by working with Hollywood producers and writers—and crafting and distributing their own—to include lived experiences and social challenges often still invisible or overlooked in TV and film. They are working within the cultural industries, not outside them.[69]

For postmillennial activists, the participatory media age has empowered creative ways of doing cultural-representation business and new Hollywood relationships to get the job done. A formalized job title has emerged for this work: narrative or cultural strategist, often used interchangeably. As a concept, *narrative strategy* is a cultural and communication practice by which social-justice practitioners collaborate with entertainment-industry executives, writers, and producers to shape positive portrayals of marginalized communities and social issues in scripted and nonscripted entertaining narratives, critique negative portrayals, and produce and disseminate their own entertainment-storytelling content.[70] The core belief holds that entertainment storytelling is meaningful to social change in its ability to shift public opinion and perceptions—and foster cultural conversation and public participation—all of which are necessary, ultimately, for supportive policy that expands equity and justice. Entertainment narratives are seen as stories that can reinforce or disrupt troubling social norms or portrayals—and thus, narrative strategists work to create enlightening and diverse portrayals, and to dismantle damaging ones.

How are they carving their own path as creative strategists, storytellers, and activists? The most effective social-justice-activism organizations collaborate directly within the entertainment industry—including comedy—instead of primarily acting as mechanisms of pressure from the outside (even though public critique is never off the table). They have figured out, through understanding the informal norms and protocols of the entertainment business, how to position themselves directly within Hollywood's social-capital networks. Social-justice organizations that practice narrative strategy carry out one or more—sometimes all—of a series of activities: working to change the pipeline of decision-making culture creators, influencing existing storylines in big entertainment programming, developing and pitching new entertainment for mainstream entertainment-industry distribution, creating self-produced content for distribution on digital platforms, mobilizing and pressuring Hollywood to change damaging portrayals of people and social problems, and participating as visible thought leaders in entertainment-industry spaces.[71] They are seen by entertainment decision makers as full creative partners and collaborators.

Color of Change, for instance, centers "Culture Change and Media Justice" as a guiding premise that shapes its work as a Hollywood collaborator and critic, but also showcases and inspires "Black joy" through entertainment, landing the group on the *Fast Company* list of "50 Most Innovative Companies."[72] As part of its efforts, the group produces its own entertainment programming through its filmed podcast, #TellBlackStories, also distributed on YouTube and Instagram,[73] pitches original storytelling content for mainstream media distribution, and partners with Hollywood producers to create and direct social-change campaigns around entertainment, such as Ava DuVernay's award-winning Netflix series, *When They See Us*. Comedy is a part of it. In the 2020 year of uprising, when media giant ViacomCBS looked around for ways to entertain and engage the public around Juneteenth, executives turned to a creative partnership with Color of Change. On June 19, 2020, comedian Mamoudou N'Diaye took over the company's social media channels with comedy material developed through the Color of Change original comedy production, *By Us for Us*, produced in collaboration with my organization, the Center for Media & Social Impact.

In yet another nod to large-scale creative and strategy collaboration between narrative-strategy activists and the entertainment industry, the MTV Entertainment Group announced its wide-ranging Culture Code initiative—training and new programming designed to bring diverse storytellers and executives into the ViacomCBS (now Paramount Global) family of networks—at the end of 2020.[74] Activist groups, working in lockstep with entertainment executives, are the co-creators and designers: the Museum of Tolerance, Color of Change, Anti-Defamation League, Jed Foundation, MPAC, RAINN, RespectAbility, Storyline Partners, and GLAAD. "We're not doing this alone, and that's important," says Erika Soto Lamb, the social-impact executive who works across Paramount Global (formerly ViacomCBS) entertainment networks, including Comedy Central, MTV, and others. "This effort is designed to result in a changed environment for content and a shift in who creates it and what stories we're telling."[75] Outcomes are not theoretical or abstract, says Soto Lamb, when entertainment-industry power dynamics and stories change. As one illustrious example, when Hispanic shoppers were the target of a 2019 mass shooting in an El Paso Walmart, she shares, Comedy Central executives rushed to cancel an episode of the comedy sketch show *Alternatino*, a Latinx take on the millennial experience in the United States, because it dealt with gun violence.[76] The sketch, she recalls, was focused on an immigrant in an American citizenship class: "The teacher says, 'Okay, now let's talk about gun violence in America.' The immigrant character played by [the show's star] Arturo Castro says, 'Wait, so it's related to cartels, right?' He keeps asking these questions from his frame of reference, and what guns are like in South America. And the teacher has to keep saying, 'No. In the US, it's just regular people going into churches, malls, movie theaters and killing people.' It just does not compute to this immigrant character."[77]

Because Mexican American former activist Soto Lamb worked inside the network in a decision-making role, she recognized the power

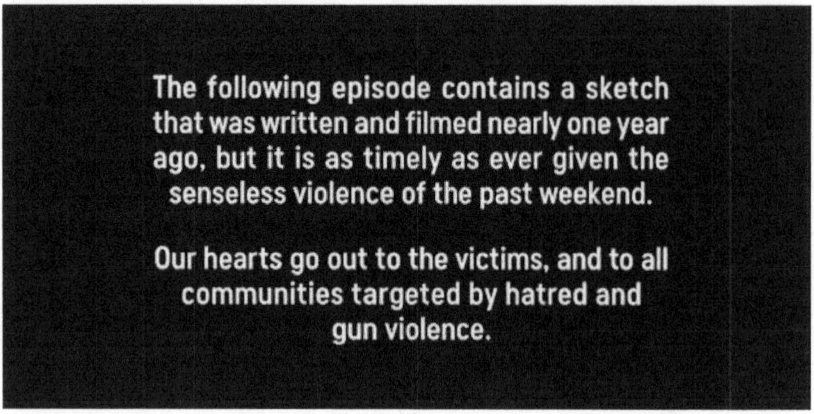

The following episode contains a sketch that was written and filmed nearly one year ago, but it is as timely as ever given the senseless violence of the past weekend.

Our hearts go out to the victims, and to all communities targeted by hatred and gun violence.

Figure 3.1: Screenshot: opening graphic for the "Welcome to America" episode of *Alternatino* on Comedy Central

of entertainment and comedy to address gun violence from an immigrant Latino perspective, which was sorely needed in that moment, she thought. With Soto Lamb's guidance within Comedy Central, the episode aired, and comedian Arturo Castro wrote an article for the *Washington Post* and spoke out on CNN and MSNBC.[78] As Soto Lamb recalls, this moment is indicative of how change manifests in a tangible way: "It became something that the company was really proud of—a recognition that what happened there was a toxic combination of both hate in America and easy access to guns that resulted in that tragedy. That sketch could have been fully scrubbed without someone who understood the experience from different perspectives."[79] Two diverse individuals—the comedian and the entertainment executive—worked together to make it happen.

In 2021, Creative Artists Agency (CAA), one of the most powerful entertainment talent agencies in the business, launched the Full Story initiative in partnership with its foundation, designed to "generate authentic narratives in television and film for a more equitable future" and spotlight marginalized creative storytellers and social issues.[80] Its creative partners? Activist groups like the ACLU, GLAAD, Color of Change, Everytown for Gun Safety, CAPE (Coalition of Asian Pacifics in Entertainment), IllumiNative, and Amnesty International.[81] Here is the key element: CAA will work with its activist colleagues not only to find and develop diverse storytellers but to source the stories from within their communities. It is unprecedented. And there are also the lists—the original Black List, expanded to inspire the Muslim List, the Indigenous List, the Latinx TV List—that spotlight overlooked entertainment stories by diverse creators, fueled by social-justice organizations now considered full members of the Hollywood ecosystem and its unwritten norms of social capital.[82]

Together, this is the cultural social-justice long game: changing the entertainment industry pipeline to lift up and ensure the success of historically marginalized storytellers, shifting on-screen portrayals of people who have been dehumanized or erased, and creating and distributing entertainment content produced from inside activist groups and the communities they represent. It is not always fast change, but it is also not invisible or marginal. As comedy producer and executive Josh Church (Apatow Productions) puts it, "Activism is essential to help Hollywood continue to move forward because without the activists pushing, it's so easy for gatekeepers to go back to historically what they thought worked before."[83] Veteran producer Deniese Davis adds, "Activism is challenging the system and the most glaring issues that, quite honestly, have been able to be swept under the rug or covered up or not really talked about in mainstream media. . . . In the era of social media, people are saying, 'We're not going to just sit around for this. We will band together and we will find ways to fight for what we feel like is right.' The fight is about challenging the system to change and be more modern to reflect the world that we currently live in."[84]

Activism for representation and justice, in small and big ways, is firmly embedded within the entertainment-industry revolution and ultimately, the images, stories, people, dreams, and worlds that will amuse us and make us think—sometimes differently than we did before.

. . . . .

Shrewd contemporary cultural activists are legitimate collaborators within the entertainment business; this is somewhat distinct from earlier antagonistic Hollywood activism that relied heavily on boycotts and letter-writing campaigns. As a GLAAD strategist put it, "We no longer have to scream at the front door; instead, we are being invited in through the back door."[85] The savviest narrative-change strategists and activists are seen by Hollywood producers, writers, and executives as essential partners in the business of creating authentic entertainment that appeals to a full range of audiences. To be sure, the industry as a whole is not necessarily motivated by a burst of moral consciousness (even if, on an individual level, this is often true) but rather by smart business savvy in the face of social media and other public dissent that can make or break a show. There is also the omnipresent real danger of vocal, visible pressure moments evaporating into performative activism at best; as Kristen Marston notes, "It's interesting that Black Lives Matter only became cool for some people during the summer [of 2020], which is disturbing."[86]

For their part, collaborative relationships aside, social-justice groups also know full well that playing nice is not their only possible path. Mobilizing organized public dissent is a threat they can employ at any moment—and the entertainment industry gets it. Collective, vocal, visible outrage is still effective. Women, people of color, the disability community, and queer folks are vocal about their erasure or mistreatment in entertainment; silencing them while conducting business as usual is not a task that Hollywood can manage effectively in the wild, open chaos of the social media landscape. As Sue Obeidi memorably puts it, "Today, if a TV show has a Muslim character praying, and she's praying all wrong, you're going to be called out on Muslim Twitter."[87]

How does this backdrop matter when it comes to entertainment that spotlights the hilarious lived experiences of comedians with something to say about injustice? Between their increasing creative skill as entertainment storytellers and strategic know-how as advocates, the culture-focused social-justice activists have positioned themselves as Hollywood insiders, partners, and peers. And from collaboration comes co-creation, a merger of entertainment artistic process and social-change strategy. Comedy, given the universal affection for it in the marketplace and the entertainment business—and the increasing value of humor for social-justice groups who see its ability to cut through polarized divisions and capture widespread attention—is the fresh opportunity. Making co-creation happen, though, is not necessarily an automatic reflex on the part of comedians or social-justice activists. In the next chapters, we travel into the adventures of intentionally bringing comedy and social justice together as both entertainment and activism.

4

"You Learn to Be Racist from People You Love"

Co-creating Comedy for Antiracism Public Engagement

When comedian Corey Ryan Forrester—homegrown son and lifelong resident of Bible-Belt Georgia's northern parts—heard about the lesbian couple in his community who couldn't find a preacher to marry them, his initial response was not shock. "Yeah, I mean, that checks out. I don't know what they thought," he said to himself at the time.[1] After all, he lives in a region made famous by a few notable personalities: the redneck good ol' boys of *The Dukes of Hazzard*, who raced around the backwoods of 1980s TV in a Confederate-flag-painted hot rod called "the General Lee"; and Congresswoman Marjorie Taylor Greene, the bigotry-spewing politician who arrived on Capitol Hill in a cloud of racist, homophobic commentary and far-right conspiracy theories.[2]

But he kept mulling it over. "I'd had a couple of beers, and the thought kind of came across my mind, like, huh, if they're a lesbian couple in my area, there's probably a good chance that I know them. And then I thought, well, you know what, I don't know who it is, but I'm going to try and make this right." A few Facebook and Twitter posts later, and the word was out: "I just said, look, if you're gay and you're in my area and you are struggling with a place [to get married], I've got a pretty yard, you can come over here and I'll marry you." Timing didn't work with the original couple, but others were interested. Corey Forrester, newly ordained internet preacher,[3] was all in: "I was so excited. I was like, 'Okay, how many people are going to be here? I'll make some quiche.'" Eventually, he officiated the union of an older lesbian couple in his living room—one of the women hooked up to an oxygen tank—fulfilling their wish after decades together.

Should we be surprised by this story about a southern-born-and-bred comedian like Forrester—with his Coors trucker hat and deep affection for all things WWE (World Wrestling Entertainment, Inc.) and University of Georgia "Dawgs" football? It is tempting, maybe. But not if we listen carefully to his comedy, and not if we strive to resist a binary, reductive view of humans and their motivations, a task surely made more difficult in divisive political times. And then there is the thick southern drawl: that detail can be the trickiest. It triggers all kinds of assumptions about ignorance and racism, Forrester says. But a few things he has known practically his whole life: comedy is his thing, and so is a streak of radical independence and impulse to push hard against entrenched bigotry and rote thinking. He loves the Deep South—the food, folkways, football, music, beer, whiskey, weather—but he wants it to be better. His comedy is fertilized in this place and its cultural specificity, rich with possibility born of absurdity and hypocrisy, carefully peppered with social criticism and pointed corrections of racism and homophobia. Even conservative southerners trust him at some level, he says, and this is key:

> From my earliest comedy days, I knew that I had something that I want to say and I know that I inherently want to shock people. And the way to shock people where I'm from would be to say things that go against the Bible and straight, White, heterosexual . . . but then I also had to be very mindful. I'm like, okay dude, but you have to talk about all these things in a way that will not get your ass kicked. Which means, number one, it's got to be funny. It's *got* to be funny. . . . People down here are like, "Oh, hell yeah, Corey. He thinks different than we do, but he's still funny."

From the beginning of his paying stand-up comedy career at age sixteen, Forrester has gleefully played with subversive social-justice commentary, even if he doesn't use those exact words. His comedy is designed to shock, as he says, but also to enlighten, joke by joke. It is an intentional approach: "I'm a fucking renegade down here. People just don't talk about this shit like this. . . . I can make these points as long as I don't talk down to people. So I always try to flip the joke back on me and use the 'we are so stupid,' not 'you all are so stupid.' Because at the end of the day I've still got this Georgia accent and I'm still one of y'all and that's how I've been able to play with it." Comedy is the sneaky Trojan horse he trots out to audiences:

> I remember the first big type of joke like this that I did was when "Don't Ask, Don't Tell" was still a thing. I had this joke that I would do always at the end of my set, and it was about how ridiculous I thought it was that gay people couldn't be in the military. Basically the punch of it was like this: I'm on one knee pretending like I'm in a foxhole, and I'm like, "Just imagine this scenario, you're sitting in a foxhole, bullets are flying past your head, bombs are going off everywhere. You can barely hear, there's that moment where it's like the scene from *Saving Private Ryan*. And you see one of your buddies, and you look at him, and you grab him by the face and you go, 'Bill, I'm so scared, but I sure could suck your dick right now if you'd let me.'" And of course, everybody laughed, and in that one tiny moment they were like, "That is ridiculous, that would never happen." When I did that joke to a majority conservative crowd, almost every time I would have dudes come up to me after the show and be like, "Man, I never thought about it that way."

In 2016, Forrester's career took off with fresh energy when he joined forces with fellow southern comedians, Trae "The Liberal Redneck" Crowder and Drew Morgan, to coauthor *The Liberal Redneck Manifesto: Draggin' Dixie outta the Dark*. The book has been described as "whip-smart, hilarious, and incisive . . . The Liberal Rednecks are lifelong, down-home Southern boys who aren't afraid to call out the outdated traditions and intolerant attitudes of their native land—while also shining a proud light on the most misunderstood region of the country. Their mission: to provide a manifesto for young progressives south of the Mason-Dixon line to rise up and claim their homeland—without abandoning the best of their culture."[4] The book was a hit, and the WellRED Comedy Tour was born: three self-described rednecks popping up all over the country with their hilarious southern stories and take-downs of homophobia, bigotry, and hypocrisy.

Between the stand-up gigs, the book, and TV writing opportunities, things were going well. And then, the COVID-19 pandemic arrived. Comedy shows were sidelined for the foreseeable future. Forrester fought a wave of depression while he tried to adjust to a temporary life without live audiences and touring, his life blood. He had to imagine his comedy away from a stand-up stage. "I wanted to figure out an angle to talk about depression and to kind of break the stigma of men, especially Southern men maybe, talking about depression. So, I had this idea for a series called Wrestling with My Emotions." He played around with draping his professional wrestling belt over his shoulder, a gift from wrestling referee "Super Dave" aka "Pond Water Dave," and speaking directly to his iPhone camera as in a classic wrestling challenge. His creative lens was wide open: maybe he wouldn't end up talking only about depression—all kinds of topics and observations were possible through this new character he called "The Buttercream Dream," an affectionate send-up of professional wrestling and a wacky southern persona who comments on the minutiae of daily life, but also current affairs and injustice. Forrester's first comedic sketch video, the debut of the Buttercream Dream, hit Twitter in June 2020. It was a viral success, and to be sure, no one was more surprised than Forrester himself: "I'd never really made a video. I have never been a video guy and now I can't deny the fact that I'm definitely a video guy, you know?"

Other comedians took notice. In 2021, fellow funny person and fan Leslie Jones invited him onto the MTV Movie & TV Awards to perform a bit as the Buttercream Dream. On May 16, 2021, less than a year after he appeared as a character on Twitter, the Buttercream Dream made his official TV debut. Audiences loved him. Buttercream Dream resonates broadly because he is funny, but he hits close to home because he is such a recognizable kind of character to millions of southern WWE fans, including those who are not necessarily seeking social commentary about mental health, racism, politics. "When I do the Buttercream Dream character," says Forrester, "nobody goes, 'He must hate wrestling, because he made fun of them.' No, they're like, 'This guy fucking loves wrestling, that's why the character's good and that's why he does it well, because it's a celebration of it.'"

On the surface, it would be easy to regard Corey Ryan Forrester as merely a talented entertainer, doing his thing on the stand-up tour circuit, making TV appearances, writing TV pilots. It is true, of course, but we might miss a bigger truth if we stopped there. We might obscure the bigger potential in Forrester's comedy and the audiences he can reach, given his thoughtful strategic approach to humorously nudging new thinking in and about a region that feels maligned and misunderstood—the opposite of a TED Talk, he says:

> If you sign up for a comedy show, you're going to see a comedy show and then, boom, here we go, we're hitting you with this. None of those people are going to sign up for a TED talk that says, "We're discussing critical race theory." They're going to be like, "Yeah, pass. I'm out." But if you're a comedian and you go up there and you find a way to talk about it, then they'll be like, "Well, we're already here and we liked the first joke about how he was lactose intolerant, and I disagree, but okay, I agree with that part, that was kind of funny. Damn, that was funny too, holy shit."

In the summer of 2021, Forrester and his Buttercream Dream tackled structural, systemic racism and the particular cultural realities that can make this topic painful and delicate to broach in the American South and well beyond. What follows is the journey of how and why that came to be, through the Comedy ThinkTanks model of co-creation comedy for subversive public engagement—a gathering that brings together diverse, multiracial comedy talents and social-justice organizations to work together for the first time. At the heart of creating comedy is a radically open process for innovation, which matters a great deal in contemporary creative social-justice work in the participatory media age. Through the following pages, I welcome readers backstage into an immersive understanding of and appreciation for the inside experience of making comedy, and the ways in which an open artistic process, a diverse spectrum of comedy minds, and subject-matter experts—all infused with elements of radical play—can combine to create hilarious new ways to look at old, persistent challenges.

"I Want All of Your Terrible Ideas": Harnessing Innovation and Play to Create Comedy for Social Change

"I was a thirty-year-old babysitter," says multihyphenate comedy writer, performer, and producer Bethany Hall. "I remember turning thirty and thinking, 'Every decision that I've made has brought me to becoming a babysitter in my third decade.'"[5] It is not entirely accurate, but then again, every comedy person has a day job (or three) on the hustle. For a while, Bethany's happened to include a nanny gig, but she was also a performer on Tina Fey's hit NBC show *30 Rock* and a regular cast member of *The Chris Gethard Show* (where she met and married a fellow comedian known to the audience as Bananaman). In the daylight hours, she worked in the communication department of a billion-dollar foundation, Atlantic Philanthropies, and by night, she sprinted over to the *Gethard Show* to play and dance and improvise with a wacky ensemble of comically misfit toys. On the weekends, she worked on her own comedy writing. And so it goes for most comedy writers and performers on the rise. But Bethany's motivations, sparked by professed childhood aspirations to become both a comedian and a minister, are a little different: her other passion is social justice. Her worlds were colliding, day by day:

> I've always wanted to leave my fingerprint on the world. I want to try to leave the world a little bit of a gentler place. That has always been really important to me. . . . It came very naturally that these worlds of social justice and comedy were merging just actively in my life, on a day-to-day basis, because I would jump from the Gethard show to a meeting with Caring Across Generations the next day to trying to write a report on undocumented folk in California, and then back to set the next day.

Bethany and I crossed paths in 2016 at a pivotal time for both of us: I was spending a lot of my time writing and publishing research about comedy and social change, but I was wholly uninterested in parking that knowledge on a virtual or physical shelf to collect dust. Wearing my producer and strategist hats, I had the goal of encouraging social-change communicators, strategists, and justice movements to consider using comedy in their work. It was slow going. I found myself giving passionate, research-based talks to various organizations, where the inevitable comedy-killing question would come from the audience: How do you control the comedy or make it safe? Clearly, my research alone was not convincing enough, because comedy still felt scary and risky to people. Even open-minded, creative social-change professionals were not sure how to collaborate with comedy writers and performers, or even how to find them. And many definitely did not know how to enable the radically open artistic ideation process comedy needs in order to breathe and find hilarious and creative new way of seeing. In the few exceptions to the rule where comedy and social justice had somehow collided intentionally (as in a public service announcement or a comedian acting as an attention-grabbing stunt for a charity fundraiser, for example), the humor often felt flat and controlled. I call it "conference room comedy," manufactured far too carefully in a room of serious people dictating the creative rules of engagement to comedians, rather than the other way around. Something was missing in the process.

Around the same time, Bethany was completing a successful run of *Thanksgiving*, an eight-episode ensemble comedy she created and executive-produced with Dan Powell (producer of *Inside Amy Schumer* and *Sarah Cooper: Everything's Fine*).[6] As luck or the arc of the universe would have it, we met at one of my public talks in 2016. We bonded immediately over the irresistible prospect of bringing comedians and social-justice organizations together in some way—to help them find one another and learn how to collaborate and, ultimately, to spark an entirely new cross-sector body of work in subversive comedy that could be watched and shared and remembered. Her vantage point as a comedy writer and performer was delightfully different from mine, and she brought something new to the thinking: the insight that comedians were ready and willing and excited to do social-good work, but they didn't know how to go about it. So much opportunity lurked in that reality— and thinking about how to solve it.

Two years and many stories later, Bethany became the first-ever creative director of Comedy Initiatives at the Center for Media & Social Impact, and we got to work creating comedian-architected programs to bring our research to life. In true comedy style, sometimes we bombed. We toiled away on some early ideas that stuck, and some that didn't. We embraced failure and the chance to learn. For comedy and social-change collaborations to work *and* expand, it became clear that the "doing" was the missing piece. Talking about these ideas was not enough. Demos were needed. How could we get comedy people and serious social-justice people to play with one another and learn from it? That was the key.

From Bethany's comedy experience and deep personal motivations, along with our shared recognition of the challenges inherent in getting comedy people and social-justice people learning to trust and work in harmony, the Comedy ThinkTanks model for comedy co-creation was born as a "co-creation workshop initiative that pairs professional comedians and social justice organizations to create entertaining comedy to spark public engagement in social issues."[7] The foundational ideals within the process borrow from the best traditions of a comedy writers' room and the science of creativity and innovation—specifically, comedy's devotion to wild play and embracing failure to generate ideas, which requires (and enables) a very open artistic space; diversity of lived experiences as key to the creativity; and co-creation principles that include expert facilitation and a shared mission and contributions from each person.

Through Hall's skillful direction as lead writer and facilitator, and ability to "speak natively" to comedy writers and performers, this kind of open workshop approach provides a safe, artistic environment for social-justice leaders and comedians to shape new comedy that can engage and mobilize people in weighty social problems. For a week or more, comedians will absorb the gravity—sad statistics, dire facts, and stories from lived experience—of the given challenge. And social-justice advocates will agree to suppress any hesitation about comedy's unpredictable deviance, following a path of humorous creative power. It is a bargain we strike at the beginning to make sure our creative sketchpad is a wide-open zone for learning and play. The communal task: find an artistic, entertaining way to communicate an issue fraught with pain and trauma. And make it funny. The comedians and social-justice experts collaborate in "directed creativity," known in creativity and innovation science as "the deliberate mental action needed to produce novel ideas in targeted areas . . . by action-bent people who need to get something done."[8]

In a collaborative comedy-generation process, we heed principles of co-creation practiced in participatory documentary and community media—that is, building a shared multi-author space for story collaboration. During the course of this specialized writers' room experience, the comedians are directed through a series of open-sky creative brainstorm exercises designed to unlock new ways of talking about the social-justice realities shared by the collaborating organization. There are characters, sketch ideas, one-liners, jokes, movie ideas, "this reminds me of that one time . . ." story snippets, laughing over shared experiences and new ones. Bethany, as facilitator and director of the creative experience—acting akin to a head writer in a TV writing room—carefully guides them from one task to the next, moving from solo contributions and writing to several days of group collaboration, where comedians work together to punch up jokes, write scripts, and flesh out ideas. All of it centers the insights they have gained from invited social-justice leaders and issue subject-matter experts. In other words, the final comedy embeds facts, challenges, and information from the activists, even as the humor is protected from the potential weight of it all.

Co-creation protocol ensures that ideas are heard and embraced by multiple members of the curated team; a horizontal process for generating ideas is favored over a top-down or single-author approach, even while a trusted guide moves the creators through assignments and expectations to provide structure.[9] And we are making comedy, after all, so we are adding a distinct complicating layer onto ideals of co-creation that largely originate from documentary and community media practices. It is easy for comedy about social justice to become didactic and boring, which renders it useless. The comedy must be funny, not sacrificing humor for shared factual information and framing. It is a no-judgment zone, all ideas are welcome, and nothing is off limits on the way to arriving somewhere palatable for public consumption: "I want all of your terrible ideas" is Bethany's standard opening line at the beginning of a new workshop room.

In this scenario—a collaboration between social-justice activists and issue experts and comedians—we trust and give space for the disparate "sectors," even as they work together, to do what they do best: issue experts provide the facts and deep insights, and comedians create the comedy. This is a key point and worth emphasizing: comedians have full creative reign here, and this is part of the innovation. It is tempting for serious advocates to get nervous about comedy along the way, and the urge to "control" or "hold back" the comedy stops the innovation—and the truly funny material—from taking place. In this environment, constructed to engender trust, each sector gets to absorb and take on the other role: comedians become crash-course issue experts who find play in the somber facts, and the social-justice advocates are creatively empowered to imagine and find absurdity alongside the artists. In this way, we combine the wild-idea-generation open space of comedy improv and the shared-vision practices of participatory documentary media. Together, they work with a shared mission and goal for the outcome: truly hilarious, subversive comedy that includes embedded factual information from the subject-matter experts, shaped primarily by the diverse lived experiences of the creative people.

At the end of the week-long co-creative writers' room experience, the comedians pitch their final comedy ideas to their social-justice partners, just as they would pitch a sitcom idea to a TV network. Together, they choose which ideas to produce and distribute via social media and YouTube, and which ones to develop further and pitch to the formal entertainment business as TV projects. In the participatory media age, after all, the reality of self-distribution and Hollywood's more frequent (and willing) creative collaborations with activists opens a full range of possibilities for where and how the final comedy projects (videos, TV show ideas, campaigns) can be disseminated.

Why and how does this kind of approach to creative comedy collaboration with activists seem to work so effectively? We use theory and science from arenas of creativity, innovation, and play to build and explain. The dominant concept is this: creativity lies at the heart of comedy, and it needs careful nurturing. Creativity, simply put, requires an open, nonjudgmental space in which to play, and yet, "play" is not necessarily the process employed by social-change strategists and communicators who carefully craft message-tested language for public consumption. "Creative ideas thrive on openness of thought," according to creativity research.[10] To shape material that sparks laughter and provokes public curiosity, comedians employ unbridled creative process and play to foster innovative thinking. In turn, such thinking disrupts the status quo precisely because the humorous lens with which to see reality can be simultaneously so true and yet unexpected (not to mention outrageous). Comedians are divergent, deviant thinkers, uniquely suited to find an untrodden path into an old problem. They flex muscles of imagination to create their art, but also to invite the audience to play along, imagining with them. And imagination, as renowned "play theorist" Bernard De Koven explains, "offers us the ability to connect compassionately. It helps us understand and relate to other people's lives and loves, regardless of social strata, ethnic inheritances, physical or mental abilities. . . . It is a gift that restores us to the best of our humanity."[11] Ultimately, as he writes, "It is in these infinite playgrounds, in the very nature of infinite playthings—in the things we make up, pretend, imagine—that we play with the powers of the soul."[12]

To generate the incongruent ideas at the heart of humor, comedians work from a place of possibility, not fear or limits.[13]

Comedians adhere to consistent motivations, values, and ideals in their artistic work: creatively deviant thinking, unfettered and open-minded space, and more recently (and ideally), co-creation with a diverse ensemble. Improv comedy, the backbone and training system for so many other mediated comedy genres (notably including sketch, sitcoms, and even satirical news), is based on seven core principles: "Yes, and" (the additive and open creative process that builds on ideas rather than stopping them), ensemble, co-creation, authenticity, failure, "follow the follower" (shared "leadership" in a creative process to allow the best ideas, regardless of hierarchy), and listening.[14] While precise habits of individual comedians vary, of course, this framework is the heart of comedy's creative process.

Why might all of this be relevant to shaping an equitable world? It matters because deviant creativity and play, and unusual, divergent ways of seeing are essential elements of innovation, which powers social progress. Comedy is a manifestation and expression of these ideas. Across disciplines and sectors of contemporary life, creativity is attributed to innovation and problem solving—the act of creating is the business of conjuring the new: "Creativity is a process involving the generation of new ideas or concepts, or new associations between existing ideas or concepts, and their substantiation into a product that has novelty and originality."[15] Ideas germinated by creative process are, therefore, originals—totally fresh and unexpected,[16] as well as surprising and valuable.[17] Forms of creativity vary, but all focus on finding what is new and unexpected, including "making unfamiliar combinations of familiar ideas," "exploring conceptual spaces," and "transforming the space."[18] The stakes are high: "Creativity, or the generation of novel ideas, is essential to our survival as a species."[19] An unrestrained exchange of ideas, or seeing without limits, is vitally important to this continuance.[20]

Beyond celebrating creative artifacts that delight and entertain us, comedy is meaningful because it fuels innovation—new methods, new ways of thinking, new material things. Traditional, somber thinking alone does not power innovation: "There are limits to traditional analytical thinking when it comes to solving nagging problems or generating breakthrough ideas. What we need, it seems, is the ability to be analytical when the situation calls for it and creative when the situation calls for that. Both skills are critical for success."[21] Playing it safe, or doing only what has been done before, is the opposite of new thinking and innovation, a force incited by creativity.[22] Comedians are motivated precisely by these ideals. The new way of thinking generated by comedy is necessary also as a counter to existing media reflections.

Individual creative minds also matter here. Creativity, while inherent in all humans at a base level, is stronger in some people than others. As pathbreaking creativity psychologist J. P. Guilford put it, "Individuals with recognized creative talent simply have 'more of what all of us have.'"[23] Within the complex span of human intelligence, there is a commonality among these supercharged creative people, and it does not come from upbringing or educational opportunities or other such predictors, but instead, from an innate way of looking and thinking. Highly creative people possess a greater ability to use and exhibit "divergent thinking," which leads to originality.[24] They literally think and see differently; divergent thinking is a special skill. Characteristics of divergent thinking that connect with creativity include "*fluency* (the ability to produce great number of ideas or problem solutions in a short period of time); *flexibility* (the ability to simultaneously propose a variety of approaches to a specific problem); *originality* (the ability to produce new, original ideas); *elaboration* (the ability to systematize and organize the details of an idea in a head and carry it out)."[25]

Following these principles, comedians are what I call "creatively deviant" thinkers—not only do they possess divergent thinking skills, clearly apparent in the unexpectedness and incongruence of funny material and jokes, but they take this idea one step further. Creative deviance, an explicit departure from the norm, requires the ability and desire to see things differently, and to do so in ways that also delight and amuse other people—an incredibly tricky task both in the process of making comedy and in the final outcome of audience laughter. In a successful comedy writers' room, Sasha Stewart (*The Nightly Show with Larry Wilmore*), for instance, sees the creative deviance of "yes, and" as essential to the process and final material:

> I'll come in with my prepared pitch, and what can be really fun is if the room really responds to your pitch and then starts to joke on top of your

jokes and say, "What if we had Michael in a bear suit?" What, oh my gosh, now he's in a bear suit. And then he's holding a bunch of tampons. And then, oh my gosh, we rain tampons from the ceiling. This is an actual skit that we did on *The Nightly Show* once. And then tampons are raining down from the ceiling and then suddenly it's a tampon parade and now it's a period parade. We're all having so much fun.[26]

Certain conditions help foster creativity: the ability to conjure and share open thoughts; working in a climate of open-mindedness, not a controlling environment with proscribed notions about precise outcomes; often (but not always) as a part of group collaboration, particularly when that co-creative experience includes a full diversity of life experiences and vantage points.[27] All modes of creative thinking require focused *attention* (on the thing being created or the problem being solved with creativity), the ability to *escape* one's present thinking patterns, and constant *movement* and exploration of various thoughts.[28] What creativity needs, then, is the ability to explore, to imagine wild new ideas without boundaries, and, often, to connect with others in the process. Creativity needs the ability, in other words, to play, because "play is disruptive . . . disrupting the normal state of affairs."[29] Play is "both escape and engagement,"[30] and "through play, we experience the world, we construct it and we destroy it, and explore who we are and what we can say. Play frees us from moral conventions but makes them still present, so we are aware of their weight, presence, and importance."[31]

And finally, often overlooked, and yet central to comedy collaborations, diversity and diverse thinking in creativity are vital. These are essential ingredients of creativity and innovation. Even as TV comedy writers' rooms remain notoriously challenged when it comes to including a broad spectrum of writers—women, BIPOC, disability community, queer, among others, still left on the margins far too often—diversity is vital to fostering the kind of creativity that leads to breakthrough ideas in group process.[32] At some level, it should be obvious: if the same brains and lived experiences are generating and reconfiguring all of the ideas over and over again, how innovative can we really be?

Imagination, open space, and silliness are invited into the room when comedians co-create with each other and social-justice thinkers. They have explicit permission to play. These are concepts that comedy people understand well, even though overt play and silliness (at work! during the day!) can feel new or possibly uncomfortable for noncomedy folks at first. For Noam Schuster, a peace activist turned popular stand-up comedian in the United States and Israel, the jokes come from play and interaction with a live audience: "With every audience, I have a little bit of a different dynamic and maybe the jokes will come in a new order because of the way that the conversation will happen. Staying playful for me personally, it is the best. . . . I'm playing games, moving jokes, discovering new ones while I'm playing."[33] Acceptance and open space matter, says Prashanth Venkataramanujam, head writer and showrunner for *Patriot Act with Hasan Minhaj*: "Joking is making an attempt to form a connection, to form a bond. . . . But if [comedy writers] are too self-conscious or if you've tightened up the room or made them feel self-conscious, you've snuffed out any future opportunity for that."[34] Ultimately, as theorist De Koven reminds us, through the process of play, "the things we can imagine can become the world."[35]

And here is where we return to Corey Ryan Forrester and his proclivity for using his sneaky, subversive, disarming comedy to poke a stick at racism and homophobia. With these ideas in mind about comedy's inner workings and possibilities, what might happen if we invited him in—along with other professional comedy folks with different lived experiences, racial backgrounds, and vantage points—to work intentionally in antiracism work from a social-justice perspective? A group of co-conspirators and I—comedy people and social-justice people—decided to find out.

Leveraging Culture and Creativity in Racial-Equity Work

Mitch Landrieu is part of a royal political family in the Deep South, the son of beloved former New Orleans mayor Moon Landrieu and brother of former US senator Mary Landrieu of Louisiana. His notoriety breached southern borders during his own stint as New Orleans's mayor from 2010 to 2018. He was steeped in the aftermath of Hurricane Katrina in 2005 when he served as Louisiana's lieutenant governor; as mayor, he inherited the disastrous 2010 BP oil spill. His trademark style works well in those parts—blunt, direct, friendly, colorful, a storyteller—and he spent his time in office with a dogged focus on uniting a divided, wounded city. As he toiled from one challenge to the next, meeting after meeting made it clear that race and racial reconciliation were central to every aspect of building and rebuilding—the very heart of it. Pretending not to see the trauma of the past and present was a nonstarter.

In 2017, New Orleans became one of the first cities in the country to remove Confederate statues and monuments from its streets and public squares, a move proposed by Landrieu and cemented by a city council vote a few years prior.[36] He called the statues part of a long-standing American tradition of racial terrorism, erected after the Civil War to reinforce White supremacy and racial control, operating at the same level as burning crosses on lawns. Confronting hard truths and pain, in his mind, is essential to building a path to real progress, as he said in his speech as the last statue was removed:

> New Orleans is truly a city of many nations, a melting pot, a bubbling caldron of many cultures. There is no other place quite like it in the world that so eloquently exemplifies the uniquely American motto: e pluribus unum—out of many we are one. But there are also other truths about our city that we must confront. New Orleans was America's largest slave market: a port where hundreds of thousands of souls were bought, sold and shipped up the Mississippi River to lives of forced labor, of misery, of rape, of torture. America was the place where nearly 4000 of our fellow citizens were lynched, 540 alone in Louisiana; where the courts enshrined "separate but equal"; where Freedom riders coming to New Orleans were beaten to a bloody pulp. So when people say to me that the monuments in question are history, well what I just described is real history as well, and it is the searing truth. . . . It is our acknowledgment that now is the time to take stock of, and then move past, a painful part of our history.[37]

The monument effort arose, in part, from extensive cross-racial networking and community-engagement work Landrieu and his team launched from within New Orleans City Hall. They came to refer to their efforts as "a racial equity agenda," and the deeper in they went, the more they learned and observed, recalls Ryan Berni, a key member of Landrieu's team: "This started with a project called the Welcome Table, which was community-based groups, people, individuals, organizations, meeting and just talking about having a safe place to talk about race and problems in their community and then working to address a problem with a creative project."[38] It was clear, says Berni, that inviting people to really talk and hear one another was key, and so was working across racial lines as allies—hard grassroots labor, neighborhood by neighborhood.

Inspired by progress from the perch of City Hall, Landrieu knew he wanted to build upon the city's racial-equity efforts after he left office. And to be sure, New Orleans is not unique in its particular experience with racial trauma; states across the Deep South face the continued legacy of slavery and Jim Crow. In 2018, Landrieu founded a new racial-justice nonprofit advocacy organization designed to reach across southern states: E Pluribus Unum (EPU), "out of many, one," was founded, according to its mission statement, "with the premise that we must confront the issue of race head-on if we are to move forward."[39] And as perhaps only a born-and-bred southerner can do, Landrieu located the South as a particular target for intervention, given its unique role in upholding the institution of slavery, as EPU's founding documents make clear: "We cannot break down the barriers of race and class as a divided nation. We can only fulfill America's promise of justice and opportunity if we are united. This work begins in the South, where we have seen the darkest side of America's history."[40]

Landrieu and his E Pluribus Unum staff and advisors knew they were embarking on a complicated obstacle course in a political climate that seemed increasingly divisive by the day. For two years, they hit the road, visiting upwards of thirty vastly different communities across thirteen states across the Deep South, talking to more than a thousand people in interviews, focus groups, and community gatherings, and in countless follow-up conversations held to dig in even more. They wanted to get underneath the polite talk and feeling of taboo—but also the well-meaning tendency toward color-blindness espoused by progressive White folks in the region—to learn what it would take to build a future founded on racial healing and equity, to shape a new American South (and well beyond into other regions of the country that are certainly not immune to the legacy of America's original sin). Even the word "racism," in this political and cultural moment, was sensitive, they learned; on the one hand, people of color shared story after story about their daily lived experiences with structural racism and a system built upon it, but on the other, White people were often defensive and confused about their own complicity and concepts like systemic racism. As EPU's managing director, Scott Hutcheson, wryly recalls, "We met with so many people who said they 'know a racist person,' but would you believe we didn't meet a single racist in all of these focus groups?"[41]

At the end of their exploration, key themes were evident: harnessing the power of creative culture and narrative was going to be essential in the team's multiyear efforts to build racial equity in the American South. As Berni puts it, "The overarching theme is that we are divided by design, and if we are to be reunited, one of the things we have to do is find places where we can come together more often." And, according to EPU's internal campaign-strategy document, "One of the most common recurring themes in our research was the lack of truth in narrative around the vestiges and lasting impact of slavery, Jim Crow, and segregation, and the actual weaponization by White southerners of narratives around people of color in the South."[42] Among the core conclusions that guide EPU's strategy: "Southern Whites have long used myth and misinformation to suppress or deny social and economic mobility for people of color, particularly African Americans. These false narratives allow many White people in the south to avoid the truth and to feel better about their personal racism and bias."[43] The most essential target audience in this particular ally work, they concluded, is White people, given that "they and the institutions they created are the holders of most of the misinformation and untruths." There is work to be done in moving them out of their natural comfort zones to talk and listen—to reach people without judgment, to find new ways to get past echo chambers where like-minded folks likely have not agitated or challenged their own often deep-seated family perspectives about race. But how?

When the E Pluribus Unum team reached out to us at the end of 2020, beleaguered by the pandemic but ready to keep moving forward, they were open to new ideas. They had never tried to incorporate comedy into their multicultural antiracism efforts, but they had a strong hunch it might help nudge past the entrenched defensiveness and sensitivity expressed by passive White audiences. Our team was up to the task, and we felt equally passionately about EPU's motivations to incorporate multiracial organizing and allyship into building an antiracist future. But how would we pull this off in the middle of the pandemic, with a shuttered entertainment industry and elusive vaccine? No one was traveling anywhere anytime soon, much less coming together on a tight and sweaty production set.

Necessity, of course, is the mother of invention, and the COVID-19 crisis sparked all kinds of new creativity among comedians—and inspired millions of bored, stressed-out people to laugh at and share whatever it was that funny people were willing to make. SNL released Zoom-filmed sketches, Jimmy Fallon played around in his car with his kids and wife as his production crew, and comedians like Corey Forrester—touring stand-up comics who had never really thought about video—experimented and unwittingly fueled the development of an entirely new genre: front-facing comedy. With distribution platforms like Twitter, TikTok, and Instagram at their disposal—and plenty of unexpected time on their hands—comedians grabbed their iPhones and started playing around with characters and satire, performing directly to camera at close range (à la "front-facing").[44] Those with a natural knack for characters and quick scenarios—and finding the extra silliness in a particular kind of editing—found viral success immediately, including funny women like Sarah Cooper, Blaire Erskine, Rachel Wenistky, and Alyssa Limperis, who wrote and filmed front-facing character sketches with shocking rapidity; as journalist Clare Martin wrote for *Paste* magazine in 2020, front-facing comedy is its own art form, but clearly also a pretty decent strategy for comedians to remind audiences (and network development executives) that they are still here: "It's clear these comedians create these videos not with the sole aim of garnering a larger audience—though it has, in Wenitsky's words, become a 'calling card' of sorts—but mostly because it's just another way of being funny . . . a medium that also brings the viewer and the performer closer in an unexpected way."[45]

Much in the same way viral spreading happens with a poignant or particularly funny clip from satirical news shows like *The Daily Show* or *Full Frontal with Samantha Bee*, millions view and share the best of the front-facing comedy videos on Twitter, Instagram, and TikTok (Facebook, which changed its algorithm a few years ago to ensure that only Facebook-native videos show on the platform, ironically shut itself out of that potential for traffic and engagement). The stunning distinction, of course, is the idea of a homebound solo comedian and video novice like Corey Forrester on equal footing alongside a network-produced TV show with a full writing staff and production crew. Well, the conditions are not precisely equal, of course, but the point is that audiences find and share what is funny, production values aside.

It was possible in this new reality, we realized, for front-facing comedy sketches and character bits on social media to enjoy a similar level of audience reach and influence as clips from legacy comedy TV programs. We had our big idea: create front-facing comedy produced by southern-born comedians and writers with huge, diverse followings. Our challenge was to bring a diverse group of hilarious comedy writers and performers together with serious minds working in racial justice, find pathways into the topic that feel authentically fresh, and create conditions that can lead to new discoveries and realizations. And make it funny.

"The Hammer Will Get You Yours": Co-creating Antiracism Comedy for Public Engagement

In March 2021, we opened our E Pluribus Unum Comedy Think-Tank creative room on Zoom with a loud, hilarious, diverse cast of characters—the beginning of a two-week immersive workshop and artistic creation space. As guides into the South and the complexity of wildly divergent lived experiences, it is hard to imagine a funnier or more unlikely duo than our two performers: Corey Forrester, the White, self-described Georgia redneck; and Jay Jurden, a gay Black comedian from Mississippi featured on *Vulture*'s "Comedians You Should and Will Know in 2020" list, whose comedy album, *Jay Jurden Y'all*, premiered in the number-one spot on iTunes.[46] Imagine them side by side: Corey's trucker-hat-wearing bombastic silliness and huge laugh, and Jurden, the genteel, classically trained theater actor with an MFA from Ole Miss. We had invited a handful of successful southern-born comedy writers and performers to fill out the collaborative virtual room, an equally colorful mix of experiences and styles and personalities to work alongside Forrester and Jurden: Mark Agee, Kenice Mobley, David Purdue, Ashley Brooke Roberts, and assistant writer Amma Marfo.

It was the first time we were all together: a wildly diverse group of people born in different parts of the South (including me) with varying degrees of comedy experience, including stand-up and TV writing gigs. And unlike the usual comedy writers' room experience, this one would begin with a series of intense visits from a multiracial network of leaders and thinkers working in antiracism organizing and culture throughout the South. We carefully curated this network of thought leaders and subject-matter experts: Victor Atkins, a jazz musician and professor at the University of New Orleans; Sho Baraka, hip hop artist and faith leader based in Atlanta; Whitney Buggs, consultant for the national racial-justice group Color of Change; Natalie Bullock Brown, film producer and professor from North Carolina State University; Rebecca DeHart, CEO of Fair Count, the Georgia-based social-justice organization founded by political powerhouse Stacey Abrams; Rev. Ryan Eller, a Baptist minister, community organizer, and cofounder of the New Moral Majority, based in Kentucky; Jeffrey Jones, native Alabamian and University of Georgia professor of politics and comedy; Shakita Brooks Jones, Lisa Flick Wilson, and Vanessa Jackson from Atlanta and Montgomery, Alabama, who together lead the Radical Optimist Collective, an antiracism training organization; Stacy Reece, owner of Down South House and Home in Georgia; and Saket Soni, founder of the Resilience Force, an immigrant-organizing organization based in Louisiana. Our team and the EPU core strategy team were there, including founder Mitch Landrieu, managing director Scott Hutcheson, and advisor Ryan Berni, joined later by Donnie Charleston, director of policy and advocacy. Suffice it to say, a group like this—an unusual collection of humans, jobs, racial backgrounds, lived experiences—had never gathered before in the same room to co-create, of all things, antiracism comedy. We were off and running.

To recount the scene properly, it is worth centering the idea that arriving at revelatory thoughts about social-justice topics—particularly one as fraught with pain, rage, sensitivity, and trauma as racial injustice embedded in the very operating conditions of the United States—feels nearly impossible when the rooms we create to discuss them in are either uniformly similar in outlook or background or are set up in lines that are already antagonistic (as in voting patterns), or in which the power dynamics already imply who is permitted to speak and share and who should remain silent. Too often in social-justice spaces, and even well-meaning "diversity and inclusion" trainings and seminars, this is the case. For better or worse, then, this particular curation of comedy people and social-justice people was a microcosm of the challenge itself. There is simply no way to find new ways to communicate about structural racism—particularly to audiences that might be naturally resistant—without creating space for everyone to contribute, to acknowledge either their ignorance or their pain, depending on lived experience and expertise. As Vanessa Jackson, part of the Radical Optimist Collective, which deals with racial trauma and healing primarily in Atlanta and Montgomery, Alabama—and increasingly around the country—sees it, "The thing that stands out for me, and I think it's something I've been reflecting on more and more, is it's the challenge of holding people with care, White folks with care, other folks of color with care, while holding people accountable." In terms of creative fodder, Jay and Corey needed and valued the differences in the room as a necessary part of incubating comedy in the first place. Jay puts it like this: "The challenge from a humor standpoint is how do a group of White writers and Black writers talk about this taboo thing in a way where we give everyone space to talk about the thing? We have to say, 'What's the funniest way to present the thing?' but then also, 'What's the most honest way to present the thing?' And that was a conversation we had a lot in the room."[47]

Corey agrees: "When it's me and several White people in the room who definitely mean well . . . we mean well, but it's like, we don't fucking know what we're talking about. We know these things are bad because Black people told us they were bad, but until you admit that you don't fucking know that there's no way that you, a White person, can know everything about all of this, and because you grow up in this society, you sometimes unknowingly harbor some racist tendencies."

To echo Dr. Martin Luther King Jr.'s famous admonishment of silent White people as the greatest deterrent to racial progress, finding ways to bring passive White folks into the real fold as active, vocal allies doing the real work—moving past what the EPU team calls "exit ramps for White people" when it comes to conversations about race—is difficult, to put it mildly. How do you reach so-called neutral people—to use EPU's research-based audience-targeting language—who are not willing or able to have a conversation about structural racism, and thus, remain unwilling to be part of the work to solve it? This was a challenge for the eventual comedy we would create together, but also one to fully unpack together in artistic process as people with diverse lived experiences. Says Berni, "White people have generally been unwilling to have these tough discussions, and as a result, many just shut off or they find exit ramps. Often they will say that they feel set up for some kind of blame or guilt especially about discussions about history or slavery where it might've been something ancestral." We made this a central idea in the eventual comedy, given the potential for comedy to invite new listeners.

In the comedy co-creation room, this idea of exit ramps for multiracial conversations about structural racism felt revelatory to the comedy folks and the social-justice leaders. There was a raw honesty in the room: it felt unusual. "Racism is taught to you by people you love," said Stacy Reece.[48] Lisa Flick Wilson from the Radical Optimist Collective sees and communicates this idea similarly in her own racial-justice work: "I'm a White person who was raised in the United States. Therefore, racism lives within me because this is our system. And once I can get through that statement, it allows all these other things to happen versus the active denial piece or back to let me just blame someone in Georgia, or Alabama, or Tennessee."[49] Jay responded to this idea of racism as sin: "Why don't we think of racism like Christians think about sin? They ask for forgiveness and work daily to be better." It was a new way in—that is, racism is a task to work on daily, not a binary idea of who has it and who doesn't. And with comedy, maybe we might find a gentler way into talking about lived differences and experiences, stopping even so-called well-meaning White people from stepping onto those exit ramps.

Was comedy uniformly embraced in the room? Not necessarily. It would be dishonest to say that all our invited social-justice leaders were fully on board with the humor route; a few were hesitant. How is it possible to give proper weight to these difficult ideas while finding ways to communicate about them through humor? It's tricky. Comedian David Perdue reflects, "I appreciated being reminded to not take any of this lightly. There are people behind these ideas and people doing the hard work, so [we have to] make sure you honor them in the comedy. And then again, comedy has this amazing ability to be like, 'Hey, you see that?' Comedy is like a kid. You know how kids just point out things and they don't know they're not supposed to say that in public?"[50]

And yet, as Jurden says, comedy can be precisely the way in: "I've talked about race, racism, and the tension between races in America particularly in the American South on stage for a while now. There's a deep well of humor there just because through that tension, you can find some humor." Finding new ways to talk about race—constantly and consistently—is hugely important, says Perdue, because "people want to believe that racism is over. And why wouldn't you want to think that?" Perhaps a different way to talk about racial injustice and structural oppression is not only by finding ways not to let people take "exit ramps" out of the conversation but also by helping them to see and understand, as EPU's policy and advocacy director Donnie Charleston shared in the co-creation room, that structural racism is an interdependent system that hurts all people, not only people of color. "'A story of interdependence' I thought was so elegant but also so tactical," says Jurden. "And Donnie talked about how racism is ever-evolving, so the ways that we combat it and strategize against it have to be ever-evolving. I thought that was so important and interesting." At the end of the day, as Vanessa Jackson put it, new angles are important, but also, "We need laughter because it's very easy to become a humorless activist."

What did the comedy team do with all of this deep contemplation? Working solo, as teamed writers, and as group writers, the participants were guided by Bethany Hall through an open creative process for the week: they developed characters, shared one-liners and stories, created ideas for sketches and stories based on what they learned and shared—funny bits like "you might be southern if . . ." or "what if Memaw goes to an HBCU?" (David quipped, "I went to an HBCU. But I never heard about a Memaw until I was in my twenties and knew some White people," to which Corey retorted, "I don't know shit about any kind of college, but I do have a Memaw.")[51] or reparations through the prism of a personal injury lawyer, and more.

All of it was open material for comedy. Maybe most importantly, the material was collectively created in the grand "yes, and" tradition, in a free creative environment that honored the distinct voices and experiences in the room. As Jay said, "There was never a moment where I felt pushed back for a pitch of a sketch or a joke would result in people shutting down. The environment was nurturing and cultivated a really good dialogue between everyone who was in the room." In his trademark direct style, Corey agreed: "I liked the fact that this was a no-judgment zone and I was able to be like, 'Look, here's a dumb thing I thought at one point.' Or this is a thing I had no fucking idea about. And for everybody to be like, 'Yeah, why would you have known?' You know?" Open space for play and admitting to not knowing created new opportunities for jokes and funny ways to invite people in. Some fifty individual comedy ideas later, the team settled on final production ideas. The comedians got to work writing the final ideas, and then pitched in a hilarious final session with Mitch Landrieu and the EPU team.

"RACISM, listen here, you antiquated prick! It's your boy, the Buttercream Dream, and I'm coming to you today to let you know that us sane people are trying to have, like, a decent civilization and stuff, and you're putting a HITCH in our proverbial GIDDY-UP . . . SKEW! . . . Only dipshits and assholes find you appealing, and the rest of us wish you'd get shot out of the sun. Skew!" In the style and fashion of the straight-to-camera WWE challenge, wrestling belt draped over one shoulder, aviator glasses firmly affixed, Corey yells through a ramped-up screed at "your casual racism at parties and your whole stable: structural racism, systemic racism, ALLLLL that horseshit."[52]

So opens the Buttercream Dream in *A Message for Racism*, the premiere of the #RacismIsNoJoke social media campaign, a collection of eight front-facing short-form comedy videos distributed across YouTube, Twitter, and Instagram in the spring of 2021.[53] The concepts from the co-creation room are embedded in each of the front-facing videos, which range from straight-to-camera character delivery to Jay and Corey playing several characters at once, made possible through quick jump-cut editing. There is Jay's *Plea to White Women*, which hilariously invites White women to be part of antiracism work; *I'm So Southern*, which intercuts between Jay and Corey establishing their cultural common ground as a precursor to explaining antiracism ally work; Jay's *Auntie Racist*, which lays out structural racism through a series of characters, and *Let's Get Real Estate*, which humorously helps to explain structural racism through the legacy of discriminatory housing policy, and more.

Based on social media response alone, though, the pièce de resistance is easily *The Hammer*, where Corey Forrester, in a dead-on satirical

Figure 4.1: Screenshot: "Comedian Corey Ryan 'Buttercream Dream' Forrester Has a Message for Racism" (YouTube/E Pluribus Unum)

send-up of a personal-injury-lawyer low-production-style TV commercial, sneaks in a brilliant metaphorical understanding of and explanation about reparations for slavery—both hilarious and frame shifting at the same time:

> Have you been the victim of an accident or some corporate malfeasance? Got mesothelioma or some other disease that you can't spell? . . . Hi, I'm Corey "The Hammer" Forester and I will get you what's rightfully yours. . . . If you or a loved one has been hit by a car, electrocuted by a malfunctioning blender, or kidnapped against your will, put on a boat, and sent across the Middle Passage where you had to work for four hundred years with no pay, you may be entitled to a cash settlement. . . . Did you slip a disc at your job or get your head stuck in a tilt-a-whirl, or suffer a legacy of pain that left your ancestors with no generational wealth and a shorter life expectancy? You deserve cash.[54]

Together, the videos and social media reach totaled in the millions of views, and engagement on Twitter was rich and lively, particularly from people who said they did not see the various twists and deep and

Figure 4.2: Screenshot: "Plea to White Women: Comedian Jay Jurden" (YouTube/E Pluribus Unum)

provocative truths about racism coming. "Corey, you're a fucking genius! I was good with it being a take on all the lawyer commercials we see in the South, but then you threw in the Middle Passage. Great way to explain it and I love the sneak attack," said one Twitter post in response to *The Hammer*. "I was not expecting the swerve in this, but this is magnificent in every way," said another. Reaching people where they are, using a medium with far-reaching potential, seeing them sharing and talking, feels like success to Ryan Berni: "The number of folks being self-reflective on social media chat comments [in response to the videos] is the whole point of doing this." And as the E Pluribus Unum team sees it, this is only the beginning of inviting comedy into antiracism public-engagement work.

. . . . .

At the end of the day, can comedy "fix" racism? Of course not. Yet breaking through the clutter with comedy is valuable within the broader cultural landscape. And so is comedy that explicitly works within a multiracial allyship framework. As Jay Jurden says, "For the longest time, it was Black people talking to White people [about antiracism]. But telling White people plainly, 'you should talk to other White people,' over the past five years maybe, people have started to do that more. I think it's a good approach. It needs to happen more." Further, as he reflects, using comedy to agitate old thinking and share new insights—and to build solidarity and traction for antiracism thought and work—is a strategy worth trying over and over:

> Comedy offers people a chance to laugh at something, share it, and then hopefully change their interaction with certain topics. And the more people that like it and laugh at it and share it, maybe they will start to change as well. It's not making someone go, "Oh, I'm not going to be racist anymore." It's making someone say, "Wow, that is rooted in some stuff

Figure 4.3: Screenshot: "The Hammer: Comedian Corey Forrester" (YouTube/E Pluribus Unum)

that I don't like. And I didn't even know that. I'm going to tell one of my friends about this. It's also really funny." There's enough of a desire for dialogue in this country that I think things do spread like that.

David Perdue also summed it up: "There's not enough Black people to do the things that need to be done in this country. It has to be allies, so you just have to wake people up. I enjoy doing that with comedy because it's somewhat more palatable than some sort of speech or whatever." And in the tradition of co-creating, learning and exploration happen, as Corey Forrester reflected: "I learned a lot [from this experience]. I've actually thought a little bit about some old stuff that I did, and I thought, 'if I'd been in this room before I did that, that joke would've been different.' It's changed the way I've looked at a lot of things. It reinforced the importance of different perspectives."

Comedy meets social justice in these ideals—in shared missions to help others see concepts differently and to participate. When it comes to finding new ways to interrogate climate change or racial discrimination or homophobia, for instance, open-minded mental dexterity and creativity seem urgent requirements. Traditional ways of engaging people—through numerical facts, somber information, and even anger and demands in protest—are not enough. The struggle to create an equitable society demands that we embrace culture and creativity to power innovation, which itself can be fostered simply by the act of bringing together professional sectors and thinkers from wildly different vantage points. When comedians address social topics and neglected lived experiences, by highlighting new angles from serious facts shared by topical experts, they are doing more than entertaining us—they are inviting us in to play and imagine along with them; after all, we are already actively participating in order to understand the joke. The outcome is new power for each group as they meet in the middle: creative power for a civil society organization that recognizes the need for cultural outreach, and civic power for comedians who think about their work a little differently as they move forward.

Comedians insist that we open our own minds and hearts, and as play expert De Koven writes, "We can't deny the impact of 'failures of the imagination.' . . . Often the failure here isn't that we imagined something and imagined it wrong. Often, the failure is that *we didn't even try*."[55]

Comedy helps to realize this imperative through play and creative deviance and imagination, embedded in the final product we enjoy on a screen or a stage, but also in the process of germinating and shaping it. At the end of the day, comedy is valuable in social-change work not only because of how audiences may experience and choose to share it but by what it takes to make it in the first place.

5

"Invisibility Is Not a Superpower"

Asserting Native American Identity through Humor

From an early age, activist Crystal Echo Hawk knew she came from a family of warriors. It was deeply embedded in her genealogical story, after all: one of her Echo Hawk ancestors got his name after returning from battle, regaled as a fierce fighter for his people, the Pawnee Nation. "Our proud family tradition," says Echo Hawk, "has always been about that warrior being of service for our people. That's deeply ingrained in our family."[1]

Over the years, the Echo Hawk warrior impulse expanded against the backdrop of the 1970s movement for Indigenous rights in the United States. With new opportunities for Native people to attend college and law school, her relatives became attorneys, legal scholars, organizers, and leaders in tribal organizations, always fighting to protect and expand opportunities for their communities. They were prolific, focused, and vocal—and seemingly everywhere. At one point, the *Denver Post* published a story about the Echo Hawk family as "the Kennedys of Indian Country." It was fertile ground, as she recalls: "Growing up in that family, it was really all about Native American rights and throwing down—growing up in the '70s in this remarkable time."

Despite the power of her lineage, discrimination was not far behind. The legacy of mistreatment of Native peoples, a long-standing tradition steeped in the original sin of the American experiment (if we can look past the gross understatement of the word "mistreatment" in this context), also appeared in Echo Hawk's early life. This, too, informed the perspective that would shape her work years into the future. Flash back to Crystal in second grade, living in the Virginia suburbs of Washington, DC, where her father was working as a young attorney in the

Indian law division of the Department of Justice. Stuck in a classroom with a slur-hurling racist teacher among primarily Black and Brown students, she says, "I used to throw up every day before I'd go to school, because I was so terrified. Then, she turned her sights on me and started terrorizing me. I went home and told my dad what was happening." The next day, her dad showed up after school to meet with the teacher—in full 1970s business garb, giant Department of Justice credentials hanging from his neck. She remembers, "I couldn't hear a word they said, but they had a nice little conversation for about fifteen minutes. Then, he just said to me, 'Let's go. It's going to get better.' Then, the next thing I know, boy, we were studying Native Americans in class. She had a whole kit. . . . I just knew that my Dad was a fucking superhero. I didn't totally understand everything he did, but that was such a catalyzing moment—including the experience of suddenly understanding the intensity of that racism."

Jump ahead nearly two decades into the future. After writing her master's thesis about the indigenous Zapatista uprising during the mid-1990s, she moved to Mexico and joined their efforts, quickly becoming an essential organizer and connecter. A contemporary Indigenous social movement had captured the world's imagination, and the immersive training was invaluable: "Through that work, I learned so much about activism and organizing. It was actually the first place I learned about the importance of narrative in cultural strategy and bringing that into grassroots organizing and thinking about national organizing." Moving between Mexico and Los Angeles, she also found a passionate artistic community: "It was the most transformative chapter of my life . . . being in Los Angeles at the time, bands like Ozomatli used to come over and throw concerts to help us pay our rent. Zack de la Rocha from Rage Against the Machine was our benefactor who helped to fund our community center where we worked. All of a sudden, we were working with all these amazing artists and activists and organizers."

Days were full but intense, and eventually, Echo Hawk moved to a reservation in Minnesota, got married, and had a baby. She found quieter ways to serve: working for her tribe, raising funds for Indigenous youth programs, taking a position with the Native American Rights Fund. Her life continued in a constant trajectory, as she describes it, "building power for our people and Native life solutions. . . .

The hallmark of everything is this deep passion and sense of responsibility and commitment to working for our people." But then, her activism took a new turn, sparked by a repeated pattern of structural discrimination that faced her and her teen daughter during a mental health crisis, not unlike her own childhood experience. It was a pivotal moment: "I suddenly realized, in more ways than I'd ever experienced in my entire life, watching what was happening to my daughter and the way that we were being treated. It just hit me so hard about the level of discrimination and racism that is so pervasive. When I look at any moment in my career, that was the most catalyzing moment. I knew I had to fucking do something about it. That's where my activism took a whole different trajectory."

She felt new inspiration for the next chapter, motivated by the power of her past activism experience, but also by frustration at the seeming invisibility of Native American peoples in the broader culture. "Invisibility," she says, "is not a superpower." Lack of Native American visibility in American popular culture and news—and, equally damaging, destructive stereotypes and tired old tropes—were hardly a mere "cultural" problem. The toxic mix of dehumanizing images and relative absence of Native stories contributed deeply to structural challenges facing tribal nations—but also, to how Native individuals were often treated in their daily lives, which Echo Hawk certainly knew firsthand. "We felt we [Native peoples and communities] were just not being seen and heard or understood on a range of issues we were working on," she says.

After a series of conversations with friends and colleagues, she crafted what would become the manifesto and strategic plan for an unprecedented effort to understand the scope of the present-day "invisibility" problem facing Indigenous communities, to identify points of intervention and a pathway to broad social change. Echo Hawk knew they needed data at the heart of the effort; the scope of the challenges facing Native American people—in terms of cultural erasure and destruction—had never been documented before. At the same time, she was inspired by the incredible transformation in public perceptions around LGBTQ+ rights and marriage equality that culminated in the historic 2015 *Obergefell v. Hodges* Supreme Court decision, and, as she recalls, "how that movement had really moved both hearts and minds over time." The core mission was set: endeavor to learn exactly what a broad swath of the American public thinks about Native American peoples—dominant narratives, beliefs—and how those thoughts affect public opinion and policy about Indigenous communities.

It all came together in the form of Reclaiming Native Truth,[2] a $2.5 million sweeping strategy and research initiative led by Echo Hawk and the First Nations Development Institute, along with a coalition of advisors, both Native and allies, launched in June 2016, coinciding with the early days of the Native-led Standing Rock uprising. It took two years to complete the research and shape the strategic path it suggested, working with more than two hundred leaders and other stakeholders to identify and reflect shared interests among tribal nations and multiple Native organizations. The Reclaiming Native Truth findings themselves were daunting—much of it hard to process, and yet instructive and eye-opening: "For the first time ever, we know what different groups of Americans—across socioeconomic, racial, geographic, gender and generational cohorts—think (and don't know) about Native Americans and Native issues. We have learned how biases keep contemporary Native Americans invisible and/or affixed to the past and are holding back Native Americans from achieving political, economic and social equality, as well as accurate and respectful representation."[3]

Among the core conclusions of the research, which included extensive surveys and focus groups with Americans across the country, nearly four in ten respondents did not even believe Native American people still exist, and two-thirds said they did not know a Native person. While a majority of the research respondents were at least familiar with some aspects of Native history and agreed that the United States had committed genocide against Indigenous tribes, they were much less likely to agree that Natives experience discrimination in the present day.[4] The role of culture—narratives, images—turned out to be hugely significant. In general, most people only "experienced" Native people and cultures through popular culture: TV and films. As Crystal relayed in a media interview, "The only references [to Native Americans] that we continuously heard as people were struggling to make a connection were *Dances with Wolves* and *Parks and Recreation*. So these stereotypes and caricatures are really forming perceptions of Native people."[5] And ultimately, as she says, "Invisibility and erasure is the modern form of racism against Native people."[6]

In 2018, on the basis of the strategy set forth by Reclaiming Native Truth, Echo Hawk founded a new nonprofit activist organization, IllumiNative, designed to increase the visibility of Native nations, change centuries of destructive narratives, and push for, as she puts it, "a radical shift." IllumiNative's mission establishes cultural narratives at the very core of its effort:

> For decades, the lack of representation and information about Native peoples has perpetuated damaging myths and stereotypes. Native peoples rank at or near the bottom of most socio-economic indicators—such as educational attainment, domestic violence, and poverty—and are often portrayed in popular entertainment, the news media, educational curricula and other influential sources as "noble savages" of days gone by. But research shows that a more powerful, more accurate, and more inspiring narrative about the contemporary Native experience—one of innovation, creativity, resilience and community—is being overlooked and obscured by the negative one. IllumiNative seeks to change that.[7]

From the Reclaiming Native Truth research, which identified a trifecta of potent forces by which damaging images are perpetuated—K–12 education, popular culture, and media more broadly—IllumiNative focuses its work heavily around narrative culture and change, with a strong focus on the entertainment industry, to ask and answer questions like, What images persist that continue to denigrate or simply appropriate Native people and culture? Where are the Native TV showrunners, writers, creators, and film directors to be found and nurtured in Hollywood, and how can they be supported and amplified? From what they watch in entertainment and media, what do non-Natives see and understand about Native communities?

Without a focus on creative culture, as Echo Hawk and her IllumiNative team see it, social change is simply not possible. Change hearts and then structural justice and equity has a better shot of sticking, they say, in the form of public policy and other institutional decision making. IllumiNative takes popular culture seriously—it is a force that directly shapes both Native American consciousness and self-esteem as well as a corrective for non-Natives who are unaware or grossly misinformed, says Echo Hawk: "We particularly want our young people to see that we can do anything. We can do anything. Then, we want other people in this world to be able to see that. For us, I love the way Ava DuVernay talks about it. She's like, 'Fuck the table. We're remaking the table.' It's not about pushing a seat up to the existing ones. We want to make the table."

Amidst so much serious data, not to mention a pretty steep set of challenges for the IllumiNative team and their many allies in Indian Country and outside it, where does comedy fit, and what role does it serve in their social-change mission? In the context of such a somber enterprise and so many layers of long-standing trauma, we might be tempted to dismiss comedy as unnecessary or "extra." But if we did, we would miss a huge reality about humor in Native cultures, well known within Indigenous communities and families, even if still "invisible" to many non-Natives given that Native storytellers have traditionally not been invited to the table of the film and TV industry to tell their own stories. Humor is a powerful tool of resistance to and recovery from trauma,[8] and also a beloved, entrenched tradition in Native cultures. As with everything else, Indigenous folks did it first. As Crystal describes humor and comedy in Native communities, "There's over six hundred tribal nations. You're going to find something very universal in all of those different tribal nations' experiences in that comedy and humor is very central to cultural life ways in the community. Being able to laugh is such an important part of life. . . . Humor is a highly valued commodity [in Native cultures]. If you're funny in a Native community, you are supercool."[9]

Suffice it to say, Crystal Echo Hawk and her team are not what we would call "comedy resistant." Some social-justice organizations need some convincing to consider comedy in their work, but Echo Hawk was open to the idea right away when we approached her to collaborate. And yet, as she recalls, "We [IllumiNative] had never sat down and thought, 'We need a comedy strategy,'" despite working with Native comedians in the past. Together, we—Crystal, me, Bethany, our teams—sensed an exciting opportunity in front of us: How might we imagine using comedy designed to explicitly help take on some of the IllumiNative strategy to infuse the culture with powerful, realistic narratives about Native American stories and peoples? And further, how might comedy be able to push the envelope of taboo just a bit further, given its deviant, fun nature?

Armed with fresh research, a roster of Native and non-Native ally comedians and strategists who were up to the challenge of a fresh collaboration, and the excitement of co-creating between Crystal's painstaking activism and the ideation of comedy people, we got to work. On the basis of our comedy co-creation writers' room, hosted on Osage Nation land in Oklahoma—an unprecedented gathering of comedians and strategists across four tribes, along with non-Native comedy writers, culminating in an invitation to an Osage Nation ceremonial dance—we developed and produced a short-form comedy talk show, *You're Welcome, America*, centering the shared joy and resilience of Native and Black communities in the United States, hilariously communicated from the perspective of Native and Black women as cohosts. It was memorable for all of us who participated, allies included. And it was a meaningful moment amid a cultural tipping point: *You're Welcome, America* was incubated and shaped as Native peoples gained visibility through the Standing Rock movement and a blossoming of Native-led comedy on US TV, perhaps optimal timing for humor to play an overt role in the movement to acquire justice, equity, and real visibility for stories that have been distorted since the very beginning.

Cultural Reflections of Native Peoples

In the year 2021, if you were to Google "Native Americans," a curious thing would happen. Twelve of the top seventeen images are historic, pre-twentieth-century images of Native American people—regalia, feathers, arrows in hand.[10] We might think, if this were our only portal, that Native people had simply vanished long ago. Indeed, "according to most American narratives," wrote historian Philip J. Deloria (Standing Rock Sioux), "Indian people, corralled on isolated and impoverished reservations, missed out on modernity—indeed, almost dropped out of history itself."[11] But nearly ten million Indigenous people—across some six hundred tribal nations—are alive and well in the United States. What do Americans see and encounter about Natives in popular culture—TV, film, fashion? Systematic oppression, as history shows, was purposeful, and its success and implications are evident.

When it comes to the dominant reflection of Natives in US media culture, a few basic narrative tropes exist along a spectrum, each dehumanizing, each stripping dignity and agency: the "savage," alcoholic degenerate living in poverty, or the "noble warrior."[12] The images also are curiously historic in nature, as a nonscientific Google search experiment shows. Contemporary portrayals of Natives are hard to find, broadly speaking. But lest we forget, visual references to present-day Native peoples are often othering, cartoon-like renderings, including professional and college sports mascots replete with sacred feathers and tomahawk chops and the red-face slur, Halloween costumes, and appropriation of Native culture, music, art, and fashion—caricatures produced by non-Natives. Americans' view of present-day Native peoples is darkly destructive in ways that are much deeper than costumes, according to the Reclaiming Native Truth research: "It is no surprise that non-Natives are primarily creating the narrative about Native Americans. And the story they adopt is overwhelmingly one of deficit and disparity. The most persistent and toxic negative narrative is the myth that many Native Americans receive government benefits and are getting rich off casinos. Another common narrative focuses on perceptions of unfairness, in particular around false perceived government benefits to Native Americans that are not offered to other racial and ethnic groups. This narrative can undermine relationships with other communities of color."[13]

Upon learning this, perhaps non-Native readers should suspend surprise when we place extant reality into proper context: it is a purposeful dominant narrative that works well when the truth about the Native story in the United States is one of abject terror, genocide, murder, violence, broken government promises and treaties, forced relocation and erasure of languages and culture, and structural discrimination at the hands of the earliest colonizers, the US government, elected officials, and, yes, ordinary American voters. The explicit oppression of Native American people has long been structurally upheld—and in historical and political terms, portrayed as *necessary*. Deloria wrote of a longstanding "fantasy world" created and maintained by Whites, and one that served a purpose: "One of the most familiar figures in that world had been the savage Indian warrior, an image that stood at a crossroads in 1890. As long as there remained a real possibility of Indian violence, the imagery of last stands and Indian surrounds helped justify the violence wreaked on Indians during the conquest of the American landscape."[14]

In other words, here is the formula: dehumanize disparate communities of Native people—make them less than human ("savages," according to the Declaration of Independence), make genocide seemingly necessary, deport them from their land, strip them of their language—and otherwise erase their true story from history books and pop culture alike, and the American melting-pot myth of absolute harmony, kindness, and benevolence continues unabated. It should be no surprise, then, to learn in such stark terms how limited and damaging these reflections are, and the complicity of so many for so long. But then again, it *is* a shock to many, because so much remains untaught.

We should rightly regard none of this as an accident if we remember the historical origins of Native misrepresentation. Dehumanizing Native people—from celebrating the seemingly heroic violence inflicted on them to culturally erasing them to exploiting and misusing their culture—was the American plan all along, Hollywood included. Real-world genocide, violence, and systemic oppression of Natives were mirrored in the earliest pop-culture reflections, wrote Deloria: "Literature, art, film, television and other media have often invoked Indian violence in order to stage extended meditations, justifications, and celebrations of non-Indian, American violence. They have negotiated issues of social and racial difference and the violence that might be performed on Indians and others, but they have done so by continuously positioning White violence as defensive."[15]

And on the other side of the spectrum, "Pacification . . . shifted the ground: Indians might not vanish, but they would become *invisible*, as the very characteristic that had once defined them—the potential for violence—was eradicated. Even if they didn't melt away—as earlier vanishing proponents assumed—they would either melt into American society or sit quietly in the marginal distance, no longer disturbing anyone."[16] The images of nineteenth-century violence were irresistible to an early and evolving Hollywood. Literally hundreds of films during the earliest Hollywood juncture—the 1910s—portrayed storylines dealing with Indian violence.[17] And, yet, even here, while Native actors were available to play Indians, directors preferred White actors in makeup, and Natives were excluded from starring roles, even as Indian characters. The Hollywood structure "carried with it a certain racial logic as well. . . . Indians and African Americans could represent only those particular identities—which cut them out of leading roles altogether."[18] As the entertainment industry progressed, early television executives made plenty of money on negative Native tropes of the old "cowboys and Indians" variety, among other familiar portraits. In the 1950s and 1960s, negative images of Natives were so pervasive on early television that Native parents complained, and a group of Oklahoma tribes joined forces to fight negative stereotypes at the local broadcast level.[19] As Choctaw Nation leader Jack Davidson said at the time, "Television makes the younger generation think that Indians were only savages. The Indians only protected their homes. Television never tells about [that side] of the American Indians."[20] Over the decades, the original inequities of the entertainment industry deepened and took firm root, from one generation of Hollywood power moguls to the next.

For Native peoples, the toxic combination of structural and symbolic dehumanization and erasure works the way such systemic oppression is designed to function: to keep them down. Appropriation of Native culture, for instance, does not bring the possibility of equity to Native communities (i.e., it's not *flattering*, as some sports fans or fashionistas have been known to say), but instead can serve a displacement effect that sidesteps any real-world association with Native peoples. In this way, cultural oppression serves structural disenfranchisement, as in the world of law and policy. As Deloria wrote in *Playing Indian*,

> As the United States has enshrined a multiculturalism that emphasizes culture more than multi-, simply knowing about Indians, African Americans, Asian-Americans, and Latino/as has become a satisfactory form of social and political engagement. As a result, the ways in which White Americans have used Indianness in creative self-shaping have continued to be pried apart from questions about inequality, the uneven workings of power, and the social settings in which Indians and non-Indians might actually meet. . . . The self-defining pairing of American truth with American freedom rests on the ability to wield power against Indians—social, military, economic, and political—while simultaneously drawing power

from them. Indianness may have existed primarily as a cultural artifact in American society, but it has helped *create* these other forms of power, which have then been turned back on native people.[21]

Insidiously, a steady stream of negative cultural imagery impacts the self-esteem of Native peoples; it alters their perceptions of real-world success and mobility. As scholars Peter A. Leavitt, Rebecca Covarrubias, Yvonne A. Perez, and Stephanie A. Fryberg wrote in their study "'Frozen in Time,'" "The lack of contemporary representation of Native Americans in the media limits the ways in which Native Americans understand what is possible for themselves and how they see themselves fitting in to contemporary domains (e.g., education and employment) of social life."[22] Oppression logic makes twisted sense here: strip dominant media culture of real Native stories and storytellers, and we leave the cultural landscape curiously barren of their real lives. The remaining panorama distorts not only what non-Native audiences see and understand but even what Indigenous peoples believe about themselves and their futures. The cycle then continues.

And yet, hope always lurks, aided by consistent community engagement and the insistent resiliency of Native communities. The tide of invisibility started to shift just a bit several years ago, says Echo Hawk, owing to the historic Native-led Standing Rock movement in North Dakota, first launched in 2016 by Native youth activists but quickly growing to include hundreds of tribal nations. Native tribes and allies stood with the Standing Rock Sioux tribe as they fought to protect their sovereignty and block the Dakota Pipeline from permanently destroying the land and water in the region.[23] The world took notice. In TV and print news stories—generated in large part from social media and activist communication channels—Native people and cultural traditions were front and center. They were not historic figures but living, breathing leaders and community members exerting their power. It was a spark of narrative change: "We interrupted the narrative of who and what Indian people are in the 21st century," said Judith LeBlanc (Caddo Nation), executive director of the Native Organizers Alliance.[24] As attorney and playwright Mary Kathryn Nagle (Cherokee) concluded in a 2018 report, "The movement at Standing Rock significantly undermined the systemic erasure of Native peoples from the dominant American narrative."[25]

Beyond the fight itself, it was a catalyzing cultural moment with tangible implications, reflected Echo Hawk:

> I feel like something is really different with the acceleration [of awareness] around Standing Rock. So many Native people felt this sense of collective pride seeing what was happening, in people taking a stand. And now, just within the last few years, we have seen the first two Native women elected to Congress. Secretary Haaland is in the highest place at Department of the Interior, and people are starting to see that we are brilliant, capable, innovative people that are leading—and that we're all in this together now, whether we like it or not.

Standing Rock, one of countless acts of historic and contemporary Native resistance,[26] was significant, according to Echo Hawk, Nagle, and other leaders and activists, because the public narratives came from Native people. Representation—that is, Native storytellers telling Native stories—is the key idea when it comes to the cultural stage, reflected in TV and film screens where stories and images can reach millions. As filmmaker and TV producer Sterlin Harjo puts it, "It's not up to Hollywood to change Native representation in the media. They have failed at it for decades. It's up to us—Artists, Filmmakers, Storytellers and Activists. That power is ours alone."[27]

Whither comedy here? Lest we be tempted to exclude humor, given the trope of the "suffering, disempowered Indian,"[28] comedy, as it turns out, is central—a revered Native cultural tradition that has barely touched the surface of the Hollywood scene and yet, is finally finding a glimmer of light.

The Joy, Resilience, and Resistance of Native Comedy

Don't call comedian Jana Schmieding (Lakota) an overnight success; she has been toiling in the entertainment business for more than a minute. Over the years, she did the work—writing and submitting spec scripts and samples—but her Hollywood profile was relegated to "only being hired as a sensitivity reader for Native stories told by non-Natives," as she wrote in an essay for *Vanity Fair*, "sometimes for a small fee but usually for the eventual carrot, 'If this gets sold, you'll have a spot at the table.'"[29] Her world changed in 2019 when she was hired as a writer—and later, as an actress playing a lead character—for *Rutherford Falls*, the first sitcom helmed by a Native American creator and showrunner (and woman), Sierra Teller Ornelas (Navajo). For once, she was not a token Native voice; Ornelas's writers' room prioritized Indigenous comedy writers. It was, by Schmieding's own admission, life-altering, not only because of the breakthrough show on Peacock, NBCUniversal's streaming network, but because the job actually *requires* the fully embodied—and hilarious—lived reality of her and her fellow Indigenous writers' experience and comedy, rather than stuffing their insights into tired, exhausting Hollywood tropes. As she wrote,

> On *Rutherford Falls*, it's not that we are "allowed" to tell our stories or that we have been "granted the space." The messaging has always been that the impact of the show relies on the Native writers to be the cultural critics and comedians that we are. We are tasked with bringing our full, joyful Indigenous selves to this story about a Native woman and her White best friend. And although I get asked this in every other press interview—no, none of the writers struggled to avoid stereotyping ourselves. It was hard work but shameless, unadulterated Native Joy every day.[30]

Schmieding's journey should not have been this hard, and it should not have taken this long to see a comedy like *Rutherford Falls* on American television. Work clearly remains to be done nearly fifty years after Charlie Hill put Native stand-up comedy on the cultural map, inspiring others to follow and yet remaining a somewhat singular figure in the popular imagination when it comes to funny Indigenous performers. And yet, *Rutherford Falls* is a spectacular member of a boom class of Native comedy TV shows in the streaming age of entertainment. Comedy from Native storytellers—notably staffed by Native writers—is popping up across TV networks, truly for the first time in the history of Hollywood. In addition to *Rutherford Falls*, there are *Reservation Dogs* (created by Sterlin Harjo and Taika Waititi),[31] which won a prestigious Peabody Award, and the animated series *Spirit Rangers* on Netflix, directed by Karissa Valencia (executive-produced by superproducer Chris Nee, who created the Peabody Award–winning *Doc McStuffins*).[32] The newest, *Rez Ball*, directed by Sydney Freeland and cowritten by Sterlin

Harjo, is coming to Netflix.[33] All are set within Native communities, centering Native characters, stories, cultural traditions—and lots of trademark humor. None position Native people and communities as adjacent to broader story worlds. (Cynics would rightfully say, "Well, that's only four shows," and they would be right, but coming after decades upon decades of nothing, their appearance is certainly something to note.)

Articulating, with precision, the pathway to this moment is beyond the scope of this chapter and this book, but it is worth spotlighting the profound role of the Sundance Institute's Native Program and its long-running former director, Bird Runningwater (Cheyenne and Mescalero Apache). The trajectory of many Native showrunners, creators, and writers working in Hollywood today traces back to Runningwater and the Sundance Institute's commitment to mentoring Native artists and fostering relationships as a creative community.[34] One or two degrees of separation come between Sundance and Runningwater in "Native Hollywood" (or "#IndigenousFilm community," as Bird puts it),[35] including many of the writers and show creators in the current TV comedy spotlight. In this way, the foundational rules of Hollywood's social capital system are on clear display, but from the perspective of Native artists who built their own networks and power: today's breakthrough Native comedy TV shows and creators did not come from overnight success, but through talent, labs, relationships, network building, activism, and community.

In 2009, for instance, a group of Native artists and comedians came together to hilariously spoof the *Twilight* film series' egregious depiction of Native characters, and their playful satire ignited a long-lasting collaboration that wound its way into Hollywood and deeper success to follow. In their launch YouTube video, "New Moon Wolfpack Auditions," they dance around in their underwear and "do their Native thing" according to the direction of a clueless Hollywood casting director, mercilessly skewering the entertainment industry.[36] The video went viral, and "The 1491s," the Indigenous sketch comedy group, was born: Dallas Goldtooth (Mdewakanton Dakota-Diné); Sterlin Harjo (Seminole-Muscogee), alum of the Sundance Indigenous Program; Migizi Pensoneau (Ponca-Ojibwe); Ryan RedCorn (Osage Nation); and Bobby Wilson (Sisseton-Wahpeton Dakota). The 1491s, who call themselves "a gaggle of Indians chock full of cynicism and splashed with a good dose of indigenous satire,"[37] have steadily increased their cultural presence, from touring comedy shows to appearances on *The Daily Show* to a sold-out play at the Oregon Shakespeare Festival.[38] All five members are now writers, creators, or performers in Hollywood's hot Native TV comedy scene,[39] beautifully illustrating the direct connection between participatory culture and the contemporary mainstream entertainment marketplace. And as Kliph Nesteroff wrote in his book, *We Had a Little Real Estate Problem*, "The effect the 1491s are having as a sketch troupe today is not unlike the effect Charlie Hill had in the late 1970s. There is a comic voice otherwise absent in popular media."[40] Notably, as he points out, the comedy operates on a broader level to a non-Native audience, but it is always created first and foremost to get a laugh from Natives.

The 1491s are not the only Native comedians who are killing it in the contemporary scene. Other highlights include Adrianne Chalepah (Kiowa-Apache), who created the Ladies of Native Comedy group;[41] stand-up comedian and writer Jackie Kaliiaa (Yerington Paiute and Washoe), who hosts the comedic podcast *The Jackie Show* and was featured in the First Nations Comedy Experience TV series;[42] and writer and performer Joey Clift (Cowlitz), a staff writer on Netflix's *Spirit Rangers* who created the first Native comedy showcase at Upright Citizens Brigade Theater in Los Angeles and created and launched the first list of "25 Native American Comedians to Follow" for Indigenous People's Day in 2020.[43] There are many more, of course. And as Kaliiaa humorously said, "We [Native comedians] all know each other. There is one phone number where you can reach all of us."[44]

Of course, we should avoid calling today's Hollywood Indigenous comedy flurry a "renaissance," since Native comedy has been around since, well, the beginning. The roots of Native humor are deep and structurally meaningful—and well known in Native communities. In his pathbreaking (and very funny) 1969 book, *Custer Died for Your Sins: An Indian Manifesto*, the attorney, activist, and former NCAI executive director Vine Deloria Jr. (Standing Rock Sioux) was one of the first to write about Native humor:

> It has always been a great disappointment to Indian people that the humorous side of Indian life has not been mentioned by professed experts

on Indian Affairs. Rather the image of the granite-faced grunting r***kin has been perpetuated by American mythology. . . . The Indian people are exactly the opposite of the popular stereotype. I sometimes wonder how anything is accomplished by Indians because of the apparent overemphasis on humor within the Indian world. Indians have found a humorous side of nearly every problem and the experiences of life have generally been so well defined through jokes and stories that they have become a thing in themselves.[45]

Humor in Native culture, according to Deloria Jr., has never been simply about entertainment and fun, but about governance and organizational styles and getting things done—but also, an irresistible response to absurd levels of tragedy. In his book, he recalled singing "My Country 'Tis of Thee" at a Native conference and the room breaking into laughter as they realized that their fathers most certainly did die at the hands of the Pilgrims—a hilariously dark twist on the lines "land where my fathers died . . . land of the Pilgrims' pride."[46] Well before the "White invasion," Native communities used teasing and ridicule as a form of functional rebuke when people seemed to go against the broad consensus of a tribe; comedy became an important quality for effective leaders.[47] As he wrote, "Humor has come to occupy such a prominent place in national Indian affairs that any kind of movement is impossible without it. . . . The more desperate the problem, the more humor is directed to describe it. Satirical remarks often circumscribe problems so that possible solutions are drawn from the circumstances that would not make sense if presented in other than a humorous form."[48]

Comedy, not surprisingly given its structural functions in Native communities, is also found in Indigenous activism. In 1969, in one of the most successful and well-known contemporary Native-led uprisings, activists seized control of Alcatraz Island, occupying it for months and demanding rightful land be returned as the 1968 Treaty of Fort Laramie had promised.[49] As attention grew and allies and Natives arrived on site, the poet John Trudell (Santee-Dakota) "wrote a satirical manifesto that conveys the feelings of the occupation," as Nesteroff wrote.[50] He was rewarded for his efforts with an FBI file that said, in part, "He is extremely eloquent—therefore extremely dangerous."[51] Humor was embedded in the resistance itself.[52]

Cut to Native activism in the present day, where Crystal Echo Hawk, IllumiNative, the 1491s, and a network of Indigenous artists are fighting cultural invisibility and structural oppression, and in its place, asserting their identities. They are focused both on the power nucleus of Hollywood and on making and disseminating their own stories, using the participatory media tools of the digital age, striving to change the image and treatment of Native people by disrupting the narrative created by others. Comedy is meaningful here, too, says Echo Hawk: "There are times in our communities when we really faced some incredibly difficult challenges, and there are moments where dark humor is alive and well because it's sometimes just the way that we cope. It's the way that we are expressing our resiliency." As the 1491s' Ryan RedCorn says, "Almost all of my actions are designed to work in service of social justice. They are often heavily disguised."[53] Incognito activism is where comedy gets to shine. And so it was that a group of us—Natives and allies, comedians and activists—arrived in Oklahoma in the summer of 2019 to see what we might create together. Our task: imagine and produce new comedy to agitate Native invisibility and push against long-standing doors of oppression.

You're Welcome, America! Creating Comedy for Native Activism

The drive from Tulsa to the Osage Nation reservation in Pawhuska, Oklahoma, is long, flat, and blanketed with tall grass. Highway signs fall behind as prairie land gives way to smaller winding rural roads, and if there are prominent street signs to mark the path, I have missed them because we are fully trusting our guide, Ryan RedCorn, comedian and son of the Osage Nation's assistant chief, Raymond Red Corn. Ryan knows every detail and turn of this place, his lifelong home. The night before, after dinner in old downtown Pawhuska, we looked up from the bottom steps of the old courthouse where most cases of hundreds of murdered Osage—killed by envious Whites for their oil claims in the 1920s—remained unresolved, covered up by the FBI in one of the most scandalous little-known stories of violence perpetrated on Native peoples.[54]

Stuffed into two SUVs, we are a noisy and funny (literally) little caravan: nine joke-cracking comedians—half of them Native, half non-Native—and me, making our way through the plains of Oklahoma on a hot June afternoon. We have been invited by RedCorn to watch and experience an Osage Nation ceremonial ritual of feast, dance, and singing that takes place every year here. Before the dances begin, we sit down outside at a long table covered with food and drinks served on delicate, blue-flowered china plates and cups; Assistant Chief Red Corn explains this homage to the French lineage that mixed with the Osage peoples. There are talks and refills and second helpings, and plenty of laughs. The dances themselves, held in a large outdoor circular arena, are spectacular, and yet, they are respectfully unrecorded. When we leave, we will only have the memory of this experience; before we arrived, we were carefully instructed not to take any pictures or videos, or to describe the experience in written form. Photography of any kind has been strictly prohibited for decades. We are, in this way, living fully in this moment alongside the assembled families who have gathered to watch and celebrate the dancers, and to pay their respects.

Our visit was the culminating event in a remarkable week spent co-creating comedy between Native and non-Native comedians, alongside Crystal Echo Hawk and an assembled group of Native leaders, activists, and experts. When Crystal and our team discussed making comedy together as social-justice strategy, she knew immediately that she wanted to host our Comedy ThinkTank session on site in Oklahoma. The learning and the immersive experience, in her mind, would be totally different than in a writers' room in Los Angeles or New York, where this kind of work usually germinates. She was right. I learned more about Native culture as an invited guest than I had in a lifetime of living in this country, and I know the other non-Natives in our group shared my perspective. As RedCorn reflected, "It's important to understand the geographic context. I live in Pawhuska, Oklahoma, but usually the people writing about Native people or rural Americans don't live here. It's a double uphill battle for people trying to write these characters in these spaces. There are so many misrepresentations of people in these spaces. . . . These stories are totally cut off to [writers' rooms] because they don't know the rules of those worlds."

We have gathered to co-create comedy together for the first time, our effort part of IllumiNative's ongoing cultural activism and its first official foray into leveraging comedy. Our group is a real "who's who" of hot

Native comedy talent—Joey Clift, Adrianne Chalepah, Bobby Wilson, Ryan RedCorn—and some of the best non-Native comedy improvisers and sketch writers and performers in the country: Sebastian Conelli, Shannon O'Neill, Johnny McNulty, Rachel Pegram. Bethany Hall, as always, is our comedy facilitator. We begin our week together with a full day of information gathering and presentations from Echo Hawk and other Native leaders who work in and for their communities; the Reclaiming Native Truth research is the heart of our session, and there is a huge amount of information to take in. What will resonate? What is important to convey—what is even possible to transmit—through comedy? How will Native joy be harnessed and reflected even as the underlying facts are traumatic? As Adrianne Chalepah summarized the challenge, "We have to know what we're talking about if we're going to write jokes. We're not just doing it for laughs, but community is on the line, and we have to find something relatable in all of that information."[55] Producing comedy for activism purposes is a tricky balance when it comes to Native invisibility issues, as Crystal puts it, because our work has to resonate strongly with Native audiences (and they are well aware of their cultural invisibility, as Chalepah wryly pointed out) even while it reaches non-Native audiences. Non-Native people, after all, are the ones who hold and perpetuate destructive misinformation at worst, or, at best, simply don't know anything at all about Native peoples, culture, and lived experiences; the comedy has to be funny to both an inside and an outside audience. And if we are following the open artistic process of comedy—that is, not predeciding exactly what ideas should be developed, what facts to reinforce—we don't know exactly where this will go.

Following the serious information transfer, the first order of (comedy) business is an exercise in which every comedian in the room shares a story about how and where they grew up: Who were the people and characters in their lives? What is memorable? Where does their comedy derive from? It is alternatively hilarious and serious, but it definitely breaks the ice. Sebastian has us on the floor laughing as he recounts stories about "Uncle Rocky": a ham-handed, gregarious Staten Island man who would sit in his work truck to eat massive sandwiches in between shifts. (Quips RedCorn later, "I need to see better Staten Island representation in comedy!") But we have to address the truly meta idea in the room itself: non-Native comedians don't know much of anything about Native culture or lived experiences. We have to break the ice and allow people to share their stories and ask questions. An informal session— "is this racist or is this funny?"—has everyone cracking up. It is hard to imagine this level of levity and honesty happening in "strategy" rooms for activist work, but once the comedians are able to hear each other's stories and questions, it is an open playing field. As Bobby Wilson pointed out later, the really funny ideas didn't start to emerge until all of the comedy writers had created a really funny comfort zone together, once non-Native folks "got past all the guilt of not knowing," as he put it.[56] If the room had stayed "careful" as people tried not to offend one another, the funny would have been suppressed. Comedian and champion improviser Shannon O'Neill reflected, "You never know how everyone is going to get along, are people going to listen to each other, will they enjoy and celebrate each other, call each other out? That's so important. It was already a nice atmosphere to 'ask stupid questions' and give permission to ask questions that might be offensive."[57]

Diversity of lived experiences—including those among the Native comedians' disparate tribes or reservation lifestyles—turns out, once again, to be the key ingredient to fully opening the door of creativity and new ideas. RedCorn described our curated comedy creation room as "uniquely American": "I don't know if this kind of process even exists in writers' rooms in Hollywood with this kind of diversity—it's a uniquely American combination of people. . . . We don't have access to those characters and stories because media doesn't give us access to them. The only way I can hear about Staten Island is from Sebastian, and I can hear about being a Texan and African American from Rachel. The same with them [non-Native comedians] hearing from us." And as Joey Clift reflected, moving beyond the one "token" Native writer is the key to finding the storytelling, laughs, and new insights: "There were situations in the writers' room where Ryan, Bobby, or Adrianne would say something like 'all Native tribes are like this,' and I would say 'my tribe didn't do it that way.' It just further emphasized that every tribe is a little different."[58] Bobby Wilson agreed:

A lot of times, the people I create comedy with are other Native people— the same ethnicity—and while our regional experiences are vastly different, our ethnic experience is very similar. It's nice to be able to step outside of that into a more diverse writing room. The hugely beneficial thing was getting into a room of people with different ethnicities and experiences and hammering out ideas that were mostly for laughs. . . . The idea of social change through comedy is cool, but specifically making each other laugh for five days straight is really something.

Listening and creative group ideation are the very heart of a co-creative process between activism and comedy, and sharing intimate lived experiences plays a role on par with facts and statistics; this is where the comedy process might depart the most from strategy sessions outside artistic experiences. As comedy writer Johnny McNulty said, "Listening was the building block of the experience. This comedy was 100 percent built around the listening to the stories and research. Nothing we wrote didn't come directly from someone's story, but then pulling out those things that are universal."[59] Joey Clift agreed: "The stories we told, the things we shared with each other, that's where the light bulb moments happened. Our pitches and ideas were totally based on what we listened to in the room." And Conelli: "As an improviser, listening is the most important thing you can do. . . . You will feel a reaction when something happens out of the ordinary. You'll never be able to hear what's unusual and funny about someone's experience without listening."

Was it hard to find the comedy amid traumatic factual information? Not really, particularly given the long-standing role of humor in Native communities; the writers arrived with plenty of it. As Chalepah put it, "When you are dealing with systems of oppression, the comedy writes itself. It's easy to find the punchlines because we can see what's wrong with that picture." The comedy balance was really important to find, though: "People who are never going to seek out Native American facts never will unless we do it like this," said Sebastian Conelli. "It was important to make the comedy really funny rather than to work on the social-justice topics so heavily."[60]

By the end of the co-creation week, the comedians came up with easily forty different ideas: TV shows, films, sketches, jokes, social media videos. On the final day, they pitched their final loglines, all centering Native joy and hilarity. Notably, none focused on the trauma or violence reflected in years and years of American culture—but all were designed to blast a hole into the absurdity of distorted Native tropes and celebrate Native truth and stories, all responding to the factual information revealed through the Reclaiming Native Truth research. The most popular ideas came from the dynamics of the room's comedic players, which emerged in the writing process: there was *Cracker Fuck Boys*, a hilarious table-turn on Native sports mascots that took shots at White men as costume-wearing "mascots"; *Two Natives and a White Boy*, a comedic travel romp in which Bobby Wilson, Ryan RedCorn, and Sebastian Conelli make their way around the country, sharing observations and realities as they go; *Scout's Honor*, a scripted sitcom centering around scouting and its long-standing appropriation of Native customs; and *You're Welcome, America!*, a sardonic and silly talk show about the shared joy and resilience of Native and Black communities.

It was time for Crystal and Native leaders to figure out which ideas to push forward into production, and which ones to develop further into formal Hollywood pitches to become mainstream TV. This is where things get tricky and complex, given the finicky nature of the business, financing, and various complexities. But keeping in mind the holy grail of social capital in the entertainment business and how it works—that is, through relationships—the collaboration itself was meaningful. As Adrianne Chalepah summed up the experience,

> I had a moment on the last day where I felt like crying because it is unprecedented in the sense that the media industry has never wanted to open its doors to Native people. They have always wanted to take our stories and do them for us. Now we are all connected and we know each other, so we can help each other in the sense of plugging into different networks. . . . So, this to me was more than fun. It could change my life and the people around me in my communities and could open doors that have always been closed. So even though this started with a small group of people, I knew the importance of it because of the fact that it was just the beginning.

About six months later, real life took a wildly unexpected turn. The pandemic came from seemingly nowhere, and we were sidelined. Native communities were hit hard. Nearly two momentous years passed—a racial-justice uprising, attempted White House coup, and historic pandemic crisis stuffed within them. Instead of our commitment being dampened, we were convinced that comedy was perhaps more important and relevant than ever before. How else might we celebrate resilience and humanity than with humor, of course?

Cut to two years later.

Despite the ongoing challenges of the COVID-19 crisis, in May 2021, we reassembled a new writers' room with additional comedy voices: Native writers and performers Deanna Diaz (Tonawanda Seneca) and Jackie Kaliiaa joined Adrianne Chalepah, along with Black comedy writers Geri Cole, Joyelle Nicole Johnson, and Kenice Mobley. Johnny McNulty also joined from the original crew. Born from the original room, our idea was in place: a short-form comedy talk show, *You're Welcome, America!*, hosted by Chalepah and Johnson, two hilarious women riffing about the shared resilience of Native and Black communities in the United States. In six weeks, the writers and performers crafted three full-episode scripts, we booked a New York stage and crew, and we brought the group together in person—finally, after days and days of Zoom-world creation. We were back.

"Native women are marginalized. It's always important to incorporate a real-life badass woman [in this work]," reflected Adrianne Chalepah. As the cohost of *You're Welcome, America!*, along with Joyelle Nicole Johnson, Adrianne is bringing the badass to the set on the day we start filming in New York. It is June 2021, and we have finally made it to a physical set to produce the trailer and the first episodes of the show (COVID protocols firmly in place, of course). Native film director Brooke Swaney (Blackfoot-Salish) is at the helm. *You're Welcome, America!* had been ignited as an idea in Oklahoma two years prior, but it became a living, breathing, hilarious set of full scripts in the hands of talented Black and Native comedy writers, with feedback and fact dropping from Dr. Philip Deloria, a prominent Native historian from Harvard (the comedians insisted on calling him "Dr. Phil" throughout the writers' room week, and I'm happy to report he had a pretty good sense of humor about it).

The show, fashioned in the style of MTV's *Decoded*, starring Franchesca Ramsey, has a bit of the feel and tone of *Who All Over There?* and *Two Dope Queens*. Adrianne and Joyelle Nicole sit back in two armchairs, surrounded by set pieces dreamed up by the writers: a wooden

Figure 5.1: Filming *You're Welcome, America!* in New York City

eagle sculpture, some vaguely 1980s background walls, and a throw pillow with Harriet Tubman's face on it. Direct to camera and to each other, the women riff about shared and distinct cultural realities, and they perform funny bits about topics that include religious hypocrisy, mental health, and stigma in Native and Black communities—and cultural appropriation:

> JOYELLE NICOLE: Hey, everyone! You're watching *You're Welcome, America*. The show that celebrates Black and Native communities. Or disappoints them, depending on who you are. I'm Joyelle Nicole Johnson.
>
> ADRIANNE: And I'm Adrianne Chalepah. Today we're discussing cultural appropriation. White people, I can see you clicking away, but you're gonna want to see this one.
>
> JOYELLE NICOLE: Or more accurately, *we* want you to see this one.[61]

Figure 5.2: Cohosts of *You're Welcome, America!*, Adrianne Chalepah and Joyelle Nicole Johnson, on set

Watching the production and reading the scripts, it seems hard to imagine this idea has not come up before, and maybe it has, but regardless, it is something special to behold: two powerful and hilarious women, playing and cracking up and dropping serious truth bombs about Native invisibility and the shared resilience and joy of Black and Native communities that have survived generation after generation of trauma. The comedy makes it a little gentler to take in. And even so, as Adrianne shared later, a bit in the script that calls for "a moment of guilt-free rage!" (in which Adrianne and Joyelle Nicole let it all out) felt like the most fun, and also the most necessary.

· · · · ·

You're Welcome, America! made its official public debut on Indigenous People's Day 2021, part of a larger series of media content celebrating Native peoples and correcting the inaccurate narratives long projected by the old Columbus Day holiday. IllumiNative and its allies and collaborators in Hollywood are at the center of this effort, leveraging media partnerships and news outlets to disseminate authentic, funny truths about Native resilience to widespread audiences, both Native and non-Native. At the time of this chapter's completion, we (the show's creators, led by IllumiNative) are pitching the series to various media partners as an ongoing web or TV show. As these things go, the formal Hollywood development cycle can take a minute (see chapters 2 and 7), but we are hopeful. It is, after all, a new lens into a bigger conversation about resilience in communities that have been systemically traumatized by colonialism and White supremacy since the very birth of the nation. As Ryan RedCorn reflected, this kind of portrait is nowhere in American pop culture: "I can't even imagine a show where you had Native writers and African American writers in the same room. I've never seen a conversation with a Native American and an African American on screen before."

Native joy and Black joy are the heart of the show's creation and execution, and this is worth highlighting, as Jana Schmieding did when she wrote about the creative process in *Rutherford Falls*—there is no sight of the old tropes and stereotypes when the writers and creators are from the communities telling the stories. The funny factoids of *You're Welcome, America!* are instructive, yes, but the humorous tone and powerful performance and presence of women comedians reveal an entirely different set of images and ideas—and jokes—than what has dominated mainstream cultural images about Native American people and communities. By inviting audiences to experience a hilarious narrative world shaped by Native American and Black comedy writers, we blow past damaging portrayals from decades of entertainment storytelling. This is what representation means: it is not the token hires or the cultural check for errors. We are invited into connection, solidarity, and laughter informed by lived experiences: civic imagination and subversive activism at work, colorfully expressed through the unexpected lens of comedy.

6

"Maybe They Think Beauty Can't Come from Here"

Resilience and Power in the Climate Crisis

The first thing a visitor notices, walking through any door of the Vivian C. Mason Art & Technology Center for Teens—a community center in the heart of the St. Paul's neighborhood in Norfolk, Virginia—is the art. There is a back door leading to a fenced-in parking lot, a side entrance, and a front door to the busy main road that connects the brick part of the city to a leafier one. Through each portal, the potential for a joyful response has been carefully anticipated. Art greets us everywhere, regardless of how we arrive.

Self-portraits lean against easels. Paintings of brown faces and bright suns and rainbows come to life with psychedelic vibrance. Inspirational phrases, posters for spoken-word performances, framed pictures of poetry slams, and artistic flyers for workshops—film editing, writing, music production—hang on every patch of exposed wall. Mismatched chairs in every room are positioned in circles and duos, playing witness and host to artistic discovery and collaboration. And the colors: each room connected by a narrow hallway is lovingly, meticulously painted— red and orange in one, blue with hanging string lights in the next, explosions of stripes and patterns in another, each one exuding a different mood, ripe for the creative expression that will be born there. The energy is light and power and warmth.

None of this is an accident. We are there on a Sunday to film for our docu-comedy project—a group of comedians, activists, and filmmakers comprise the "we," brought together through a project with advocacy group Hip Hop Caucus—and the grand dame of this place, our host, Deirdre "Mama D" Love, is giving us a tour. Refurbished from old storage space, the center, Mama D explains, is a no-judgment zone, a retreat for artistic improvisation and discovery, a haven for local teens to create family and community together. The center is designed as a dwelling of welcome, as she says,

> The young people we serve are really searching for something more than they have. Because, the things that they want, the things that they need, and the questions that they have are not being answered for them and their lives in general at the time that I usually encounter them. . . . But the minute that the light goes on, that's how powerful they are. I watch with my own eyes in real time and it's almost like rolling the camera quickly because change happens just that fast. Quickly, I watch them transform. The minute a young person believes that somebody believes in them, then I can see this little glow thing happen. The minute that they put their hands on something and watch it change because of them and only them, they really see their part in it. . . . We welcome a person as they are. That's when they can put their shoulders down.[1]

There are big hugs and jokes all around as we meet some of Mama D's beloved young people: Malik, Alisha, and Zenaya. She has invited them to be part of our documentary with a group of comedians—Kristen Sivills from neighboring Virginia Beach, Aminah Imani from Atlanta, and Clark Jones from Chicago—to talk about what they create in their colorful space and swap stories about their lives in Norfolk, a flood-prone coastal city in the midst of gentrifying transition. Hip Hop Caucus's leaders are here—president Reverend Lennox Yearwood Jr. and executive director Liz Havstad—along with the film crew led by Elijah Karriem. It is a little weird, this stopover from comedians and activists on a Sunday afternoon, but our young hosts are rolling with it, curious and welcoming. An adventure awaits.

We film first with joke-cracking Malik, a twenty-year-old who has "graduated" from the center but finds ways to hang around. He proudly tells the origin story of the sprawling community garden and mural installation across the street, which Mama D and the teens brought to life when he was fifteen. The garden solved a real need that the city was not addressing, he explains. There are hot peppers, greens, and tomatoes for his neighborhood; the nearest grocery store is miles away, and many people don't have cars.

Figure 6.1: Community gardens at the Vivian C. Mason Art & Technology Center for Teens in Norfolk, Virginia

Through Malik's spoken word, which he performs on camera for the comedians, we are invited into life in St. Paul's: his neighbors and their strength, the time city workers arrived to cut down the one tree in the community—the tree that the kids loved and played in and mourned when it fell—and the power that erupts from young people with a voice. But "they," broader city leaders and inhabitants, do not see the community garden and the art and the teens; they call us "hood rats," he says. "Maybe they think beauty can't come from here." But if they did think so, he imagines, maybe his neighborhood would be treated with dignity and respect.

On that day, the main filming event takes a long time to set up—a kind of funny talk-show scene in the large main room. The film crew is painstakingly tricking it out with lights and filters, moving furniture around, positioning the art to make it visible from all three camera angles, situating the young on-screen "stars" in place to check their lighting and shadows. Wireless mics are attached to shirt collars and jackets, war stories about accidental microphone malfunctions—a favorite for media people—are swapped, the teens are cracking up. Music is playing and someone busts out an enthusiastic verse. More than an hour ticks by, and the sunlight starts to fade. I am impatient with the time, but I know it will be worth it: the final set is beautiful, the comedians and teens are goofing off and ready to talk, the art is on display, and everyone is excited. It is almost time to roll camera.

Five minutes out.

The sound of gunfire takes a few seconds to mentally register. "Get down! Cut the lights!" yells someone, maybe ten seconds in. We all drop where we are. One of the camera operators crawls on his belly to try to lock the community room door, but it won't close. Someone whispers in the dark, "Are the outside doors locked? Do we know if they're locked?" We don't know. Someone with a semiautomatic weapon is firing right outside the community center, directly on the other side of the brightly painted walls. And in this moment, we have no idea whether the shooter is inside or outside, targeting this place or something else, whether there is more than one person with a gun.

Somewhere within the slow-motion quiet panic of five minutes, we realize that Clark, one of our comedians, is outside in the middle of the shots. He has managed to squeeze himself under a truck in the back parking lot. He is praying and texting us. When the crew gets him inside the room, he falls apart—he is not physically injured, but he is not undamaged; tears stream down his cheeks while he holds his head in his hands. He stares blankly, trying to catch his breath. And just as quickly as it all took place, it is silent outside again. Whatever just happened feels like it's over. When Mama D calls the police, two uniformed officers dutifully show up and look around; as they leave, one reminds Clark, the out-of-towner, in a rote, matter-of-fact tone, "Sorry that happened to you, man. But it's just what happens around here." They say nothing to the teens.

Our scene is done before it begins, and we move around quietly, collecting our backpacks and phones. Elijah and his film team are methodically packing up the film gear, breaking down the lights, moving the sofas and art back to their original places. One of the teen girls walks over to our group: "Will you come back again? Will you come back so you can show them the beautiful things we are making here?" I am not sure what will happen next. We are angry for the young people and Mama D, enraged about the callous detachment of the police. The crew disperses in different cars.

This corner of Norfolk is a singular place—much of it marginalized in a complex maze of institutional racism and gentrification, and also powerful in its resilience—but it is simultaneously many communities around the country, united in legacies and contemporary realities of inequity. It is one location, yes, but it carries within it the interconnected story of environmental justice, poverty, climate change, and lower-income communities of color across the country. Norfolk is many places all at once. Hundreds of years of sanctioned structural oppression arrive at moments like this one, when the people's stress and anxiety include a kind of weary internalized resilience to violence and other chronic challenges that head their way. And yet, resilience is also an ability to survive and thrive despite the constraints—to believe in art and community and beauty and hope. We can see this pattern clearly in this story. Power lurks within it.

We have arrived here partially through the long journey of Reverend Yearwood, who knows this narrative well. "Rev" is an accidental activist and son of the Deep South traveling along an inexorable path. As an Air Force Reserve chaplain who protested the Iraq War alongside thousands of Americans—a display of inconvenient opposition to the military's rank-and-file obedience—he was led by a moral calling to activism, one thing leading to the next. In the 2004 presidential election year, music moguls Sean "Puffy" Combs and Def Jam Records' co-founder Russell Simmons created new campaigns to mobilize young Black voters through popular culture, hip hop, and on-the-ground organizing. Rev, by then a known operative who directed national grassroots strategy for both efforts, inevitably founded Hip Hop Caucus in September 2004 to leverage the power of music and pop culture to advocate year-round, not just during elections, on behalf of communities of color in matters of equity, justice, and health.[2]

Less than a year later, Hurricane Katrina smashed through New Orleans, leaving thousands of people dead or stranded—most of them low-income Black people—traumatized and dehumanized, their tragedy and desperation coarsely laid bare as spectacle for gaping news audiences all over the world.[3] The political savvy of a postmillennial activist combined with the oratorical power of a Louisiana-born minister as Rev and his Hip Hop Caucus team began years of work on Katrina recovery and environmental justice. They worked from a growing body of research about the perils of climate change and historically grounded racist policies that together threaten the lives of vulnerable neighborhoods inhabited by people of color—insights and stories that often fail to register in the larger climate movement. In its expressions of outrage and solidarity, the trajectory of Hip Hop Caucus is inseparably intertwined with the legacy of Hurricane Katrina. It was the trauma that defined its calling.

Flash forward a dozen years: an era of vocal activism and loud partisan in-fighting about climate change, and yet, a kind of day-to-day malaise on a topic that can seem, to nonscientists, abstract and diffuse. Spurred by the increasing urgency of the climate crisis and high stakes for low- and middle-income Black and Brown neighborhoods, Hip Hop Caucus launched a new "content and engagement platform," Think 100%, to inspire multicultural young people and expand climate-change advocacy to resonate with communities of color.[4] As Rev sees it, "We can't do this as a siloed, segregated, progressive kind of movement. We need everybody. We need a movement that has everyone."[5] Culture and art are requisite tools to incite digital natives who absorb entertainment and information in a near-inseparable flow of messages, and Think 100% grounds its ongoing public-engagement efforts with creative energy.

When my team first connected with Hip Hop Caucus leaders in the early summer of 2019, they had been planning a coordinated creative campaign with and for the Norfolk community—an attempt to sound a new alarm about climate change in a coastal locality that bears an uncanny resemblance to New Orleans's rising sea levels and concentrated urban population. We knew immediately we wanted to work together. We wanted to invite comedy, as yet untried within Think 100% efforts, into the movement. From the perspective of Hip Hop Caucus, the story of Norfolk, showcased through the journey of young Black comedians, has the potential to be meaningful in ways that require the hindsight vision of Katrina's history to imagine. It can provide the light and play to mobilize people. As Rev puts it, "We have tried every kind of way to bring this climate revolution to the people to get them involved—through science and scientists and news—but it cannot happen without culture and creativity and art."[6]

By the time we started filming in Norfolk in October, our team of researchers, comics, activists, and filmmakers had been working together since the summer on a climate-justice project that centers comedians of color. We began in August with a Comedy ThinkTank session between my team and Hip Hop Caucus in Los Angeles. Incubated from the ThinkTanks process, a live and filmed stand-up comedy show was produced by Hip Hop Caucus at the historic Crispus Attucks Theater in Norfolk a month after our documentary filming. A network of community leaders and organizers helped shape the film in a production process that centered local voices as guides and on-screen subjects.

This chapter shares the research and stories behind the participatory co-creation and production of the comedy show and docu-comedy project, *Ain't Your Mama's Heat Wave*.[7] Through this journey, we explore and unpack the unique potential of social-justice comedy as local community empowerment and mobilization strategy, and as disruptive creative expression inserted into a broader cultural conversation about climate change—one that often fails to center the experiences of communities of color and poor people who are "hit first and worst" by flooding and climate disasters.[8] Resilience is the emergent theme—certainly in the climate change sense, but also in the strength and people power in Norfolk. Resilience is also on display in the ability and cathartic need to transform trauma into comedy—as Clark does in the final stand-up show. The similarities between New Orleans and Norfolk provide the backdrop and urgency of the comedic storytelling, even as their shared destiny remains unclear, subject to the whims of nature and the actions of humans.

A Tale of Two Cities: New Orleans and Norfolk

In the late summer of 2005, a swirl of warm air brewing over the Bahamas quickly gained strength over the course of a week, traveling over the southern tip of Florida. As a Category 3 monster, Hurricane Katrina hit New Orleans in the early dawn hours of Monday, August 29, 2005.[9] The levees around the city were breached in a few hours, and water began to rise,[10] inch by inch, and then foot by foot. The next day, four-fifths of the city was flooded. An estimated fifty thousand to one hundred thousand people were stranded with no way out, stuck on the rooftops of houses and apartment buildings or the Superdome sports arena and the city's convention center.[11] Nearly two thousand people died, and as the weeks and months continued, almost 1.5 million residents were displaced.[12] About 60 percent of the housing in New Orleans was destroyed; hospitals, schools, and other essential facilities were lost or closed.[13]

The staggering physical, ecological, and cultural destruction wrought by Hurricane Katrina—and the delayed, inadequate response of the federal government[14]—is too extensive to cover here, although dominant themes are clear. Katrina was a historic natural disaster of astonishing proportions,[15] but low-income African American residents were disproportionately affected. They paid the highest price in lost lives, homes, jobs, chronic physical and mental health damage, and dissolving neighborhood cohesion as they were forced to migrate. Their story is Hurricane Katrina's legacy.

For decades, New Orleans—a culturally rich mecca of music, food, and local tradition—has been one of the country's most impoverished, racially segregated cities. Before Katrina hit, nearly seven in ten (67 percent) New Orleans residents were Black, up from 55 percent in 1980.[16] Concentrated poverty built up in the city's African American neighborhoods over the years. As scholar Sherrow Pinder reminds us, this was not organic or accidental; she traces a path back to 1916 laws designed to segregate and enforce Black and White districts: "Residential segregation in New Orleans took a heightened form of poverty in Black neighbourhoods, and displayed overcrowded, underserved and blighted by crime and diseases urban spaces."[17] Entrenched segregation and housing restrictions constructed a calcified barrier. This is hardly new or regionally specific: racist housing policies in the United States, by no means relegated only to New Orleans, are longstanding human constructions enabled for decades by elected officials and the voting public.

Neighborhoods with predominantly Black residents, the hardest hit by Katrina, "were concentrated in the most vulnerable parts of the city, located well below sea level and poorly protected by inadequate levees."[18] Residents of the city's Ninth Ward—the primary area devastated by flooding, where 98 percent of residents were Black—lived in crumbling, unstable housing well before Katrina made landfall.[19] Scant measures were in place to safeguard people of color living in flood-prone areas; the majority of less damaged, protected areas were white and wealthier.[20]

With decades-old racist housing policies firmly rooted, the process of recovery intensified historical inequities. Rebuilding measures favored big developers and businesses over working-class African Americans who had lost the most.[21] The impact was persistent, wrote scholar Rodney Green and his colleagues: "Blacker, poorer, and more devastated communities faced relatively low rates of return by 2007, jeopardizing their long-term ability to recover from the storm in their original homes and exacerbating pre-storm racial and economic disparities."[22]

News media coverage provided the window through which millions viewed the human suffering in southern Louisiana, and the reflections generally reinforced damaging caricatures of Black Americans. The imbalance became glaringly obvious and somewhat famous as two 2005 news photos went viral when a *New York Times* story and other media outlets picked them up: an Associated Press photo of a young Black man describes him as "looting" a grocery store for food, compared to a Getty Images picture of two White people with a caption about "finding food" from a store.[23] Similar depictions reverberated with dehumanizing media descriptions of Black residents as "refugees" in their own country,[24] and as stories showed African Americans repeatedly in negatively stereotypical ways.[25] As they tried to persevere, Hurricane Katrina's Black survivors faced continuous obstacles, even in the very public portrait of their grit and pain. They were seemingly doomed from the start.

And yet, local people and researchers knew what would happen. Only a few years earlier, scientists provided incontrovertible evidence: climate and infrastructure conditions were ripe for a monstrous storm to cause inconceivable destruction in the area.[26] Ordinary folks sensed it, too. Journalist and climate advocate Mike Tidwell wrote in 2013 in the local *Virginian-Pilot* newspaper,

A hurricane is coming, and it's going to wipe us out. Papoose Ledet, a Cajun shrimper, told me this as we rode on his wooden trawler just south of New Orleans. I was a visiting journalist, and it was the spring of 2001, more than four years before Katrina. How did Ledet—and millions of other Louisianans—know the Big One was coming prior to Katrina's actual arrival in 2005? Simple. They saw the ocean creeping steadily into their lives, for years, with their own eyes. They saw the tides grow higher and higher. They saw unusual and increasingly intense flooding of streets and homes. And they saw scientists issue study after study showing that the ocean was literally rising, an obvious threat to Louisiana's flat, watery coastal region, where some areas were below sea level.[27]

Tidwell was not just talking about New Orleans. He was pointing out a sister region—the vast coastal Hampton Roads area that encompasses Norfolk, Virginia. As director of the Chesapeake Climate Action Network, he was understandably alarmed. He had spent months in New Orleans crafting his 2004 book, *Bayou Farewell: The Rich Life and Tragic Death of Louisiana's Cajun Coast*, which virtually predicts a massive hurricane amid increasingly catastrophic climate conditions.[28] His 2013 editorial continued, "If you live in coastal Hampton Roads, take a deep breath and re-read that last paragraph. You live, right now, in a world eerily parallel to south Louisiana prior to 2005. Every time you take a different route to work—or miss work completely—due to newly flooded streets, you become more like a citizen of New Orleans."[29]

The environmental similarities were obvious in Tidwell's mind, echoed by researchers: frequent flooding, spotty barriers to hold back high water, coastal storms exacerbated by climate change. Like New Orleans, Norfolk's rising sea levels endanger all of its inhabitants, but a particular ferocity faces low-income communities—populated primarily by Black residents—thanks to the distinctive pattern of poverty and substandard housing, unprotected low-lying areas, a historical legacy of segregation, racist housing policies, and other structural mechanisms of injustice.

Bordered by the Chesapeake Bay and the Elizabeth River, Norfolk is part of a sweeping region of coastal southeast Virginia known to the locals as Hampton Roads, a composite of seven cities connected by waterways and tunnels. Each has its own cultural folkways and distinctive demographics. The most urban of the group, Norfolk, which houses the largest naval station in the world, US Naval Station Norfolk,[30] is joined by Portsmouth, Chesapeake, Virginia Beach, Hampton, Newport News, and Suffolk. Scientists and environmental-policy groups place Norfolk near the top of the list of risk-prone coastal areas due to its low development, rapid sea level rise, and frequent flooding even from normal rainfall—in fact, says the Natural Resources Defense Council, the Norfolk metropolitan area, according to the Organization for Economic

Cooperation and Development, "ranks 10th in the world in the value of assets exposed to increased flooding from sea level rise."[31] In Hampton Roads and Norfolk, the impact of climate change is clear, intrinsically linked with a host of social and human health concerns.[32]

Demographically, Norfolk is precisely the same as pre-Katrina New Orleans, but its population of African American urban dwellers is much higher than the average US population: the city is 42 percent Black and 49 percent white.[33] As in New Orleans, Norfolk neighborhoods inhabited by people of color face substantial risk from frequent flooding and the possibility of increased hurricane-level storms.[34] The city's leaders recognize the need to address looming climate-related events and to focus on strategies for resilience, a concept that encompasses various methods by which local municipalities prepare and adapt systems and infrastructure to withstand climate-change impacts.[35] In 2013, Norfolk was one the first cities chosen to participate in the Rockefeller Foundation's 100 Resilient Cities initiative, which includes funds for a chief resilience officer and invitation to collaborate with similar cities, and one of eight cities in the RE.Invest Initiative, described by the city's coastal resilience plan as an initiative that "helps cities attract private investment and use public resources more efficiently to upgrade their infrastructure," and also to "beautify the City; make Norfolk more resilient to extreme weather, more attractive to businesses and investors and save significant taxpayer money."[36]

Experts praise Norfolk's official resilience strategy as "kind of miraculous."[37] And yet, questions about equitable outcomes linger. Will predominantly lower-income African American communities, rather than being strengthened and preserved, be inadvertently pushed out to make room for high-investment retail and higher-priced housing properties that are better protected from flooding and storms?[38] Will the plan amount to gentrification through resilience planning? The complicating factor is the biggest one: local resilience efforts cannot fully move forward without the resources and collaboration of the federal government. Public engagement is key.

Only a few streets away from the city's arts-centered "NEON District" (New Energy of Norfolk) and newly refurbished downtown waterfront, we might imagine that the large, low-land St. Paul's community is similar to the Ninth Ward of Norfolk, where more than four thousand low-income residents—95 percent Black—live in public housing apartments built in the 1950s. They resemble military barracks, with no stores or restaurants or other vestiges of play and community. Regular flooding is common; the area is unprotected.[39] Norfolk's official resilience and redevelopment planning is well underway, and city leaders plan to tear down the buildings and relocate residents elsewhere or move them back into the spaces built in their place—a mixed-use and mixed-income community that promises to break up the fabric of poverty and to become, according to the city's planning documents, "one of Norfolk's most desirable neighborhoods."[40] The new community will be newly fortified against rising sea levels while the original neighborhood had been inexplicably exposed for decades. Not all of the apartments will be replaced, though, leaving open questions about future housing once rental prices increase. As the Pulitzer Prize–winning nonprofit news outlet *Inside Climate News* noted in a sweeping investigative article, "The city has a history of demolishing housing for poor, Black residents and not following through on promises to help them find somewhere better. This time, officials say, things will be different."[41]

Communities tangibly experience the manifestations of climate change as a local reality, even as it is most often discussed on a global and national scale.[42] In St. Paul's and broader Norfolk, flooding continues regularly. It feels very real, to state the obvious. And yet, climate-change alarm bells may not necessarily reach African American low- and middle-income residents of communities like St. Paul's—and across the Hampton Roads area. A local environmental-justice strategy in the area means inviting impacted neighborhoods in to build awareness and solidarity and centering social justice, which improves outcomes, as scholar Michael Paolisso and his colleagues wrote: "Research, environmental decision making, and governance focused on adaptation to climate change impacts are strengthened by an explicit consideration of social justice issues."[43] Climate resilience, if enacted on the community level to help structurally dismantle—rather than perpetuate—decades-old inequities, requires inviting impacted neighborhoods and people to have "fair participation in planning and making decisions on adaptation."[44]

In Norfolk, this means centering and thoughtfully engaging Black communities as the city prepares for coastal storms, flooding, water contamination, and daily life in a place below sea level. Social-justice organizations and environmental-justice coalitions are crucial in mobilizing local citizens, working strategically with often limited resources.[45] Navigating climate-change preparedness as an environmental-justice pursuit means acknowledging that "environmental hazards are disproportionately located in low-income communities of people of color. . . . Sometimes the product of intentional siting decisions, and it is sometimes also the result of a long historical process of industrial legacies, racial segregation, zoning regulations, and other factors that lead to the formation of environmental inequality."[46] Contemporary environmental-justice mobilizations, according to a widespread examination by sociologists David Hess and Lacee Satcher, are successful when they garner local government support and inspire substantial public engagement and civil disobedience.[47] Success is also crafted by forging thoughtful relationships between local coalitions and larger national organizations, and capturing broad, nonlocal attention.[48]

Inviting wider audiences to see and understand local environmental matters can encourage them to re-contemplate a social-justice issue often communicated in ways that seem abstract and clinical. Shaping a just future is not possible without local communities mobilizing their own people, but also recognizing the importance of the federal government—directed by the president—in unlocking massive climate-change resources that can impact local daily life. Citizen involvement matters. Voting is essential. But how can this be encouraged and made manifest?

Enter storytelling, participatory culture—and, yes, comedy.

End Times and Science Deniers: Storytelling and Comedy in Climate Change

In 2006, former vice president Al Gore reemerged onto the public scene with *An Inconvenient Truth*, a documentary about his journey to convince world leaders about the looming, incontrovertible, human-caused destruction of climate change. The film premiered at the 2006 Sundance Film Festival and opened in Los Angeles and New York later that year. Cultural acclaim followed, media coverage took off, and the public took notice. In 2007, the film won the Academy Award for Best Documentary Feature, and Al Gore, along with the Intergovernmental Panel on Climate Change (IPCC), won the Nobel Peace Prize.

Much has been contemplated, years later, about *An Inconvenient Truth* and its role in firing up the postmillennial zeitgeist around climate change. Self-described liberals and conservatives, who at that time already broadly disagreed about whether or not global warming was happening, dug in with opposing positions beginning in 2006.[49] This chasm between so-called climate science deniers and scientific consensus would prove central to the storytelling and public engagement to follow, for better or worse. Culturally, *An Inconvenient Truth* was notable and influential: it positioned climate change onto a broad media and public agenda beyond scientists' insider conversations, and it launched years of new films and TV programs about climate change. Climate change was in vogue.

Hollywood's big climate-focused stories continue to beat a steady drum about ferocious storms and fires and destruction to the natural world—an apparent visual argument to hammer home the "realness" of climate change, echoing Gore's film. A particularly well-publicized exemplar is *The Years of Living Dangerously*, the celebrity-infused, climate-change-as-heart-thumping-action-story 2014 Emmy Award–winning docu-TV series, which had a second-season run on National Geographic in 2016. Calling it well meaning but "terrifying," the two directors of the Breakthrough Institute, a climate-change research group, wrote in a *New York Times* op-ed that "a decade's worth of research suggests that fear-based appeals about climate change inspire denial, fatalism and polarization."[50] Other titles in the climate-change entertainment genre include the meticulously crafted, award-winning documentaries *Chasing Coral* and *Chasing Ice*, which emotionally invite viewers to see environmental wreckage up close. Any lingering questions about storms, ecological decay, and nature under siege should have been dissuaded by the big-entertainment portraits. Local angles, and the perspectives of people hurt "first and worst," though, are not the spotlights.

But what about humorous efforts to engage publics in climate change? Comedy is meaningful. As Lauren Feldman and I wrote in previous work, "In the face of a crisis as complex and consequential as climate change, comedy offers a valuable, if often underused, pillar of communication—one that can engage attention, offer a sense of hope and agency, and in some cases, overcome partisan resistance. In this way, comedy may help to encourage wider public acceptance of climate solutions and foster the public engagement needed to pressure policy-makers to act more aggressively."[51]

And yet, mimicking the editorial framing established by *An Inconvenient Truth* and the big nature-destruction entertainment projects that came later, climate-change denial—and its absurdity—is quite often the comedic target. But poking fun at so-called deniers as ignorant idiots who dismiss science, while perhaps cathartic for frustrated progressive-minded media makers, is useless strategy more than fifteen years after Gore sounded a cultural alarm bell. Twenty years into postmillennial climate-change awareness, the majority of Americans now agree that climate change is real and human caused,[52] regardless of how master-fully this reality is distorted by conservative elected officials whose reelection fates rely at least partially on the big energy lobby. Worse, denier-focused messages are harmful: focusing on partisan identity cues (such as Republicans as climate-change deniers) creates a boomerang effect that simply sends audiences to burrow deeper into their ideological camps.[53] For example, in a 2015 Funny or Die short video starring eco-warrior Ed Begley Jr., titled *Climate Science Denier Disorder*, the portrait of "deniers" is clear: they are stupid, according to the video's text and subtext, and they are Republicans.[54] But does this help? Not really, unless laughing within a progressive echo chamber is the goal, even if the intent is well meaning.

Climate change is a hot target for humor on *The Daily Show*, *The Colbert Report*, and *Saturday Night Live*, among other comedy shows, which generally focus on politics and Trump. Largely still missing, though, are tangible, real local ideas and angles—which can be engaging and attention-grabbing when seen through a humorous lens. Equally important, comedy can push back the hopelessness to invite in people who have the most at stake.

In a participatory-culture era, where grassroots organizations are producing their own high-production-value stories to engage audiences, we begin to find what is generally lacking in climate-change stories and comedy: people of color and local human impact that moves beyond nature portraits. For instance, in 2016, progressive social-justice group NextGen America produced and distributed *Spotlight California*, a multipart YouTube docu-comedy series that follows the journey and funny antics of Kiran Deol, a comedian of color, as she makes her way through California to visit with local experts and people feeling first-hand the effects of environmental contamination and climate change. Black and Brown communities are at the fore, which "highlight[s] the human implications of drought and lack of access to water, air pollution and health, oil policy, and more."[55] Comedy storytelling is a necessary strategy, said the organization's creative director, to mobilize young voters around the environment and climate.[56]

A scripted comedy web series, *The North Pole*, which launched its second season in 2019, centers the humor around a diverse group of friends based in Oakland, California, as they work through the hilarious absurdities and outrage of interconnected gentrification and climate change.

The North Pole merges activism and creative entertainment in its design. It is produced by Hollywood actress and activist Rosario Dawson, social-justice group Movement Generation, and Favianna Rodriguez of Culture Strike (now the Center for Cultural Power). Whimsy is essential to *The North Pole*, said comedy writer and show creator Josh Healey in a media interview.[57] To launch the second season and simultaneous grassroots mobilization campaign, *The North Pole*'s producers took the show on the road across the United States, partnering with local grassroots organizations in each city to inspire community members to get involved in local climate and environmental-justice efforts.[58]

With hilarious exceptions crafted by creatively empowered social-justice organizations, we might surmise—if we only paid attention to the main-stage entertainment marketplace—that climate change is a White people's movement, an elite problem focused on existentially huge and impossible destruction, partisan infighting, and polar bears. We might conclude, despite public opinion data to the contrary, that our time is best spent convincing people that climate change is real. We might obfuscate the extent to which many communities of color and low-income people are acutely vulnerable now and over the long term, particularly if they are not invited and supported to participate in real ways, from organizing to voting. And we might not be able to see or imagine what local climate-justice engagement looks like, and why it matters. Can comedy help empower people locally, where climate change and environmental justice are not abstract at all, but facets of daily life? We travel back into our experiment to find out.

Polar Bears vs. Black Bears:
Finding Absurdity in Climate Injustice

It is a hot, quiet day in downtown Los Angeles, August 2019. We are all meeting for the first time at Hip Hop Caucus's West Coast office, a hidden space behind a vegan deli in the heart of the fashion district, bordering Skid Row's tent cities and gentrified landscape of new juice bars and original taquerias. The "we" is a diverse mix of activists and artists. There are the professional comedy writers and performers from Chicago, New York, LA, and Atlanta—Yedoye Travis, Shantira Jackson, Clark Jones, Aminah Imani, and Tessa Hirsch—led by our fearless comedian and comedy process facilitator Bethany Hall. There are the activists and grassroots organizers: Rev Yearwood, Liz Havstad, Jazmine Williams, and joke-cracking music supervisor and producer Dejuan Cross of Hip Hop Caucus; and environmental-justice advocate Roger Kim, who directs the Climate and Clean Energy Equity Fund. Filmmaker Elijah Karriem is here, camera rolling.

Sitting around the living-room-style open space on couches and puffy chairs, we have come together to begin what will become a months-long collaboration to produce a live comedy show and collaborative documentary in Norfolk. It will be the first time (we think) that a climate-themed comedy show directly addresses communities of color, and also the first on this topic that will be performed exclusively by Black comedians. Today, we are kicking off the first day of our comedy co-creation process. After we share the expectations for the "no bad ideas" generative energy space, the workshop-style creative construction session begins with a full curricular immersion into environmental-justice and climate-change urgency. Imagine "Climate Change and Environmental Justice 101." The comedians are the students in the beginning, and the activists and experts are the professors, opening up space for questions and discussions—and yes, plenty of dark jokes and observations.

Rev is fervent and impassioned when he explains the mission of Hip Hop Caucus's Think 100% campaign: basic awareness of climate-change injustice for multicultural Americans is not enough. Mobilizing them to vote is critical. The countdown clock to irreversible damage is down to a handful of years, he says, and there is no time to waste. Liz Havstad talks about climate-change statistics in precise health and environmental-justice terms: 68 percent of Black communities in the United States live within thirty miles of a coal-fired power plant, they are dramatically more likely to suffer from asthma and other health-related impacts of environmental pollution, and they are the least likely to reap economic or other benefits from major energy companies even while they physically exist together in the same areas.[59] Historically damaged by segregationist housing policies, they are revictimized as energy companies distort truth and manipulate communities of color, suppress Black voters, and try to distract them from understanding their disproportionate health burden.[60] The 101 session is a look at campaign strategy, too, as Roger Kim talks about local policy advocacy in key states, including Virginia, and what local communities, joined by groups like the NAACP and Sierra Club, are doing to fight for clean energy futures. Voting is a central recurring theme—and notably, in local and state elections, not just federal ones.

Even in the collaborative workshop itself, comedy's potential value is clear as comic relief and catharsis and resilience. The data is enraging. The week transforms from quasi–college classroom to comedy writers' room as the comedians work through a guided, improv-based creative process to share their instinctive, personal reactions about what they learned. What was memorable? Who are the characters in their lives who combine with, or are inspired by, the factual scenarios they absorbed? What was too horrible to be true, and thus, ripe for comedy to point out the absurd? The comedians coalesce around the racial-injustice theme—summed up, as comedian Yedoye says, with the idea that the mainstream climate-change movement feels to many Black communities like it is more about aesthetics and appearances than saving lives, and that "the people contributing least to environmental decay are suffering most from it and have no ability to relocate."[61] Adds Shantira, there is power and outrage in the reality that people of color are the most culturally influential (think music, fashion), but they are the "least visible" in the movement to avert a disaster that affects them the most.

Across several days of a creative process that is both open-ended and structured into assignments and concept building, the ideas and characters flow. The comics come up with sketches about

White-people-Birkenstock-wearing Greenpeace meetings adapting for Black participants, a parody of Black spiritual music as a climate-justice song, White people buying land in urban Black communities as "beach-front property" (a biting twist on gentrification with a climate-change angle), Black Captain Planet as a sloppy and worn-out old dude in therapy to deal with his depression about the earth, suburban white polar bears vs. urban black bears arguing about who is more screwed (polar bears get great PR, say the comedians), and, "something about straws . . . we are feeling bad about straws."[62] There are stand-up jokes and characters, and in-group laughs around references to Black women wearing their hair in natural "flood styles" when the water won't stop rising in the streets. They build on each other's ideas—*yes, and*—and find ways to work in the angles that strike them as the most outrageous and funny for a predominantly Black audience.

When we see it up close, grotesque absurdity lurks in climate-change data and the unique circumstances that face many Black and Brown communities—a wrecking ball of destruction already in motion while we virtually sit still in a ridiculous swirling eddy of bureaucratic mess. Comedians are the best equipped among us to shine a spotlight on what is ludicrous, to lean into the complexity of what is often communicated in wonky or elitist technocratic terms, and to pull out the kernels of clear, outrageous truth. They are able, as scholar Jeffrey Jones asserted, to use comedy to find the breathtakingly clear *common sense* of what is wrong, thereby opening a new way for us to look at an old problem.[63]

When we come back together as a group at the end of our creative workshop week, the atmosphere is open and supportive and even a little festive. The comedians present a full show's worth of sketches, recurring characters, parody spirituals, stand-up bits, and audience participation gags—like a standard entertainment-industry pitch but infused with the facts and angles shared by the climate experts. They have, in essence, translated the material from one language to an entirely different, funny lexicon of accessible, memorable humor for an audience that is most often overlooked in climate-change storytelling, despite the egregious irony of disproportionate damage. From the language of science and doom to one of bemused common sense and play. The basic outline of the show is set, and we have about three months to pull it all together.

Producing Comedy as a Local Organizing Tool:
Ain't Your Mama's Heat Wave

Cut to October. Our group of comedians, filmmakers, and activists is tossing funny banalities back and forth over lukewarm coffee and hash browns at a Marriott Hotel in Norfolk. A persistent gray dampness hovers over the downtown panorama of war ships and a gleaming, gentrified waterfront facade prematurely draped with holiday wreathes and big red bows. The final cast members for the project are here for our 8:00 a.m. documentary production meeting—comedians Clark, Aminah, and Kristen, the local talent—along with Rev, Liz, Elijah, and me. Rev, wearing his clerical collar, gets us going with a little inspirational gravity: "If I could go back in time and tell the story of New Orleans before Hurricane Katrina, I would have called in the comedians. Norfolk is that same story. With what we do here, if we can save *one* life with this project, that would be worth it."[64]

Over the past several months, Hip Hop Caucus has fired up its grassroots organizing machine with Norfolk community leaders and other local folks, and the comedians got to work on stand-up comedy material based on the Comedy ThinkTanks. Working remotely on a live sketch variety production—through Zoom and conference calls—has been a challenge, even if fun. The kind of show we originally had in mind, a filmed Second City–type sketch and stand-up show with music and set changes, requires time physically together in one place to find the flow and humor in theatrical moments and comedic timing, so we have landed on stand-up as our show genre. We are embracing the unpredictability of artistic process in our decision making. Today, our first day of filming, the docu-comedy's logline is about to come to life: a diverse group of comedians takes a funny journey to Norfolk, Virginia, and they learn through local leaders and ordinary people about resilient community and the challenges of daily life. *Ain't Your Mama's Heat Wave* is born.

The docu-comedy is designed, from the logistics of production to what we see on screen, as a participatory project with leaders and members of the Norfolk community—to authentically share what is real on the ground and to ensure that "people [who are not usually shown] will see themselves in the climate change conversation. It's on all levels. We have folks who are kids on the block, in the community garden, to the comedians, to the mayor, so you have all levels of government, the different aspects and people who are engaged, and they will see themselves as important,"[65] says Rev. It is production process as grassroots organizing and a mechanism to build community power, telling the story of Norfolk's climate challenge through "buckets" of local-level political, cultural, public engagement, including, as Rev puts it, "the influencers, the actual culture community, the religious community, the government community, there was the civil-rights-leaders community, and media, those who got the word out."[66]

As the comedians make their way through Norfolk, meeting with people and using some of their Comedy ThinkTanks material—classic fish-out-of-water observational humor about the absurdity of reality—the cast of characters is broad and diverse, a mapping of community engagement roles: Charles "Batman" Brown, the young music marketing influencer and grassroots organizer; Gaylene Kanoyton, president of the Hampton Roads branch of the NAACP; Keja Reel, local business owner and community influencer along with her husband, a popular hip hop DJ; Dr. Tom Allen, local geography researcher and professor at Norfolk's Old Dominion University, who has been tracking the sea level rise; Deidre "Mama D" Love, founder and executive director of the Vivian C. Mason Art & Technology Center for Teens in St. Paul's, alongside the teen poets and artists Malik, Tiffany, Alisha, and Zenaya; Rev. Dr. Dwight Riddick, tenured pastor of the sprawling Gethsemane Baptist Church in Newport News, Virginia; local community network builder Toya Sosa; Mayor Kenny Alexander, Norfolk's first African American mayor; and others.

In Norfolk, everyone in this "cast" plays a role in reaching and engaging with communities who are uniquely vulnerable to climate impacts—and on the most basic level, as Keja Reel says, "the flooding is not discriminating, it floods everywhere"[67]—and yet, they are not consistently working together. Reaching out to set up documentary scenes and spread the word about the live comedy show is itself a process that convenes disparate sectors. Batman, the local grassroots influencer, says it is vital, in this community, to bring together three different "worlds" on the local level if community engagement on climate resilience is going to be effective in Black communities—social-justice activists, entertainment influencers, and the political world, which often operate in their own separate siloes, as he reflects: "You always have to create a mechanism or a platform to bring people together to have those kinds of conversations when there is a disconnect. . . . There needs to be more things done through art and through comedy to keep creating a place where everybody would want to come. . . . It's always best, I think, when those three worlds can come together and partner up. I think the problem is that doesn't happen as much as it should."[68] People are responding to the cultural spark of comedy as an unusual idea.

Clark, Aminah, and Kristen take us on a funny, accessible jaunt through a challenging topic, approaching it on screen and off as a friendly road trip—not journalistic interviews, but conversations and adventures fueled by the authentic curiosity of travelers. They visit the local music store, neighborhoods, and a club with Batman, Gaylene, Keja, and Toya; sample an area dish, "yock," with Kristen and her mom; go back to St. Paul's to hang with the young people and Mama D several days after the shooting at the community center; learn about the first enslaved Africans to step foot in the country four hundred years ago at nearby Fort Monroe; sit in church and debate Pastor Riddick about whether faith leaders or stand-up comedians are better at mobilizing the flock; splash with Tom Allen, the university climate scientist, in the casual "sunny day flooding" of a high-tide day; and meet with Mayor Alexander and the city's resilience team.

The comedic tone is not incidental, but strategic for both the organizing and the eventual audience experience of watching the final film in Norfolk and similar places. Amusing visits from funny people encourage even the experts to be conversational, accessible humans, joking back and joining in the absurdity and gravity of the facts. As filmmaker Elijah expresses it, "Climate change can be exhausting. . . . Comedy is the perfect vehicle to help communicate this issue, especially when you're dealing with people of color, you're already dealing with different layers of cultural trauma, especially in America, where you have a lot of people that have unresolved or unaddressed trauma from a historical perspective. So mixing that in with another issue—oh, we're already socially or financially disenfranchised, and now we have to deal with a global climate catastrophe on our hands? You know, it can be a bit much."[69] Gaylene Kanoyton, the local NAACP leader, a veteran of years in the trenches in the fight for environmental justice in the area, thinks comedy is particularly important for raising awareness and mobilizing local Norfolk-area Black communities:

> We know that when a crisis happens, whether it's a tsunami or an environmental crisis, climate environmental crisis happens, that African Americans and underserved are the first that it affects. . . . People remember through music and comedy or something that's memorable. But you know, we're such in a crisis age right now. People are stressed. So everything is stressful, but if you break relief through comedy, and when I say relief I'm not talking about relief in terms of, making light of it. I'm just talking about bringing relief that this is a serious matter, but we can put it in a way that you can understand it and enjoy learning at the same time. . . . If you have one more documentary [on climate change], one more article to read, it's going to tick so many people off. You've got to find creative ways to educate the people most vulnerable.[70]

But even through the light tone, the potentially dire implications for underserved, predominantly Black communities—represented through a particular spotlight on St. Paul's—are clear in the filming. Many, as she points out through her NAACP work, are not aware of how directly climate change and environmental justice impact them, and they are not included in the planning conversations, which leads to a disconnect: "It's easy for people to sit there and be like, 'oh my God why are you staying there? Why don't you move?' You need to be able to hear the barriers that prevent people from leaving flood-prone areas. It's just not that simple and we need to be able to tell our story. Nobody can tell our story better than we can."[71] Deirdre "Mama D" Love is blunt: "I think that as long as this community has been economically disenfranchised, nothing was done about climate impacts. It is the chronic crisis. . . . I think the people who suffered through it should have the opportunity to benefit from any of the improvements that are going to come."[72]

Throughout the process of producing the docu-comedy and simultaneously drumming up interest for the live comedy show in a month, Hip Hop Caucus hosted new climate-change coalition meetings between sectors—not for the cameras, but off-screen, as a way to leverage the comedy project as a mobilizing centerpiece for future voting-engagement work. One of the first gatherings of faith leaders to talk about climate change and Black communities came together in this way, and a local gathering convened young activists and an aide from the mayor's office, alongside cultural influencers. The meeting of faith leaders to discuss hurricane preparedness and climate-change impacts, says Pastor Riddick, was meaningful for area clergy: "We talked about the potential of what could happen for those in the event of having maybe a Category 2 hurricane and so I think what it was, it was a tremendous eye opener. . . . It was one of those meetings where people left saying, 'Hey, tell me more. How can I get the information about this?'"[73]

Strengthening and convening the local network, sparked by the novelty, curiosity, and entertainment excitement of the comedy, is a process by which a cultural activity can help build community power for the present and the future. Says Batman, "Energy creates momentum and momentum creates opportunity. . . . The more we are successful with this, the easier it'll be for us to build up our actual Virginia team and to partner with organizations who are like-minded and that want to do the work, as well as government entities that want to partner and help us fund and launch different initiatives around the city."[74] In this way, producing the documentary itself helps to power a local coalition that centers people of color. Creating comedy becomes a vehicle for community mobilization in a place that is not accustomed to seeing itself represented in media portrayals, admittedly not ready for the climate impacts or hurricanes heading its way—a place where many people are simply exhausted by daily life.

"Do You Know Any Sea Turtles?"

"Heyyyyyy, Norfolk, what's up, what's up?!"

Grammy-nominated singer, actress, and climate activist Antonique Smith, a longtime Hip Hop Caucus collaborator, walks on stage with Rev Yearwood. The two nights of live climate-change-themed comedy shows have arrived in Norfolk. We have reached the culmination of the documentary and comedy-show production journey, and the energy is hot—from the red carpet to the audience buzz in the sold-out six-hundred-seat historic Crispus Attucks Theater, the "Apollo of the South," built and financed by African American entrepreneurs a hundred years earlier. It is hallowed ground to jazz and comedy aficionados, a place that hosted Redd Foxx and musician Cab Calloway. The audience is nodding along to beats from music producer Cross, who is sitting just off stage left with his laptop and turntable.

Everyone is here: Mama D and her crew of teens, the mayor and his top aide, local business leaders, musicians and artists, faith leaders, curious neighbors. Hampton Roads grassroots organizer Batman has been working his connections for months, and he is pleased with the turnout—the "public engagement sectors" are all accounted for, from curious community members to social-justice leaders to artists to the political folks. It is unusual for this mix of people to come together here, he says. Elijah and his crew are filming the show, so cameras are everywhere. Rev warms up the crowd and sets the scene: "We feel climate destruction the *hardest* and the *worst* in our African American communities. It's time for us to get engaged—this *ain't* your mama's heat wave. Are you ready? Are you *ready*?" It's showtime.

Comedy host Mamoudou N'Diaye hits hard with the racial-injustice theme: "So, you know, climate change is really worrying the White people. But you know what White people care about? Here's the order: first, polar bears. Next, straws. And after that: sea turtles. Do you know any sea turtles? Do you know any? I know the Ninja Turtles, but I don't give a *fuck* about sea turtles. But way down here at the bottom, here we are, Black people—we're below sea turtles. White people definitely care more about sea turtles than Black people." Kristen, the local comedian, talks about buying a canoe for her kids' first car because of the flooding. Aminah jokes about creating a swim team for the local Norfolk State University because of the rising sea levels, working on natural hairstyles for the floods, and getting ready to visit some newly hot "climate change vacation spots." Mamoudou keeps the show moving between sets that sneak in serious material amid jokes about dating, poverty, and Clark's setup about Dr. Martin Luther King Jr., which he performs with a dead-on imitation that kills with this audience: Dr. King was ill equipped for jobs other than "inspirational speaker," Clark says, because his voice and cadence were too distracting for, say, selling food in a deli: "I . . . have a *creeaaaaaam pie*. . . . I have a number *seventy-six* . . . with marmalade . . . with *maaaaaarmalaaaaade*."

And then Clark sees Mama D and the teen community center group in the crowd, sitting near the front by the stage. He begins his new set:

Figure 6.2: Comedian Clark Jones prepares to go on stage to perform at the *Ain't Your Mama's Heat Wave* live comedy show in Norfolk, Virginia

"During my first visit to St. Paul's, I got shot at. So that was a little true story. I'm from the South Side of Chicago, so you know I'm tough. . . . I'm walking back to the community center and I say, 'Oh, let me stop at this BP real quick.'"

He pauses. The teens, who immediately know where this is going, gleefully cheer him on. Clark waits a beat for the wave of laughter to take its course. He continues, pacing the stage, warming up to the jokes:

I'll tell you who don't care that I'm from the South Side of Chicago: the dude who started shooting about three feet from me. I'm trying to get in the building and the door's locked because it's Sunday. I'm like, "This place ain't safe on the Lord's day? The community center with the garden?" Mama D didn't tell me "don't go to the BP." . . . Three seconds later, six shots, right across the street from me. We all like to think, like, we in an emergency situation, we just gonna Jesse Owens real quick. It's nothing. I ran track in high school, like if anything is ever gonna break out, I'm gonna break out. But your body gotta know you fitting to run, right? The older you get—all you young people in here, I'm telling y'all, I'm the ghost of fat-dude future, OK? You gotta warn your body that you're about to run. Now in my head, I'm gone. I hear one shot, I'm gone. But y'all know how *Boyz in the Hood* was slow motion? Slow motion was my top speed, but the volume was still the same as I was running. I made it about five steps.[75]

The crowd loses its collective mind—the young people are up out of their seats, laughing and shouting up to the stage. Clark is grinning, cracking himself up. I sneak a peek from backstage and try to find everyone who was there that day—our film crew, the teens, their mentors—and scan the crowd. Everyone is laughing and clapping, rocking back and forth in their seats, heads thrown back, a communal experience of something that seems like catharsis and connection. It is a reclaiming of a moment of trauma, and a recognition of community resilience and strength. We are in something together, he is saying, in a language that welcomes understanding through the communion of jokes, as he reflected months later:

> Sometimes truth is stranger than fiction. I didn't try to put too much sauce on [the jokes about the shooting]. I just told what happened in an elaborated way, in a detailed way, and real thoughts that I had about the situation. . . . Comedy just has to be genuine and real. There are plenty of White comedians who come from challenged neighborhoods and all of that. But you see somebody who's the same color as you, there's that natural assumption that they get it. Because no matter how rich you are in America, if you're a Black person and you have a Black family, you're only so many degrees away from certain communities. So that's not to say that a White comedian couldn't go up there and kill and do the exact same thing. But trying to comb through the world of comedy to find [that connection] is like, why make things more difficult than they have to be? . . . I'm just thankful to the community for opening up. I took away so much from this experience personally about me as a writer, me as a comedian.[76]

· · · · ·

In its co-creative process and its final product, *Ain't Your Mama's Heat Wave* was and is an experiment to leverage the attention-getting entertainment potential of comedy to spotlight local community, an attempt to illustrate the intersection of social justice and climate change beyond portraits of nature and storms, focused on people. It is about Norfolk, but it is also about places around the country—usually unseen until and unless trauma is visible—that are immediately and disproportionately affected by the interconnected complexities of environmental injustice. Big-media portraits about ecological destruction and climate change are not showing this complexity, or the areas that look and feel like Hampton Roads. As Liz Havstad points out, reflecting and centering historically marginalized people can help build civic power within their communities:

> In most places, there's a disconnect between those working through the environmental movement on climate change and the communities on the front lines—in this case, African American communities in the Hampton Roads area. And part of that disconnect is a culture of the environmental and climate movement that is just perceived as White and elitist and as an issue that isn't as integral to people's daily lives as it really is. . . . This is a quintessentially American story of public housing, racial and economic injustice, at the intersections of the climate crisis. But the climate crisis isn't just an environmental issue. It's a housing issue. It's a jobs issue. It's a health issue. It's a public safety issue. It's a national security issue.[77]

Relayed through a lighthearted humorous approach, it is a story about community resilience and solidarity, not pity, meant to forge strength and local networks to mobilize for clean energy futures. Comedy has not been leveraged for this topic through the lens of Black performers, and its cultural resonance can help build local community power because, as Liz says, "People can use their cultural expression to affect when they're participating in the political process. Culture is a shorthand for how we all relate to each other. If we want to build power through collective action, that collective action is taking place because we're connecting through that shorthand of a shared culture and identity. . . . There's a disenfranchisement of communities of color who have this shared cultural identity and we're just flipping that script and making that a vehicle for collective action."[78] Comedy is meaningful as a creative vehicle to capture attention and interest in places that do not feel seen or heard; it provides a way into a topic that has felt disconnected from many daily lives, and an entertaining reason to convene and discuss in the first place. From Batman: "We're not hitting this demographic properly. . . . The regular way of doing this a lot of times is boring. Comedy can do things that other mediums sometimes can't. I think the best comedians and writers are able to simultaneously make us laugh and pass information in that same joke. When done effectively, this is a way where it can be done to show differences, but also show our similarities. We're all in the same battle in general, but this [climate change] affects different communities in different ways. It definitely affects communities differently."[79]

To be sure, comedy is not a magical panacea for explicit disenfranchisement, gentrification, and climate change. Humor cannot convey the full scientific or sociological or policy complications of these challenges, nor would we want it to. *Ain't Your Mama's Heatwave* itself is not a perfect vehicle for both hilarious comedy and efficacious messages, and it did not turn out precisely as we had planned and designed it as a multifaceted full-sketch and variety show. And yet, as with any form of innovation or experiment, the first step starts a new idea, building to the next and the next.

Cultural products can shine a glaring spotlight to engage local and national audiences, and comedy is unexpected and disruptive. It is a critique and an invitation. In 2021, *Ain't Your Mama's Heat Wave*, as a first-of-its-kind docu-comedy special, premiered at the DC Environmental Film Festival, followed by a year of community engagement in a series of festivals that included the Charlotte Black Film Festival, the Urban Film Festival, the Oakland International Film Festival, the Detroit Black Film Festival, the March on Washington Film Festival, the Baltimore International Black Film Festival, the Climate Crisis Film Festival, and the Planet in Focus International Environmental Film Festival. But its larger destiny is its role as a local voter-organizing tool: Hip Hop Caucus and its team of local neighborhood organizers are taking *Ain't Your Mama's Heat Wave* on the road, back to Norfolk and all over as a centerpiece of its cultural efforts to mobilize Black and Brown voters around an explicit theme and call to action: "Racial justice is climate justice." With the promise of creativity and entertainment, the same local organizing machine that came together to produce the docu-comedy and fill the Attucks Theater for comedy is powering local voter-turnout actions, with the original comedians on hand to attract attention, and to infuse fun and excitement into the task at hand.

In its final manifestation as a local grassroots voter-mobilization tool that centers Black communities, the comedy here is about much more than entertainment, although the accessibility and shared cultural experience are the mechanisms by which people might be willing to engage

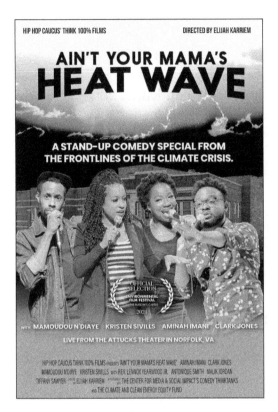

Figure 6.3: Movie poster for *Ain't Your Mama's Heat Wave*

in messages that are otherwise exhausting or, as Batman says, "boring." It is about bringing people together, reflecting their voices and their stories, celebrating their resilience and empathizing with their struggles, and inviting others along. Science says the countdown clock is ticking. Ultimately, and over the long term, as Rev says, "The number one thing that we need to do with this kind of crisis is to broaden the movement."[80] The climate catastrophe is urgent, and if comedy can play a fresh starring role, there is no time to waste in bringing it into the picture.

7

"I've Always Been a Syringe-Half-Full Kinda Guy"

Changing the Entertainment Comedy Pipeline

Comedian Murf Meyer goes for the pathos right away, but he doesn't stay there long enough to wallow: "Hey-eyyyy, I'm Murf! I'm a former heroin addict and current alcoholic. . . . I come from a big family. My mom's one of nine kids, my dad's one of eight. So I've got a lot of aunts and uncles, a shit-ton of cousins, and I'd say half of us are functioning alcoholics. Now, the other half are also alcoholics, buuuu-ut, they don't function too good."[1]

To hear him tell it, in a raspy smoker's growl laced with bemused sing-song cadence, "damn near thirty years" of addiction is practically inevitable if the lottery of your birth plops you in the middle of Luzerne County, Pennsylvania. It is the stuff of American working-class boom-to-bust struggle, the kind of place where presidential hopefuls literally roll up their sleeves every four years (for TV cameras, of course) to prove their humanity by visiting so-called hard-working Americans in diners and hardware stores. Generations of Pennsylvania coal miners bequeathed to their kin storytelling chops while, according to Murf, they tried to "drown that black lung" and wash the coal dust down with a shot of whiskey and a beer at Nana McDonough's bar ("Whaddya gonna use, water? Nah, you gotta get a little nip.").

His birthplace is the unhappiest region of the United States, says a 2014 study.[2] Murf thinks those smug nerds could have saved their research money (and did they have to call it the "Unhappy Cities" report?), but then again, they have a point even though they missed the full story:

> Why the long face? Weh-e-ell, first the coal mines dried up, then came
> the catastrophic natural disaster, plus our local economy's not worth a

dog's dick, and we've been plagued with rampant political corruption. . . . Also, for decades, we've been haunted with longstanding reports of child sexual abuse from the Catholic Church. Anyhow, four generations of all that—turns out that's kind of a bummer. Sooo, well done, you Harvard hot shots. Looks like your analysis on us sad sacks checks out. . . . I reckon that's why booze and drugs have always been pillars of our community.[3]

These days, hopelessness in places like northeastern Pennsylvania is such a rote media narrative that the stories seem to write themselves (and probably do, considering the local-news death spiral) through a repetitive template of unemployment, prescription pills, heroin, overdoses, meth labs, tragedy. Addiction- and poverty-porn headlines are steady, unrelenting, expected. Drug-related deaths are driving up the cost of morgues and cremations, even while arrests for drug possession climb higher—"and we all know that worked well in the past," says Murf.[4] There is no end in sight. If you ask Murf, this is all pretty exhausting. And victim-blaming messages about addiction are downright hilarious considering the obscenity of big pharma's bloated opioid-crisis profits in a place that needs economic opportunity more than it ever needed prisons or overprescribed pills.[5] Maybe the big cultural story is the wrong one. Maybe the punchline and the villains are backwards. Is there a new way to look at things—to cut through the daily diet of shame and stigma to give a guy like Murf a little hope?

Enter comedy.

Murf Meyer took a winding road to a professional comedy career. He worked as a bartender, security guard, psychiatric hospital orderly, pharmaceutical delivery driver, and, he adds, for "a telemarketer that was a money-laundering front, and a laundromat chain that was a front for a phone-sex business."[6] None of those jobs, he points out, required his attention more than the occupation of "full-time IV heroin user" in his late teens and early twenties: "I'll tell you what, *that* was the hardest goddamn job I ever had. I mean, you're on call 24/7. Whenever you're not shooting up, you're busy doing prep work, like haggling with someone at a pawn shop or doing maintenance work on the one dull syringe you got left. . . . It's an exhausting job with shitty benefits."[7] The comedy part, though? Not entirely unexpected. His kindergarten teacher, notes his mom, Jane, said he "show[ed] more interest in being the center of attention than his schoolwork."[8] He sat out the Pledge of Allegiance, a display of "oppositional defiance" (according to his fifth-grade report card) that checks out for a self-described "guy with an anti-authoritarian streak" who sees the humor, absurdity, and hypocrisy in institutions of power that could use a little tweaking.

Murf found his village and his calling in improv comedy classes at New York's Upright Citizens Brigade Theater, where he met comedian Chris Gethard, a fellow traveler playing on the edges of weird and funny—and, like Murf, working to stay one step ahead of anxiety and depression. As a mustachioed, hypervolume monologuing announcer dressed in a 1970s-era suit, Murf became a long-running cast member of the quirky cult classic comedy program, *The Chris Gethard Show*, which aired first on a New York public access channel and then on cable networks Fusion and truTV for a combined seven years, from 2011 to 2018.[9] Beloved by comedy luminaries and a fiercely devoted fan base, the show landed him a talent agent, a creative community of quirky and boundary-pushing comedians, and an opportunity to experiment with his own comedic voice. Keeping his head above water—treading through cycles of self-medicating and shame—had occupied some part of his brain since his first sip of booze at eleven and his first joint at thirteen. Comedy offered a way to find a laugh and cope.

The Gethard show came to a close as Murf began workshopping a comedic platform to share his story of self-medicating, mental health, and coming to terms with being sexually assaulted when he was eleven years old. Sure, maybe it was heady stuff for humor, but there was no shortage of material, he thought. He tried out jokes and storytelling on stages around New York. He took notes on what worked, learned from the bombs, and found new places for laughs. In 2019, he heard about our new initiative, which invited comedians to develop and pitch their best material that could break open real human space to talk about social issues—comedy that went to the heart of ignored lived experiences and urged its makers to creatively talk about hilarious, dark, marginalized stories and taboo or polarizing topics that are too often unseen in the entertainment marketplace. Drug addiction, stigma, and childhood sexual trauma? Perfect. He pulled together an application packet and applied to our Yes, And . . . Laughter Lab (affectionately known as YALL, an acronym that's both gender inclusive and a fun double entendre or dumb dad joke, depending on how you see it). A few months later, the news arrived: he was a finalist and then a winner—one of six projects out of nearly four hundred—in YALL's pilot year. His live comedy show idea, *Murf Meyer Is Self-Medicated*, had a place to build and possibly find a home with an audience.

And so it was that Murf Meyer found himself on a dusty basement comedy stage in New York's Lower East Side in the summer of 2019, pitching his project and telling his story to a carefully assembled audience of fellow funny people, entertainment industry executives—and, for the first time in a room like this one, leaders of major foundations and social-justice and humanitarian organizations. *Murf Meyer Is Self-Medicated* was a hit. Hushed reverence hovered over the painful bits, and well-earned laughter came when his careful timing brought the audience back into the safe place of comedy just when it felt too dark to giggle. After all, he reminded us, "I've always been a syringe-half-full kinda guy."

Things moved simultaneously quickly and slowly after Murf's pitch presentation at YALL, as entertainment projects tend to go. A flurry of TV network meetings followed. Production companies wanted to meet and talk about the project: could it be a TV show *and* a live show? What was possible? As Murf recalled, the usual entertainment path certainly opened up, but it fell a little short: "There were a million meetings. And we spent some time in LA pitching different stuff at different levels of the development ladder and whatnot. But there are always a lot of snakes in the grass in that process . . . and on this topic [in the entertainment industry], there's some fetishizing." And then, a new twist to what might have been a classic entertainment industry story: executives from the global Open Society Foundations (OSF), a long-running philanthropic funder for mental health and addiction who had watched Murf's pitch in the room, took notice immediately. Comedy about self-medicating, intentionally designed by a former heroin user to address stigma and provide hope to people who needed it? They had never seen or imagined anything like it. Comedy was not something they had ever considered, but Murf's story and funny delivery of hard truths was compelling and evocative. The foundation gave *Murf Meyer Is Self-Medicated* a sizable grant—the first for Murf, and a very notable comedy first for OSF.

With his new foundation funding, Murf got to work creating the show. He honed the sharp bits of comedy and dedicated himself to learning more about the harm-reduction movement, a growing body of science and practice in addiction treatment that takes its cues from historical movements for oppressed peoples, like the women's movement and the Black Panthers—social-change efforts Murf calls "grassroots mutual aid work." After years of battling stigma that made his own addiction harder to confront, finding a community of people pushing for safety over abstinence, care over shame, was a revelation: "When people are kind of shoved aside and pushed into the shadows, they still take care of each other, and I think that's the one big thing even for addicts." Comedy is new for the harm-reduction movement, just as it is for the philanthropic sector that supports it. They are learning from each other, says Murf: "The harm-reduction folks are like, oh, so there's a *clown* at the party now. All right. Let's see what his deal is."

In March 2021, *Murf Meyer Is Self-Medicated* launched first as a podcast, the first leg in a longer entertainment journey that is building to become a live comedy tour of treatment and recovery facilities and communities across the country—and maybe TV in the future. In his entertaining, intimate, comedic storytelling style, Murf takes listeners deep into his own story while he interrogates the injustice and scandal of the opioid crisis and interviews a cross-section of people like harm-reduction experts, drug users, people in recovery, former police officers, and even his mom. It is stand-up comedy meets *This American Life* meets *The Moth* story hour, weaving in snark and sarcasm with revelatory moments and discoveries, story by story. His is an anti-stigma look at addiction and mental health, science and access to treatment, and the underlying roots and effects of trauma.

Comedy is desperately needed in this topic, if you ask Murf, to "normalize" the very human path from mental health trauma to self-medicating. Humor can also take away the shame and victim blaming that keep addiction in the shadows: "People just don't want to be talked at. . . . In the drug issue, there's a power dynamic going on here and there's people hoarding resources and they're exploiting the rest of us. It is that simple at the end of the day. I feel like you've just got to find the humor in that to keep people's interest."[10] As he says on the podcast's first episode after rattling off the names of the thirty-plus substances in his past, rapid-fire as in the style of pharmaceutical-advertisement side-effects disclaimers, "To be clear, I'm not glorifying any of those drugs.

Figure 7.1: Comedian Murf Meyer stands in front of a hometown (Luzerne County, Pennsylvania) billboard for his comedy podcast, *Murf Meyer Is Self-Medicated*

I'm also not stigmatizing them. They're just chemical substances, and people who use them are just human beings, so there's really no need for outside judgment in any direction."[11]

Audiences love it. On a regular basis, Murf hears from addiction counselors and people struggling with their own trauma, self-medicating. He is offering, after all, a fresh and funny and very open take on pain and internal shame, and they see themselves in his story. The laughs create a different space for reflection than finger-shaking victim blaming or guilt. For Murf, the project has even opened up a conversation in his own family—hard to imagine without comedy as the mental cushion and soft landing place, he says. He recalls the response from his father, who witnessed the darkest years of his teen addiction:

> When I showed my dad the Laughter Lab video of my presentation, we watched it together in my living room. He was like "OK," and then he kind of left the room. And then he came back, though, and he was just like, "Listen, I don't know if I'm ever going to watch any of this or listen to this. But I know why you're doing it and it's to help people and I love you and I support you." And he hugged me and we had a quick cry. It's the first time I've seen him cry in decades.

Is this the standard process for developing and launching a comedy project to reach wide audiences? No, at least not in the usual way entertainment is developed, produced, and distributed in the Hollywood pipeline. And that is precisely the point. These are questions and challenges posed and interrogated throughout these pages, and here is where it all comes together in some ways. If we agree—hopefully in part on the basis of the evidence shared in this book—that comedy is a powerful force for social change through which to open up space for cultural reflection about people and ideas and lived experiences, then we might also find it provocative to imagine how to change the cultural pipeline for humor work that brings marginalized voices and social topics to the fore. Opening up different creative avenues for comedians to develop their unique visions is part of that aim. This is the story of the Yes, And . . . Laughter Lab,[12] and the final stop in our journey.

Disrupting (Comedy) Business as Usual: Innovating for Social Change

From vaudeville stages of the 1920s to the live clubs and records of the 1950s to the earliest days of television sitcoms, American comedy as monetized entertainment has been incubated along somewhat paradoxical lines. At its core, it is alternative and rebellious independent art that is then discovered and molded into palatable (less offensive?) shape to make money for advertisers in the commercial entertainment marketplace. Sometimes, the comedian becomes famous, and the entertainment doors open further. A career is born. What most of us vaguely understand and accept about comedy we experience on TV—in the form of stand-up shows, satirical news programs, sitcoms, episodic dramedies, and even live show tours—is that it all arrives to audiences as part of a Hollywood undertaking. As millions of us experience comedy that is packaged and shared by big media companies, comedy contributes to shaping our views of each other, our problems and dreams and realities, and the world around us. Meanwhile, as the wheels of the entertainment-media business turn, people and groups pushing for public participation in democracy or addressing social challenges are toiling away in the streets and working hard to empower historically marginalized communities, often supported by a nonprofit philanthropic sector that sees the work as serious and worthy.

In both cases, we have limited the potential for creative expression with an eye toward shaping a pluralistic, just society. We have relegated comedy's development and expression to the commercial entertainment marketplace alone, failing to see it as art that might also need the public-interest values of philanthropic support in order to find the fullest creative—and societal-. public-good—potential. And at the same time, the serious business of informing a populace and encouraging us to participate in public life (and efforts for equity and justice) is too often seen as somehow a separate, somber, droning exercise in old-school civics and the broccoli messages we know are "good for us" but not fun to eat. Who wakes up with excitement to read a new white paper, really?

But what could happen if we mash it all up and flip this equation? What is possible if the entertainment industry is invited to meet and witness the raw comedic power of stories and ideas that explode with creativity because these stories and ideas have *not* been designed to appeal only as a "purchase" in the marketplace? And what if those stories and ideas come from people who bring the newness Hollywood needs so desperately, since marginalized voices have a harder time breaking in? What if entertainment-industry executives also share physical and virtual space with philanthropic and activist organizations, and topical subject-matter experts, to hear their perspectives on comedy that brings social issues and lived experiences to life in funny and original ways? And what could transpire if philanthropy and humanitarian leaders and organizations meet and hear from comedians for the first time— talking about the issues and communities they care about in ways that cut through the numbing sameness of echo-chamber messages and can grab audience attention through the human, emotional lens of comedy and play? Pushing and prodding decision makers in the media marketplace to reflect diverse, marginalized comedic voices requires much more than simply pressuring the entertainment industry through activism. At the same time, developing comedians as powerful artists who can work within social-justice efforts also means introducing them to the civil society leaders and sectors that normally do not consider comedy in their serious efforts. These are the ideas behind the scenes of a dark comedy club in New York in 2019, when Murf Meyer stood onstage and elicited chuckles and tears from a group of people who do not normally find themselves in the same rooms together.

How did we all arrive at that moment? There is, as always, a back story.

Cultural strategist Mik Moore and I met in the summer of 2017 after I wrapped up a public talk at the first global "Comedy for Social Change" gathering hosted by the *Onion*, the Center for Media & Social Impact (which I direct), and Open Society Foundations. Mik, whose creative projects included a successful 2008 voter-engagement initiative with Sarah Silverman, *The Great Schlep*,[13] and a Muslim American comedy web series, *Halal in the Family*,[14] was rapidly developing a full comedy practice at his narrative-strategy agency, Moore + Associates. At the same time, I was several years into a new body of research into the powerful intersections of comedy and social change, sparked by producing the documentary *Stand Up Planet* starring Hasan Minhaj, and, of course, years of collaboration with legendary comedy TV producer Norman Lear. I was looking for a way to put research into real practice, painstakingly building deliberate bridges between professional comedy writers and performers and the social-justice organizations working hard to engage people in community challenges such as racial equity, environmental justice, and more. It was slow going. The pipeline for producing powerful, hilarious, subversive comedy about topical social issues—shared by a full range of diverse creators—was nonexistent, and yet, the changing entertainment industry was fluid and ripe for disruption. Social media and streamers were shifting the old Hollywood rules on a daily basis. And at the same time, the creative, effective postmillennial leaders in the social-change sector seemed open to working with comedy. But these are strange bedfellows who do not naturally intersect or run into each other. Comedy people and social-change people move through pretty distinct professional subcultures. How would they even come together? As we talked more, an idea came into focus: if we took all we knew, individually and collectively, about how comedy works for social change, about the challenges of representation and closed entertainment pipelines for discovering and distributing amazing and diverse comedy, and about the potential of the participatory media era to break open old models, what might be possible? A new idea was born.

The Yes, And . . . Laughter Lab is an innovation in comedy development that intentionally aims to lift up and inspire diverse comedy writers and performers whose stories are hard to find in the entertainment marketplace, and whose humor addresses social topics in entertaining, enlightening, deliciously subversive ways. We also invite philanthropy and social-justice players to have an equal seat at the creative table. In part, this kind of approach and innovation is needed, to use Aymar Jean Christian's parallel arguments about developing independent online "Open TV," because, as he writes, "Corporate development processes [in the entertainment industry] make it difficult for executives to satisfy multiple constituencies—producers, brands, and audiences. Balancing what is marketable, engaging, and artistically or culturally viable, development executives only occasionally satisfy all three criteria, prioritizing marketability and profit potential."[15] In other words, truly original creativity and artistry are not centered in contemporary industrial production of entertainment—or at least, not unless some existing market trends or executive's hunches have ensured its guaranteed viability for profit. To extend Christian's arguments into the comedy realm in particular, it is clear that the economics and norms of developing mediated comedy in the United States, traditionally speaking, tend to live and die in the hands of commercial entertainment conglomerates. But what comedic stories are we missing when product packaging and selling are the primary—indeed, the *sole*—forces at work in the culture business, even at the level of financial resources for developing the ideas in the first place? Whose perspectives are cut out—or muted in the process of assimilating diverse voices or little-heard creative points of view to make them marketable to the mythical mass audience?

Although the cultural landscape of American entertainment is more diverse than in decades past, making a career in entertainment and comedy remains more exponentially difficult for women, people of color, ethnic and religious minorities, creators with disabilities, people from lower socioeconomic backgrounds (er, or just people without trust funds or wealthy families?), and LGBTQ+ and similarly marginalized communities.[16] In film and TV, the underrepresentation of racial and ethnic minority creators is well documented, and gender imbalance in creative decision-making roles persists.[17] But this equation *can* be—and increasingly *is*—disrupted in the participatory media age and its many possibilities that allow new audiences to discover and support disparate talent.

This thinking extends scholar Stuart Cunningham's assertion that "innovations" in creative industries must necessarily expand to center social and public benefit of creative work as a "value-driven orientation,"[18] rather than incentivizing media businesses only to go with the same sure thing based on economics alone. To be clear, I am arguing not that entertainment-industry executives should forgo the basic economic realities of their decision-making processes where comedy is concerned, but the opposite: that in lifting up and hearing the unfettered creative comedic voices of diverse writers and performers, they have a better shot at the Next Big Thing. It's a win-win: good for the entertainment business, good for supporting a pluralistic culture.

The Yes, And . . . Laughter Lab is best understood if we situate it within a broader cultural and entertainment context: it resides among a growing list of creative media disruption initiatives and practices aided and abetted by the power of the participatory media age. In the rapidly changing entertainment industry, new models for finding and developing brilliant creative material are on the table: "This means that different forms of production, distribution and consumption are stimulating emergent new markets for screen content even as traditional ones weaken. It means changing costs of production and lowering barriers to entry for those prepared to experiment with form, content and market," wrote Cunningham on the topic of innovation in creative industries in transition.[19] YALL is an innovation that applies these ideas to comedy—nearly always ignored in discussions about cultural interventions that power social justice and progress. Within the vast scope of entertainment and popular culture, comedy deserves unique care and attention, particularly when we consider its power for representation and social change.

The Yes, And . . . Laughter Lab model is based on fundamentals echoed throughout this book. A wholesale approach to developing and supporting comedy for social change and civic power requires changing social capital within entertainment-industry ranks, building networks of like-minded people who start to know and work together (and thus, construct their own social capital together), centering and honoring diverse representation among creative voices and perspectives, and offering comedians the open creative space to develop and showcase their talents to the entertainment industry and civil society. And providing ways to interact with new collaborators and allies from social justice and philanthropy can expand comedy's reach and deepen its impact. In a kind of "indie" creative setup that centers representation, we help foster the kind of space at work behind the scenes of important representational comedy like Issa Rae's Peabody Award–winning *Insecure* on HBO, and *Broad City* on Comedy Central, both of which incubated first as open creative projects before networks decided they were market-worthy.[20] The comedy writers and performers who participate in YALL overwhelmingly come from diverse communities often overlooked or typecast in Hollywood, including immigrants and refugees, women, queer and trans people, BIPOC, and religious minorities.

In practice, the Yes, And . . . Laughter Lab model includes four main components: a competitive application and selection process to curate strong, unique comedy ideas from diverse comedy writers and performers; a pitch training program to strengthen comedy creators' abilities to attract supporters, financers, and collaborative partners; pitch showcase events held in New York and Los Angeles, where a carefully assembled room of entertainment-industry executives, subject-matter experts (on the topics of the comedy projects), and movement and social-justice leaders gather to experience and give positive feedback to the top comedy selected that year; and entertainment-industry and social-justice partners. We begin the YALL "season" with a call for the most original, hilarious comedy that centers social topics and lived realities in the work—sketch, stand-up, live shows, sitcom pilots, feature film scripts. Following a competitive process with a professional comedy and social-justice selection committee that includes diverse comedy writers and performers, successful showrunners, entertainment execs, and social-justice leaders, we invite twenty finalists to participate in a two-day training program, where they strengthen their projects and learn how best to pitch them to both the entertainment industry and nontraditional collaborators and partners in philanthropy and social justice, working with diverse comedy professionals and luminaries. Then, the final winners from across the country pitch their comedy projects—six in New York and six in Los Angeles—to a room of hand-picked television and streaming network development executives, comedy producers and directors, cultural strategists, nonprofit leaders, and foundation representatives. A veritable village of people ends up touching and enriching the comedy ideas—and supporting the creators—by the time the experience wraps up.

The full YALL cycle takes place over about nine months. Diverse comedy and entertainment executives help review projects and work with our comedy community from time to time throughout the year, from powerhouse comedy producers like Dan Powell (*Inside Amy Schumer*, Sarah Cooper's *Everything's Fine*) to comedy performers and writers like Franchesca Ramsey, Roy Wood Jr., Chris Gethard, and many more. Entertainment-industry and social-justice leaders act as partners. The list is long, from the networks like NBCUniversal and Comedy Central to Amazon to Netflix to powerhouse production groups like Apatow Productions to the most effective social-justice organizations working within entertainment advocacy today: Color of Change, Define American, Muslim Public Affairs Council, GLAAD, RespectAbility, Pillars Fund, the Coalition of Asian Pacifics in Entertainment, and others. For the first time, like-minded comedy writers and performers come together to develop and refine their best socially conscious comedy, collaborating and networking along the way with social-justice leaders and entertainment-industry insiders. The room feels like magic, we like to say, when it all comes to life in the pinnacle pitch showcase events—live, on stage, under a spotlight, as comedy is meant to be experienced.

In the Room Where It Happens (and Why It Matters)

Norman Lear used to say that there was nothing quite like the feeling of watching a whole audience of people experience a joke at the same time. They rock forward and then backwards in their seats in one wave, he says, throwing their heads back in unison before they recover and settle down. It is a physical act as much as an emotional one, this communal delight. He was fond of sneaking around to the back of the studio when his various sitcoms were filmed before a live audience, where he could anticipate and experience the ripple of laughter that brought a disparate group of people together as one temporary community, united in their delight and recognition of something ridiculously true, profound, and silly.

I was reminded of this communal joy and feeling of solidarity at the first Yes, And . . . Laughter Lab comedy pitch showcase in the summer of 2019, and I felt it again at the gatherings in Los Angeles and New York that have followed. The pilot showcase event launched at Caveat, a basement comedy club on the Lower East Side of New York City that is straight out of central casting for "comedy club" of the Mrs. Maisel/ Lenny Bruce variety. It is dark, intimate, slightly sticky, and damp: in other words, it is perfect. It is no conference room in the tower of a fancy appointed office. We have assembled a very unusual list of people— comedy producers, entertainment-industry executives, social-justice and movement leaders—to watch and offer feedback and commitments (for meetings, resources, connections) to the winning comedians, and the air is anticipatory.

One by one, the comedy creators come to the classic stand-up stage, where they offer a ten-minute "pitch" that is equal parts classic comedy performance plus confessional plus an unusual twist by entertainment-industry standards: a direct set of asks for the "pitch tables" that have been curated to hear from them. The performances are distinctive in the grand scheme of either Hollywood-business or social-justice inner workings—they are hilarious, personal, vulnerable. Alongside the funny bits, they weave in stories about why this material matters, and how it connects to broader lived experiences and social realities. The audience laughs as one, of course, and this is truly something to behold, particularly when we have people in the room working in the depths of social challenges: racial injustice, addiction, mental health, Islamophobia, and on and on. But they also listen carefully when the performances turn serious, connecting the need for levity and unique story lenses with real urgency.

Figure 7.2: Marcos González and Gabe González pitch their comedy project, *Los Blancos*, at the launch of the Yes, And . . . Laughter Lab at Caveat in New York City, 2019

What kinds of projects and comedic storytellers come to the stage here? A glimpse into only a few 2021 YALL projects offers a closer look:

Camp by Air Durnell and Maddie Smith is a thirty-minute comedic television series about married lesbian couple Leo and Jo Powers, who reopen their inherited gay "conversion" camp as a secret queer utopia for children who were originally sent to pray the gay away.

Getting Schooled, hosted by high school teacher Chris De La Cruz, explores the intricacies and inequities of American education policy with plenty of humor to help the learning go down. In Mr. DLC's class, an array of monologue jokes, celebrity guest speakers, and out-of-studio "Field Trips" will show students young and old that it wasn't just you—it was the system all along.

The AzN PoP! Show by Anna Suzuki, Iliana Inocencio, Maya Deshmukh, and Angel Yau: After being scorned by the same woke White man, four vastly different Asian American women in their thirties decide to form the "Dove campaign" of pop groups. A half-hour scripted comedy.

Native Comedy at the Rock by Jackie Keliiaa is a multiday comedy festival featuring Native comedians, sketch comedy groups, and improvisers from all over Indian Country, who perform on a central stage on Alcatraz Island, home of the Occupation of Alcatraz by Indians of All Tribes from 1969 to 1971. The festival is a celebration of Native comedy that blends humor with history, highlighting important Native activists and movements that have brought Native issues to the forefront.

CameronTown by Sheri Bradford: After living (and metaphorically dying) in LA for over a decade, Shannon Cameron, a millennial Black woman, returns to her conservative South Carolina hometown to start a cannabis farm on her family's historical land.

Lifeline by Meredith Casey is a serialized dark comedy about a depressed young woman from a dysfunctional family who has to do community service at a suicide hotline after her own suicide attempt goes hilariously wrong.

Momo's Amerika (animated series) by Abdallah Nabil and Ayman Samman: A jovial immigrant with a short attention span works various odd jobs to support his family while chasing the American dream as he creates his own version of America.

Bendecidas y Afortunadas (Blessed and Highly Favored) by Julieta Messmer and Marianne Amelinckx: Two spoiled immigrants come to the United States determined to make it in the Hollywood industry, but when their destiny—and their visas—are held hostage by Immigration Services, they decide to make ends meet by taking a cash-paid job on a marijuana farm in Northern California.[21]

Change happens well beyond the room, even as it begins there. A snapshot of successes from YALL winners and finalists: comedian Carla Lee and her team raised enough funds to shoot and produce the pilot for *Nice Tan*, an intersectional sketch comedy show; Gabe González, cowriter of *Los Blancos*, a scripted comedy that explores the complexities of Latinx politics, secured a manager; Murf Meyer is planning a second season of *Murf Meyer Is Self-Medicated* while he continues to work on the

Figure 7.3: Poster for the 2021
Yes, And . . . Laughter Lab
NYC Pitch Showcase. Artist
credit: Bekah Malover

touring idea for the show; Thaddeus McCants secured a BET pilot deal
for *Lit Lounge*, which turns the tables on the drug wars in a workplace
comedy about the politics of new weed economics; Lorena Russi secured
a production partner, Wise Entertainment, for *Hilo*, her show about a
queer Latinx soccer player; Joey Clift produced a short film with Comedy
Central about Native mascots and continues to curate the first-ever "Funniest Native Comedians to Watch" list with IllumiNative. And in 2021,
Carolyn Pierre-Outlar, a budding writer and physician's assistant, joined
forces with *The Daily Show*'s Roy Wood Jr., a YALL selection committee
member, to sell her show, *Rhonda Mitchell, MD*, to NBCUniversal. The
scripted comedy, moving into formal development with a major network,
shares the funny and poignant stories of a Harlem-based doctor who hilariously balances her community health practice and patients with her

real life.[22] In video remarks delivered at the 2021 Los Angeles pitch show-case, Wood Jr. addressed Pierre-Outlar, his new creative partner:

> You're a part of a very small and select group of people that have a story that matters, that speaks to something very specific, that a lot of people may not understand and know a lot about. And that's what attracted me to this project. . . . This is something unique, because it's cool to have a way to speak to an issue while at the same time, it's still gotta be funny. . . . I think it's dope that the Laughter Lab brought us together. . . . I saw your [application] packet and thought about healthcare in the Black community, and about Black women getting misdiagnosed. I knew this is something that had to be made, and I'm happy to be on this journey with you, Carolyn.[23]

Inspiring success stories aside, it would be tragically reductive, however, to say that the Yes, And . . . Laughter Lab is solely focused on the

Figure 7.4: Yes, And . . . Laughter Lab on the marquee at Dynasty Typewriter, host of the 2021 Los Angeles Pitch Showcase

individual comedy projects and their precise outcomes—that is, ultimately whether or not each one makes it fully on TV (or touring stages or movie screens) intact as it was presented in the room. The experience also is not merely about a pitch process in a standard entertainment industry sense. The Lab is about the individual comedy people and how they connect and build community with each other through the process. It is also about how much that sense of validation and creative space can mean for comedy careers moving forward. We have come to call it the YALL community and family, and it feels that way. And here is where we find the most powerful—and for me, at least, somewhat unexpected—lessons about culture change work at a broad scale beyond individual anecdotes (i.e., beyond one particular TV show at a time): observing what YALL means to its participants and what this discovery suggests about how to help foster a pluralistic cultural space for comedy to work its magic.

A story, as usual, helps bring this idea to life: in September 2020, as we wrapped an exhausting (but hilarious!) two days of the Yes, And . . . Laughter Lab virtual pitch showcases on Zoom—let's call it the "pandemic edition"—we invited all of the participating comedy writers and performers to hang out for a little while. We intended it as an informal, noncompulsory space to talk, have a cocktail, and compliment each other. We expected a few people might hang out for five perfunctory minutes before logging off; after all, we had just spent a full two days looking at screens. Instead, though, the Zoom room was completely full: every comedy performer and writer from the 2020 YALL cohort joined. With beers and wine glasses and vodka tonics in hand, we toasted our little group, all of whom we had never even met in person because of COVID-19.

What followed was a wholly unexpected series of what I can best describe as "testimonials," which the comedians shared with great animation and expression over more than an hour, about what the experience had meant for them—the "them," of course, almost without exception a group of wildly talented people who felt generally unheard and unseen in any meaningful, authentic way in their craft when it came to the entertainment industry. Even at the unit of standard industry meetings, they felt repeatedly marginalized—sometimes in cloaked ways, sometimes overtly. And often, the "diversity showcases" from the industry were no better. (As one participant put it, one of the most prominent Hollywood diversity comedy showcases was "the most tokenizing, racist, homophobic place I've ever spent time in Hollywood. Like: 'You're Latina. Can you be a little more sexy and more Latina in your routine?'") Many had also never shared space with subject-matter experts and movement leaders who passionately expressed how much their comedy would mean for the actual social challenges they addressed, from mental health to drug addiction to racial justice. Not only was their work validated in an unusual room of cultural decision makers and world changers, but the comedy creators could sense how much their individual voices mattered—some for the first time.

One by one in our Zoom after-party, they shared stories that coalesced around similar themes: they had generally never had the experience of an audience truly rapt with their genuine creative ideas in all of their authentic, hilarious glory. The YALL experience and community felt life-changing, even, as some shared. There were tears all around the room, mine certainly included. It was a stunning highlight and manifestation of several ideas, centering around the ways in which the decision-making machinery of the cultural landscape has systemically pushed out so many diverse and funny voices and stories, but also how it has stolen confidence from swaths of brilliantly creative people who might hesitate to move forward after being told "no" in so many subtle and not-so-subtle ways. And in the lens of hope and optimism, this realization also helps solidify convictions about how to build from here.

The power and intent of YALL, ultimately, is focused on individual comedic artists, listening to and honoring what they have to say through their comedy. We have watched as they create their own collaborative, supportive ecosystems while they push further into the social-capital networks of both the entertainment-industry and social-change sectors. As Carla Lee said, "We emerged from the Lab with new partners who are really excited to see what we come up with next, and are super supportive of our efforts."[24] In so doing, the program creates and strengthens a community of comedy people invested in social change and one another as creative talent—a community now in touch with philanthropy and social-change leaders, and decision-making Hollywood executives across the industry, from powerful showrunners looking for writers to networks looking for new content. As 2019 YALL comedy participant Mamoudou N'Diaye reflected,

> This experience let me just expand kind of my circle of other people doing this sort of work. . . . [The Laughter Lab] gave me a little bit more confidence. And then to meet all those other comics who have been feeling like they're trying to be representative of not only our marginalized identities but also representative of our POV in a comedic and fun way, and being very meticulous and very smart with the way they went about doing it was super impactful. And now I'm sitting at this very nice intersection that I've always wanted to be at with social justice in one hand and comedy in the other. I think the lab was instrumental in opening up that door. Like my foot was in the door but it wasn't quite open for me.[25]

The networks continue well beyond the YALL experience, and perhaps this is where the greatest potential for change comes in. Joey Clift helped put this idea into context:

> A really big benefit of the lab for me is that it just got me in front of a room of a hundred people, really cool execs and funders, nonprofits, and now I'm on their radar and they're also, by seeing my pitch, just more aware of Native American issues. If my manager emailed out to set up a pitch for something and the person that she's emailing hasn't heard of me, then they're probably not even going to read the email. Whereas this really boosted up my project, and also just my story and the things I'm passionate about in such a way that when my manager sends that email, people are like, "Oh Joey Clift, he did the Yes, And . . . Laughter Lab!"[26]

What YALL means, structurally and individually, is the value of supporting new opportunities for talented creative people to break into elusive networks and build their own social capital. At the same time, the experience is designed to provide a genuinely safe, caring, and open creative space for them to craft *their* best and most hilarious work—notably, not versions of their ideas that the industry seems to regurgitate over and over again as "safe," but what comedy people *actually* want to do and create when granted freedom to be authentically themselves. When we move beyond thinking only about the business of entertainment and instead celebrate and support the open creativity it requires in the first place, real space opens up for storytellers and creatives who have been shut out. These ideas, in turn, become the fresh content Hollywood needs, reaching audiences that are hungry to see them. As for the process itself, by curating pitch tables that place entertainment-industry executives shoulder to shoulder with the social-justice leaders, we invite people to bring the best versions of themselves. They are gently pushed to think beyond terms of commerce and business and instead, to collectively consider the powerful function of culture in creating a more just and equitable future. They listen to and learn from one another in an affirming, creative space.

Moving well beyond this one particular model and thinking more broadly about changing and expanding the pipeline for comedy, this is ultimately about inviting comedians into professional communities and spaces that have been hesitant to let them in, but also supporting conditions to help incubate comedy well beyond the decision-making processes of the commercial entertainment marketplace. Properly resourcing and supporting diverse comedy storytellers—that is, the *actual world we live in*—also means that Hollywood executives will make good on their promises to create diverse comedy writers' rooms and greenlight programming from voices that still remain on the outskirts, despite a blip of recent hope.[27] Art and commerce, new ideas and hilarious storytellers: they are all possible to incubate in one shared space if we remember that open creativity and unusual ways of thinking are not only what engage audiences but also what can help move the world forward, inch by inch.

Conclusion

Taking Comedy Seriously

Laureano Márquez walks onto the stage and reaches for the mic. A spotlight tracks his path as nearly every phone stretches up into the air—it is a rare opportunity to get the best photo of a man infrequently seen in public in 2021, much less performing stand-up. His comedy descendants regularly refer to him as a legend and a hero, and it is clear that his fans and compatriots feel the same way.

The applause erupts and carries on, rippling and regenerating as he scans the crowd. He takes a long beat to smile down at the front row and every corner of the room, delighting, perhaps, in the warmth and electricity that fill the space, not a single empty seat to be found. Laureano Márquez is, after all, one of Venezuela's most beloved sons, albeit Spanish born—a renowned humorist who won the International Press Freedom Award in 2010 for his funny, pointed critiques of then-president Hugo Chavez;[1] author of three political comedy books (one, *El Código Bochinche*, a national bestseller in 2004); and a former star of Venezuela's long-running comedy sketch TV show, the wildly popular *Radio Rochela*, a cousin of *Saturday Night Live* known for its hilarious political and social commentary and characters.[2] He is, to use a comparison that American readers might understand, a kind of "Jon Stewart of Venezuela"—a comedy entertainer, yes, but also a voice of bemused moral consciousness and outrage in the face of the staggering injustice, poverty, and political corruption that hold his country hostage. "If there were an Algonquin Round Table in Caracas, Laureano Márquez would have a seat," wrote the Committee to Protect Journalists in 2010.[3]

This is a special (and indeed, historic) evening and event—a gathering of Venezuela's hottest comedy voices performing stand-up together for the first time: Ricardo Del Bufalo, Rolando Diaz, Neisser, US-based Joanna Hausmann, and, of course, Márquez as the kind of godfather.

The crowd settles down as he launches into his act, a hilarious observational set of bits and jokes ranging from passport woes to musings about American life and Venezuelan culture and politics. The audience, primarily Venezuelan, loves him—they are shouting and laughing, poking each other in the arms with recognition, rocking back and forth in their seats, calling out. It is rowdy and joyful. He uses his animated face and a complex range of vocal inflections as tools to bring the people along, waiting patiently to slip a new joke into a wall of laughter at the exact right moment. We are all watching a comedy master, with precise timing honed from decades in his craft.

And then it is time to close, and Laureano Márquez does something unexpected: he asks the crowd to listen carefully to a different kind of story. They giggle at first, not sure how to respond, but they follow his direction, somber and respectful. His father, he tells them, once planted the seed of a fig tree during hard times, and his neighbors thought it was ridiculous. "You will have to wait for such a long time to eat the fruit from that tree," they said. His father was unmoved and unbothered. Someday, he said, others will eat from this tree, and even more will be able to enjoy it many years from now. The seed is the beginning. It is the hope and anticipation for what will follow, even if the fruit is not intended for the person who planted it. "I believe the situation will be bad in Venezuela perhaps for many years," Márquez said to the audience, "but we must remember the fig tree seed and the hope for the future, and we must work together to keep it alive for those who will follow." We can never give up hope, and we can never accept this situation as the way things should be in Venezuela, he told them.

In comedy parlance, every performer killed it that night. The event was a massive success—huge laughs every minute, a spontaneous standing ovation, and a sold-out venue. Even so, a show like this one should not have happened where it did, in a comedy venue in Brooklyn, New York. It should have taken place in Caracas or Maracaibo, Venezuela's metro centers. But it is impossible, at least for the time being. Comedy laced with much political or social commentary is not welcome in Venezuela—at least in any official entertainment-industry terms—a consequence of political corruption, authoritarianism, and fear. Not only is it unwelcome, but it is dangerous.

Figure c.1: Laureano Márquez performs comedy in New York City in December 2021

Venezuela's human-caused humanitarian crisis tracks back to the Hugo Chavez regime in the late 1990s and continues under his successor, Nicolás Maduro, elected to presidential office in 2013 and reelected in 2018 through a process widely regarded as unconstitutional and fraudulent.[4] In this century, Venezuela has declined on every level of human survival at an unbelievable rate: since 2014, nearly six million Venezuelans have been forced to flee conditions with frequent blackouts and lack of access to food, water, and medicine; the number of Venezuelans seeking asylum has increased by 2000 percent, continuing at a rate of five thousand per day, comparable to the Syrian refugee crisis.[5] Since 2010, the proportion of Venezuelans living in poverty has increased from an already high 33 percent to a stunning 93 percent (with more than six in ten people, or 64 percent, living in extreme poverty).[6] These are published figures, of course, but Venezuelans say that the real numbers are likely much worse—and yet, they will never know because of the absolute silencing of journalists and others trying to tell the real story. It is a dire situation incubated and supported by a political system that lost its way, falling deeper into corruption and authoritarian control, year by year.

And here is where the comedy comes in. Democracy—with a life force that requires, at a basic minimum, freedom of expression, social critique and dissent, and the people's access to information—is in dire straits in Venezuela.[7] On the absurdist end, this means that talking about the constitution or human rights is off limits. Even the rolling electricity blackouts can only be discussed as "the situation that happened" (truly ripe for comedy).

Of a more insidious nature, though, are two regimes in a row—Chavez and Maduro—that have slowly but surely crushed political dissent, journalistic institutions, and, yes, comedy.[8] *Radio Rochela*, the popular political and social commentary sketch comedy show that made Laureano Márquez a household name and legendary TV star, was canceled in 2007 after the Chavez administration refused to renew the license of its parent network, Radio Caracas Televisión (RCTV), known for its politically and socially critical content.[9] Márquez found himself in danger after he wrote a humorous column in the publication *Tal Cual*, fashioning his critique of the oppressive Chavez administration as a plea for help via Chavez's young daughter.[10] After fining the publication and Márquez with a staggering sum of money, the administration called for criminal prosecution, "describing the column as an assault on the country's democracy and a coup plot disguised as humor."[11]

As authoritarian power and corruption continued in Venezuela, dismantling fair voting processes and fostering a climate of danger for journalists and others speaking truth to power, socially critical comedy disappeared from TV networks. Even after migrating to radio, the remaining comedy programming has gradually ceased political or social commentary for fear of government retribution, including impossible monetary fines, jail, or worse. Today, humorous resistance to political oppression and human rights catastrophes—necessary as both information and dissent—is hard to find in Venezuelan media. A few years ago, Laureano Márquez, under threat and unable to continue his livelihood, left the country. He does not know if he will ever return—or if he can.

This is a stark and obvious cautionary tale, and yet, it is not the only example. This one lives and breathes in the current day, not historical terms. It happened quickly—Laureano Márquez watched his country change dramatically within his adult lifetime. In the United States, where we generally take our democracy and right to critical creative expression for granted—where we spend time wringing our hands about whatever offensive things comedians say (remember when journalists and politicos were angry at comedian Michelle Wolf for her "vulgar language" at the White House Correspondents Dinner instead of focusing on her accurate critique of the cozy relationship between commercial news profits and the Trump administration?)—we seem to still not fully grasp the immense cultural power comedians can wield, and the precarious nature of our own freedoms. Too often, we falsely believe that journalism and access to rational information and facts are the sole (or dominant) routes to social progress. Taking comedy seriously means a lot of things, but surely—if nothing else in this book sticks—we can grasp comedy's influence when we contemplate a story like this one. Comedy is so powerful, so subversive, and so crucial as a tool that inspires and sustains dissent or hope that it has been removed from the people's ability to see and hear it in Venezuela. It happened right in front of their faces—and ours. But "it's just comedy," right?

Taking comedy seriously means intentional efforts to alter the underlying mechanisms by which cultural territory is availed and ceded to funny artists with something important to say—particularly the voices and experiences of people who have been and are systemically oppressed. Contemplating comedy for social change means that we believe in the vital importance of humor as a formal mechanism to help strengthen democracy and build an equitable society that honors its pluralism, rather than seeing comedy as frivolous dalliance in that pursuit. In this spirit, before we depart from these pages, let us consider final summative points—the underlying connective threads of this book—to punctuate why comedy matters.

Comedy as Culture

The ebb and flow of political struggle finds us in a constant state of hand wringing, and rightfully so, about the precarious state of democracy and our ability to see our fellow humans' basic shared humanity beyond our voting patterns. Our ideological identities are fueled by regional affiliations—how our neighbors and communities think—and increasingly by divisive partisan news. In the meanwhile, popular culture, operating on a different frequency when we think about how beliefs and attitudes are shaped, speaks to us on a daily basis not only through what reality it depicts and how, but by what it ignores or dismisses. Culture is the very essence of how we know and understand our own values as a society, what we believe and long for, what we revile and hold dear, the people we care about and the ones we seem to easily discard. Culture is created by all of us—rippling across communities and gaining meaning not only through institutions of power, and certainly not only through more serious forms of information like journalism, but in artistic expressions and our conversations about them, and our human connections to them.

Popular culture still has a shot at bringing us together. This is real, tangible, tactical stuff. It is not theoretical. When Ryan Berni told me about E Pluribus Unum's focus groups with more than a thousand people across the Deep South region of the United States, he recalled how hard it was to find common ground in any topic that hinted of politics; discussions about race were particularly uncomfortable. People remained stiff, careful, guarded. But, he said, the one topic where everyone came together—consistently, without fail—was popular culture, including comedy. Popular culture was the only arena where all kinds of different folks could find one another despite political differences or levels of discomfort talking about taboo or painful topics. Here, in the space of discussing culture, people could laugh together, and they could share moments of recognition. We need this desperately.

Surely there are grounds for a dystopic lens on a bleak future. Much is broken. When it comes to contemporary media as a central institution of power and control, we might easily feel hopeless—after all, corporate consolidation of entertainment media and big tech (including social-media behemoths) continues unabated, misinformation runs rampant, and journalism seems to lose more public trust and money every year. We are surveilled and sold to across a dizzying array of corporate-controlled platforms and devices. Ideologically slanted news and pseudo-news outlets are radicalizing many of us. It is all enough to make any reasonable person want to opt out of any information-seeking or participatory activity. And this, then, will be the death of a civic-minded and civilized society. What is to be done? I would argue that we should never neglect dystopia's counterweight. We cannot afford to focus only on what is broken, working nearly exclusively from the inevitably toxic and draining emotions of rage and hostility and frustration and futility. Fueling social change through the civic imagination is a parallel pursuit that deserves equal resource and attention—the process of inviting people in without shaking our fists and wagging our disapproving fingers at them. We need a utopic lens, too, embracing the superpowers of hope, optimism, and play in shifting culture. Comedy can help us precisely in this way.

Comedy's Societal Influence

At a basic, fundamental level, some ideas about social change are straightforward. Communal buy-in with certain values and beliefs is a requirement: we must be able to see one another and our shared humanity. We also need to be able to talk about tough topics together. We need to be able to dissent and critique the absurdity of injustice. In all of these areas, it is hard to find a more effective mechanism than comedy. When we experience comedy as audiences, we experience a kind of stress relief and relaxation that comes through hope, optimism, enjoyment, and entertainment value.[12] Comedy is often uniquely able to broach taboo and painful topics that are otherwise polarizing. Humor opens new ways to see old problems. We are persuaded through comedy, we are more likely to remember even serious messages when they come through comedy, and we are also much more likely to share comedic media material than other forms of information or genres of entertainment, thus amplifying the reach of ideas.[13] When we apply these known influences of comedy to matters of representation, equity, oppression, and social-justice issues, it is powerful stuff. Comedy's ability to aid equitable social progress is profound, both because of how we receive and interpret and respond to comedy as individuals and also because of the ways in which comedy can set media agendas and diffuse messages throughout our cultural landscape.

Resourcing Comedy for Social Change

Despite what we know about how comedy works as a persuasive, mobilizing, amplifying force for messages about historically marginalized people and social problems, comedians are still not resourced consistently by the sectors that explicitly work in social justice and change—large global philanthropies and social-justice-advocacy organizations among them. Looking at the roster of any given social-justice or cultural event will bear out this reality. When comedy *is* included, it is often present as a kind of bonus sidekick, as in a hired performer at a charity event. And yet, within social-change sectors, we are fond of pointing out examples like *Modern Family* for its role in softening public opinion around gay marriage, or satirical news progenitors like *The Daily Show* for helping to civically activate a generation of young people, or pathbreaking shows like *Ramy* for inviting audiences to learn about often-maligned Muslim culture, or *Black-ish* for taking on racial violence and police brutality through a gentler lens of comedy, thus inviting incongruent audiences to contemplate ideas they might not understand. Despite these examples, we leave comedy solely to the commercial marketplace for its development. This is a missed opportunity for social justice and cultural power. Bobby Wilson, founding member of the 1491s, the Native sketch comedy group, and writer on Peacock's *Rutherford Falls*, reflects, "It's crazy that comedy is not generally recognized as an art form. Social-justice groups are usually looking at music or poetry and the visual arts [to be part of their work]. Comedy is left out of that conversation a lot."[14]

If we take comedy seriously as a compelling and gently persuasive (and sometimes sharply critical) form of art that works symbiotically alongside the efforts of humanitarian groups and journalists to provide vital information and facts, powerful social-change professional sectors would stop regarding comedy as a "risk" or an extra in the pursuit of building an equitable world. We should see comedy as *vital*. As this book reveals, comedians are ready, willing, and creatively able to do so much more in social-change missions and spaces. By inviting comedy people in and funding their work, we can intentionally expand the possibilities spotlighted throughout these pages, breaking through the clutter of anger, rage, or even "serious but boring" information to engage publics in fresh new ways.

The Revolution Will Be Hilarious

Stories about the convergence of comedy and activism, as well as the transforming entertainment business, reveal the potency of this burgeoning arena of participatory culture and its potential to foster social change and build civic power. An amazing thing happens when social-justice organizations collaborate with, and learn from, comedians: they embrace creativity and creative process more than they did before. They talk about how much they actually *need* comedy in order to help build resilience for their hard work, or to invite people to see their communities as fully realized, flawed, hilarious people—the opposite of othering, and the counter to finger pointing. When they choose to contemplate comedy seriously, and to co-create and celebrate comedy in a deliberate way, social-justice organizations speak of building civic power through flexing their creative muscles: they choose comedy for its ability to spotlight hope, light, optimism, and above all, to invite play.

And let us not forget the comedians themselves in this interplay—or, that is, the ones devoted to punching up and enlightening, rather than tearing down. They are already doing the work: making fun of stereotypes, inviting audiences in to giggle and agitate their own views, taking up full space, hilariously critiquing injustice, sharing their lived experiences. When they are invited to collaborate with social change makers, they are open and ready and willing. The aftermath of their enthusiasm, perhaps, is where the most profound cultural impact may continue to unwind, embedded in a comedy writer or performer who has explicitly considered the societal importance of their work. As co-median Shannon O'Neill said after she worked in our Native activism comedy writers' room (the focus of chapter 5), "Now I realize how important these issues are, and it's going to be really important for me to not just think my work is done. I know I will be thinking more about other marginalized groups and doing something positive with my comedy in the future. The experience was overwhelming."[15]

We may never know the full influence over time as a comedy professional makes their way through the entertainment industry and their career, creating characters and stories that reflect the world differently than they might have before they were invited into community with people and sectors working for justice and equity. We should value comedy, in other words, not only because of how it works as it permeates cultural spaces but also due to what lives inside it—innovative creativity and artistic process, play, and deviance that can disrupt the steady hum of status quos that need agitating. Comedians themselves, particularly those who have been traditionally excluded from entertainment-industry culture, center a lens that is so meaningful to social justice. The innovative forces of creativity and play at work in comedy help provide a potent mechanism by which to assert cultural and civic power.

As we look toward the future, the lessons of this book are intended to remind us that comedy's unique creative traits help to build civic power by providing fresh and entertaining ways for communities to see themselves represented in the cultural landscape, and when broader swaths of the population can see and connect with the shared humanity and lived experiences of all kinds of people. Comedy—not in spite of its irreverence and silliness but because of these delicious qualities of play that can beckon audiences to move past their calcified identities or identity politics or ignorance, or at least soften them—is uniquely positioned in this way. Creativity opens doors to innovation, and the deviant thinking and cultural affection for comedy can provide a mobilizing source of optimism and fun alongside the hard, somber work of pushing for progress against daunting odds: dark and light, serious work and creative play, all coming together to make change and disrupt the grotesque absurdities of injustice. The revolution *must* be hilarious—because our challenges will always be ridiculous.

ACKNOWLEDGMENTS

It takes a village to write and publish a book, and I am grateful for the people behind this one. My heartfelt thanks and admiration go first to the comedians and the folks who believe in them. One of the greatest joys of crafting this volume was the conversations I had with so many inspiring individuals: comedy performers and writers, social-justice warriors, community leaders, and entertainment-industry executives. In all, I interviewed close to eighty people, always for at least an hour, sometimes stretching into two and beyond. Many of them were my active collaborators during our interviews, so the hours extended exponentially. These conversations never, ever failed to brighten my day and motivate my work. Without exception, every person offered an insight I had not considered, an experience worth contemplating, and too many stories and jokes to possibly recount. (Suffice it to say, rereading some of the transcripts often had me laughing out loud during 6:00 a.m. writing sessions, and something has to be *really* funny to get a laugh before sunrise.)

I regret that I was unable to directly quote or cite every single interview and person in the book, and yet, *all* of these diverse brains and perspectives shaped this work. I can never properly offer enough gratitude to this remarkable assemblage of humans, including Niles Abston, Jose Acevedo, Ryan Berni, Ellen Bravo, Charles "Batman" Brown, Gloria Calderón Kellett, Jandiz Cardoso, Chaz Carter, Adrianne Chalepah, Kesila Chambers, Erin Chan, Marie Cheng, Josh Church, Joey Clift, Geri Cole, Sebastian Conelli, Ryan Cunningham, Deniese Davis, Rebecca DeHart, Philip Deloria, Deanna Diaz, Crystal Echo Hawk, Ryan Eller, Corey Ryan Forrester, Molly Gaebe, Makiah Green, Bethany Hall, Liz Havstad, Josh Healey, Jeff Hiller, Dawn Hucklebridge, Vanessa Jackson, Joyelle Nicole Johnson, Clark Jones, Shakita Brooks Jones, Jay Jurden, Jackie Kaliiaa, Gaylene Kanoyton, Elijah Karriem, Michael Kayne, Janet Kim, Andrew Kimler, Rob Kutner, Kathy Le Backes, Una LeMarche,

Steven Levinson, Alyssa Limperis, Deirdre "Mama D" Love, Kristen Marsten, Thaddeus McCants, Johnny McNulty, Murf Meyer, Fawzia Mirza, Kenice Mobley, Mamoudou N'Diaye, Sue Obeidi, Shannon O'Neill, Rachel Pegram, David Perdue, Sally Rashid, Ryan RedCorn, Keja Reel, Rev. Dr. Dwight Riddick, Lorena Russi, Noam Schuster, Rashid Shabazz, Roger Smith, Erika Soto Lamb, Ishita Srivastava, Achilles Stamatalaky, Sasha Stewart, Mahyad Tousi, Yedoye Travis, Prashanth Venkataramanujam, Bobby Wilson, Lisa Flick Wilson, and Rev. Lennox Yearwood Jr.

Beyond those essential voices, this book was enabled by a handful of supportive colleagues and friends, and I offer them my profound thanks. My friend and collaborator Henry Jenkins—a comedy person all the way—inspired me to imagine this set of ideas as a book, and it became one in large part due to his own pathbreaking scholarship in participatory culture and politics. Thank you to Henry and fellow Postmillennial Pop series coeditor Karen Tongson (whose witty Twitter feed regularly makes me giggle) for believing this volume could join their illustrious curation of titles. I am grateful to NYU Press editor Eric Zinner for offering the dream publishing home for an unconventional passion book, and also to the press's Furqan Sayeed for his friendly support throughout the process.

On both professional and personal levels, my beloved professor friends and role models, Leena Jayaswal and Pallavi Kumar, make me feel loved and supported on a daily basis (er, talk to them about sitting next to me in meetings, though), and I am enriched beyond measure by their friendship. Also, my collaborator, friend, and muse Jeffrey P. Jones—whose unique lens and early scholarship about comedy and political engagement inspired many others to follow his lead—is an unwavering source of encouragement, brainstorming, and improvisational "yes, and" ideation. How fortuitous to find a fellow traveler who uniquely understands the scholarship *and* the deviance, creativity, and gravitas of comedy as an art form that matters a great deal in public life.

As for the enterprising labor of researching, incubating, and creating media and new pathways for social change, this book—and the ideas within it—absolutely would not have been possible without the smarts, creativity, ideas, and incredibly hard work of my core comedy collaborator friends and colleagues: Bethany Hall, Varsha Ramani, Clare Kenny,

Kenice Mobley, Mik Moore, and also Sabrina Bleich and Sarah Vitti, who were essential to the Yes, And . . . Laughter Lab in earlier junctures. I am truly awed to work with—and learn from—such a generous and wildly talented group of people, and I am stunned by what we have managed to build together as a scrappy team of believers and doers. Their profound contributions are embedded in this book in a thousand large and small ways, for which I am very thankful.

Similarly, I am indebted to several philanthropic supporters of my (and my collaborators') various comedy projects and machinations. It is no small thing for serious foundations and media organizations to believe in unconventional ideations enough to financially support them, particularly when they are early ideas. These are leaders I respect and admire, well beyond our work together, and I am indescribably grateful to each of them for believing in comedy as a tool for social justice and civic power, including Zeyba Rahman and Linda Artola, Doris Duke Foundation for Islamic Art's Building Bridges Program; Taryn Higashi and Adey Fisseha, Unbound Philanthropy; Bridgit Antoinette Evans and Tracy Van Slyke, Pop Culture Collaborative; Jennifer Humke and Kathy Im, the MacArthur Foundation; David Morse and Elizabeth Cahill, formerly with Atlantic Philanthropies; Nishant Lalwani, Felipe Estefan, and Deepa Iyer, Luminate; Felipe Cala, Open Society Foundations; Aprile Age and Johnny McNulty, McNulty Foundation; Jeneye Abele and Shirley Hamilton, Argosy Foundation; Daniel Green, Gates Foundation; and Erika Soto Lamb, Comedy Central and Paramount Global. When they read these pages, I hope they see and celebrate their roles in breathing it all into real life.

Finally, my amazing children, Elias and Simone—who patiently play with (put up with?) their mama's silliness on a daily basis—are my very favorite comedy viewing partners and targets of my goofy "mom jokes." I thank them for the endless fun and happiness they bring to my life. Making them laugh is my greatest joy, and their love makes everything possible.

APPENDIX

LIST OF INTERVIEWEES

Niles Abston

Jose Acevedo

Ryan Berni

Ellen Bravo

Charles "Batman" Brown

Gloria Calderón Kellett

Jandiz Cardoso

Chaz Carter

Adrianne Chalepah

Kesila Chambers

Erin Chan

Marie Cheng

Josh Church

Joey Clift

Geri Cole

Sebastian Conelli

Ryan Cunningham

Deniese Davis

Rebecca DeHart

Philip Deloria

Deanna Diaz

Crystal Echo Hawk

Ryan Eller

Corey Ryan Forrester

Molly Gaebe

Makiah Green

Bethany Hall

Liz Havstad

Josh Healey

Jeff Hiller

Dawn Hucklebridge

Vanessa Jackson

Joyelle Nicole Johnson

Clark Jones

Shakita Brooks Jones

Jay Jurden

Jackie Kaliiaa

Gayle Kanoyton

Elijah Karriem

Michael Kayne

Janet Kim

Andrew Kimler

Rob Kutner

Kathy Le Backes

Una LeMarche

Steven Levinson

Alyssa Limperis

Deirdre Love

Kristen Marston

Thaddeus McCants

Johnny McNulty

Murf Meyer

Fawzia Mirza

Kenice Mobley

Mamoudou N'Diaye

Sue Obeidi

Shannon O'Neill

Rachel Pegram

David Perdue
Sally Rashid
Ryan RedCorn
Keja Reel
Rev. Dr. Dwight Riddick
Lorena Russi
Noam Schuster
Rashid Shabazz
Roger Smith
Erika Soto Lamb

Ishita Srivastava
Achilles Stamatalaky
Sasha Stewart
Yedoye Travis
Mahyad Tousi
Prashanth Venkataramanujam
Bobby Wilson
Lisa Flick Wilson
Rev. Lennox Yearwood Jr.

NOTES

INTRODUCTION. "IT'S LIKE TAKING YOUR VODKA WITH A CHASER"

1   A note for reading: I change tenses from time to time, but the shifts are meaning-
    ful and intentional. In the ethnographic and storytelling components—that is,
    where a story is unfolding—I use the present tense as a device to bring you, the
    reader, right into the action. But the present tense is not where I stay throughout
    the book. You'll get the hang of it.

2   Associated Press, "All Aboard P. Diddy's Party Plane," *Today*, October 27, 2004,
    www.today.com.

3   Gary Younge, "Hip-Hop Message to Young: Get Out and Vote," *Guardian*, June 19,
    2004, www.theguardian.com.

4   Henry Jenkins, *Convergence Culture: Where Old and New Media Collide*
    (New York: NYU Press, 2006), 238.

5   Jeffrey P. Jones, *Entertaining Politics: Satiric Television and Political Engagement*,
    2nd edition (Lanham, MD: Rowman & Littlefield, 2010).

6   "Help America Vote Act," US Election Assistance Commission, accessed January
    15, 2020, www.eac.gov.

7   Wired Staff, "Profiting from Political Urgency," *Wired*, June 23, 2004, www.wired
    .com; Cokie Roberts and Steven V. Roberts, "Year of the Net," *USA Weekend*,
    July 18, 2004.

8   The Declare Yourself/Comedy Central 2004 voter-registration-campaign PSAs are
    not widely available online as of the time of this writing, but several can be seen
    courtesy of the Internet Archive, including Wanda Sykes, Molly Shannon, and
    Amy Poehler (https://archive.org).

9   The 2004 Declare Yourself campaign included other entertainment-related
    activities and PSAs, not only the Comedy Central effort, so comedy was a major—
    but not the only—effort to which we can attribute the voter-outreach campaign
    successes.

10 "The 2004 Youth Vote," Center for Information & Research on Civic Learning &
    Engagement, accessed January 15, 2020, https://civicyouth.org.

11 See, for instance, Caty Borum Chattoo and Lauren Feldman, *A Comedian and an
    Activist Walk into a Bar: The Serious Role of Comedy in Social Justice* (Oakland:
    University of California Press, 2020).

12 See for example, Adrianne Chalepah (#InTheTimeItTakes), Twitter Post, Septem-
    ber 20, 2020, 1:06 p.m., https://twitter.com/adriannecomedy/status/13080902364
    13460480?lang=bg.

13 K. Sabeel Rahman and Hollie Russon Gilman, *Civic Power: Rebuilding American Democracy in an Era of Crisis* (New York: Cambridge University Press, 2019).

14 Borum Chattoo and Feldman, *A Comedian and an Activist Walk into a Bar.*

15 Eric Liu, "Why Ordinary People Need to Understand Power," TED Talks, September 2013, accessed January 15, 2020, www.ted.com.

16 David Bornstein, "A How-to Book for Wielding Civic Power," *New York Times*, April 5, 2017, www.nytimes.com.

17 Eric Liu, "A Cure for Post-Election Malaise," *Atlantic*, December 10, 2016, www.theatlantic.com.

18 Adrienne Day, "Can a Nonreligious Church Save Politics?," NationsWell, December 5, 2018, https://nationswell.com.

19 Stuart Hall and David Held, "Citizens and Citizenship," in *New Times: The Changing Face of Politics in the 1990s*, edited by Stuart Hall and Martin Jacques (London: Verso, 1990), 175.

20 Gianpaolo Baiocchi, Elizabeth A. Bennett, Alissa Cordner, Peter Taylor Klein, and Stephanie Savell, *The Civic Imagination: Making a Difference in American Political Life* (Boulder, CO: Paradigm, 2014), 1.

21 William V. Flores and Rina Benmayor, *Latino Cultural Citizenship: Claiming Identity, Space, and Rights* (Boston: Beacon, 1997), 29.

22 Flores and Benmayor, *Latino Cultural Citizenship*, 27.

23 Baiocchi et al., *The Civic Imagination*, 8.

24 Rahman and Gilman, *Civic Power*, 9.

25 Baiocchi et al., *The Civic Imagination*, 7.

26 Rahman and Gilman, *Civic Power*, 24.

27 Rahman and Gilman, *Civic Power*, 47.

28 Sarah J. Jackson, Moya Bailey, and Brooke Foucault Welles, *#Hashtag Activism: Networks of Race and Gender Justice* (Boston: MIT Press, 2020).

29 Rahman and Gilman, *Civic Power*, 30.

30 Rahman and Gilman, *Civic Power*, 79–80.

31 Rahman and Gilman, *Civic Power*, 51.

32 Henry Jenkins, *Participatory Culture Interviews* (Medford, MA: Polity Press, 2019), 3.

33 Jenkins, *Participatory Culture Interviews*, 149.

34 Steve Dubb, "Interview of Ai-jen Poo, Director, National Domestic Workers Alliance," Community-Wealth.org, May 2014, https://community-wealth.org.

35 David Morse, "Social Innovation Blog: Colloquy on Power and Narrative at the SoCal Symposium," USC Sol Price Center for Social Innovation, 2018, accessed January 15, 2020, https://socialinnovation.usc.edu.

36 Ishita Srivastava, "One of my all time fav quotes from @rashadrobinson: 'Let's not mistake presence for power. Presence is visibility; power is the ability to change the rules.' #normalizinginjustice @ColorOfChange #culturechange #Sundance2020," January 24, 2020, https://twitter.com/ishthebish/status/12208284 49280905216?s=09.

37 Henry Jenkins, Sangita Shresthova, Liana Gamber-Thompson, Neta Kligler-Vilenchik, and Arely Zimmerman, *By Any Media Necessary: The New Youth Activism* (New York: NYU Press, 2016), 29.

38 Borum Chattoo and Feldman, *A Comedian and an Activist Walk into a Bar*.

39 Stuart Cunningham and David Craig, *Social Media Entertainment: The New Intersection of Hollywood and Silicon Valley* (New York: NYU Press, 2019).

40 Aymar Jean Christian, *Open TV: Innovation beyond Hollywood and the Rise of Web Television* (New York: NYU Press, 2018).

41 Amanda Nguyen, phone interview with the author and Lauren Feldman, November 18, 2016, for Borum Chattoo and Feldman, *A Comedian and an Activist Walk into a Bar*.

42 Borum Chattoo and Feldman, *A Comedian and an Activist Walk into a Bar*, 153–55.

43 Amanda Nguyen, phone interview with the author and Lauren Feldman, November 18, 2016, for Borum Chattoo and Feldman, *A Comedian and an Activist Walk into a Bar*.

44 Jenkins et al., *By Any Media Necessary*.

45 Suzanne Nossel, "Introduction: On 'Artivism,' or Art's Utility in Activism," *Social Research* 83, no. 1 (2016): 103.

46 Stephen Duncombe, "Does It Work? The Æffect of Activist Art," *Social Research* 83, no. 1 (2016): 118.

47 Nossel, "Introduction," 104.

48 See Caty Borum Chattoo, *Story Movements: How Documentaries Empower People and Inspire Social Change* (New York: Oxford University Press, 2020).

49 Henry Jenkins, Sam Ford, and Joshua Green, *Spreadable Media: Creating Value and Meaning in a Networked Culture* (New York: NYU Press, 2013), 193.

50 Manuel Castells, *Networks of Outrage and Hope: Social Movements in the Internet Age* (Cambridge, UK: Polity Press, 2012).

51 Matthew Hindman, *The Internet Trap* (Princeton, NJ: Princeton University Press, 2018).

52 See, for example, Stacy L. Smith, Marc Choueiti, and Katherine Pieper, *Inclusion or Invisibility? Comprehensive Annenberg Report on Diversity in Entertainment*, University of Southern California–Annenberg, February 2017, https://annenberg.usc.edu; and Maureen Ryan, "Showrunners for New TV Season Remain Mostly White and Mostly Male," *Variety*, June 8, 2016, http://variety.com.

53 I employ the language, ideals, and similar practices of "engaged scholarship" described in Sasha Costanza-Chock, *Out of the Shadows, into the Streets: Transmedia Organizing and the Immigrant Rights Movement* (Cambridge, MA: MIT Press, 2014), 4.

54 Meredith D. Clark, "White Folks' Work: Digital Allyship Praxis in the #BlackLivesMatter Movement," *Social Movement Studies* 18, no. 5 (2019): 519, https://doi.org/10.1080/14742837.2019.1603104.

CHAPTER 1. "DESPERATE CHEETO"

1 "Randy Rainbow Dates Mel Gibson," YouTube, Randy Rainbow, July 18, 2010, www.youtube.com; "Randy Rainbow Works at Chick-fil-A," YouTube, Randy Rainbow, August 1, 2021, www.youtube.com/watch?v=jiZLFjbqDxQ&t=18s; "Kanye West Kicks It with Randy Rainbow," YouTube, Randy Rainbow, November 18, 2010, www.youtube.com/watch?v=icVRIlknohk&t=98s; "Anthony Weiner Is Dating Randy Rainbow," YouTube, Randy Rainbow, August 1, 2013, www.youtube.com/watch?v=3BBiN98XVvE.

2 Michelle Ye He Lee, "Donald Trump's False Comments Connecting Mexican Immigrants to Crime," *Washington Post*, July 7, 2015, www.washingtonpost.com; MPower Change, "86 Times Donald Trump Displayed or Promoted Islamophobia," *Medium*, April 19, 2018, https://medium.com.

3 "Randy Rainbow Performs at a Donald Trump Rally," YouTube, Randy Rainbow, January 18, 2016, www.youtube.com/watch?v=jDxSg1fSrws.

4 "Ted Cruz 'GOP Dropout,'" YouTube, Randy Rainbow, May 5, 2016, www.youtube.com/watch?v=vdB9nTe4ldE&feature=youtu.be.

5 "BRAGGADOCIOUS! Randy Rainbow Moderates Debate #1," YouTube, Randy Rainbow, September 18, 2016, www.youtube.com/watch?v=ldfF6chin5s&t=98s.

6 "Desperate Cheeto," YouTube, Randy Rainbow, October 11, 2017, www.youtube.com/watch?v=LTosB6V_V24.

7 "Randy Rainbow Upcoming Tour Dates," RandyRainbow, accessed January 4, 2021, www.randyrainbow.com/tour.

8 "Randy Rainbow w/Guest Star Patti Lu Pone. Fundraiser for the ACLU, If Donald Got Fired," *Daily Kos*, October 7, 2020, www.dailykos.com.

9 David Artavia, "Randy Rainbow on Emmy Nom and Resurfaced Racist, Transphobic Tweets," *Advocate*, August 20, 2020, www.advocate.com.

10 Margaret Sullivan, "Journalists, It's Time for a Cold-Turkey Breakup with Trump," *Washington Post*, December 16, 2020, www.washingtonpost.com.

11 Steven Levitsky and Daniel Ziblatt, *How Democracies Die* (New York: Crown Publishing, 2018).

12 Levitsky and Ziblatt, *How Democracies Die*, 5.

13 Daniela Diaz, "READ: Brief from 126 Republicans Supporting Texas Lawsuit in Supreme Court," CNN, December 11, 2020, www.cnn.com.

14 Zack Stanton, "How Trump's Attack on the Post Office Could Backfire," *Politico*, August 13, 2020, www.politico.com.

15 Christopher Ingraham, "New Research Explores Authoritarian Mind-set of Trump's Core Supporters," *Washington Post*, October 12, 2020, https://search-proquest-com.

16 Ingraham, "New Research."

17 M. J. Sorensen, "Humor as a Serious Strategy of Nonviolent Resistance to Oppression," *Peace & Change* 33 (2008): 167–90. https://doi.org/10.1111/j.1468-0130.2008.00488.x.

18 George Lakey, "How to Fight Fascism from a Position of Strength," Waging Nonviolence, February 15, 2019, https://wagingnonviolence.org; Srdja Popovic

and Mladen Joksic, "Why Dictators Don't Like Jokes," *Foreign Policy*, April 5, 2013, https://foreignpolicy.com.

19 Popovic and Joksic, "Why Dictators Don't Like Jokes."

20 Nicholas Kristof, "To Beat Trump, Mock Him," *New York Times*, September 26, 2020, www.nytimes.com.

21 Christopher Ingraham, "GOP Efforts to Overturn Election May Do Lasting Harm to Democracy, Political Scientists Warn," *Washington Post*, December 14, 2020, www.washingtonpost.com; Christopher Ingraham, Twitter Post, December 15, 2020, 11:59 a.m., https://twitter.com/_cingraham/status/1338529140211810304?s=09.

22 Stephen Duncombe, "Does It Work? The Æffect of Activist Art," *Social Research* 83, no. 1 (2016): 118.

23 Duncombe, "Does It Work?" 120–23.

24 Duncombe, "Does It Work?" 123–25.

25 Sorensen, "Humor as a Serious Strategy of Nonviolent Resistance to Oppression." See also Barbara Fultz (ed.), *The Naked Emperor: An Anthology of International Political Satire* (Cambridge, UK: Pegasus, 1970).

26 See also Michael Moore's news magazine–style television vignettes with costumed characters attacking the gun lobby and corporate corruption, as well as other forms of street-theater spectacle Moore employed. Jeffrey P. Jones, *Entertaining Politics: Satirical Television and Political Engagement* (Lanham, MD: Rowman & Littlefield, 2010).

27 David Brandenberger (ed.), *Political Humor under Stalin: An Anthology of Unofficial Jokes and Anecdotes* (Bloomington, IN: Slavica Publishers, 2009).

28 Rollo Romig, "The Eastern Bloc's Chief Export," *New Yorker*, August 12, 2008, www.newyorker.com.

29 Jonathan Gray, Jeffrey P. Jones, and Ethan Thompson (eds.), *Satire TV: Politics and Comedy in the Post-Network Era* (New York: NYU Press, 2009).

30 Another Soviet-era joke that captures this point nicely: "Don't think. If you do think, don't talk. If you do talk, don't write it down. If you do write it, don't publish it. If you do publish it, don't sign it. If you do sign it, write a denial." C. Banc and Alan Dundes, *You Call This Living? A Collection of East European Political Jokes* (Athens: University of Georgia Press, 1990).

31 Todd Gitlin, *The Sixties: Years of Hope, Days of Rage* (New York: Bantam Books, 1987), 233.

32 Gitlin, *The Sixties*, 234.

33 John Bell, "The Bread and Puppet Theatre in Nicaragua, 1987," *New Theatre Quarterly* 5, no. 17 (February 1989): 8–22. For a documentary of the performance, see www.youtube.com/watch?v=aRbecb8Nlbs.

34 Kenneth Best, "'Upset-ness' Feeds Bread & Puppet Exhibit at Benton," *UConn Today*, June 3, 2015, https://today.uconn.edu/.

35 Marwan M. Kraidy and Marina R Krikorian, "The Revolutionary Public Sphere: The Case of the Arab Uprisings," *Communication and the Public* 2, no. 2 (June 2017): 111, https://doi.org/10.1177/2057047317717499.

36 Sabine Damir-Geilsdorf and Stephan Milich, *Creative Resistance: Political Humor in the Arab Uprisings* (New York: Columbia University Press, 2020).

37 Sharif Paget, "Bassem Youssef: The Wild Story of 'Egypt's Jon Stewart,'" BBC, January 10, 2018, www.bbc.com.

38 Marc Owen Jones, "Satire, Social Media, and Revolutionary Cultural Production in the Bahrain Uprising: From Utopian Fiction to Political Satire," *Communication and the Public* 2, no. 2 (June 2017): 138, https://doi.org/10.1177/2057047317706372.

39 Jones, "Satire, Social Media, and Revolutionary Cultural Production," 138–41.

40 Hassan Abu-Hussein and Alexi Peristianis, "Why Iraqi Comedy Shows Are Booming," BBC, May 23, 2019, www.bbc.com.

41 Abu-Hussein and Peristianis, "Why Iraqi Comedy Shows Are Booming."

42 David Zucchino, "Great Read: Iraqi TV Comics Make Fun of Islamic State at Huge Risk," *Los Angeles Times*, October 29, 2014, www.latimes.com.

43 Adam Gallagher and Anthony Navone, "Not Just a Punchline: Humor and Nonviolent Action; How Comedy Can Provide Relief and Promote Resistance in Authoritarian Environments," U.S. Institute of Peace, May 16, 2019, www.usip.org.

44 George Lakey, "How to Fight Fascism from a Position of Strength," Waging Nonviolence, February 15, 2019, https://wagingnonviolence.org.

45 "The Finger Awards," accessed January 10, 2021, http://thefingerawards.org.

46 Josie Thaddeus-Johns, "The New Guard of Female Twitter Comediations," *Wall Street Journal*, June 23, 2020, www.wsj.com; David Lindquist, "Indianapolis Comedian Brent Terhune Has Much Bigger Plans Than His Viral MAGA Character," *IndyStar*, October 1, 2020, www.indystar.com.

47 Stephen Duncombe, *DREAM: Re-Imagining Progressive Politics in an Age of Fantasy* (New York: New Press, 2007), 19–20.

48 Caty Borum Chattoo and Lauren Feldman, *A Comedian and an Activist Walk into a Bar: The Serious Role of Comedy in Social Justice* (Oakland: University of California Press, 2020), 25.

49 Borum Chattoo and Feldman, *A Comedian and an Activist Walk into a Bar*, 25–26; M. Heath, "Aristotelian Comedy," *Classical Quarterly* 39, no. 2 (1989): 344, https://doi.org/10.1017/S0009838800037411; Cyrus Henry Hoy, "Comedy," *Encyclopædia Britannica*, accessed January 25, 2019, www.britannica.com.

50 Sigmund Freud, *Jokes and Their Relation to the Unconscious* (Harmondsworth, UK: Penguin, 1976); Borum Chattoo and Feldman, *A Comedian and an Activist Walk into a Bar*, 25–26.

51 This way of thinking is primarily the focus of Borum Chattoo and Feldman, *A Comedian and an Activist Walk into a Bar*.

52 Simon Critchley, *On Humour* (London: Routledge, 2002), 1, https://doi.org/10.4324/9780203870129; Michael J. Apter and Mitzi Desselles, "Disclosure Humor and Distortion Humor: A Reversal Theory Analysis," *Humor: International Journal of Humor Research* 25, no. 4 (2012): 417–35.

53 Borum Chattoo and Feldman, *A Comedian and an Activist Walk into a Bar*, 26.

54 Michael J. Apter and Mitzi Desselles, "Disclosure Humor and Distortion Humor: A Reversal Theory Analysis," *Humor: International Journal of Humor Research* 25, no. 4 (2012), 417–35.

55 Borum Chattoo and Feldman, *A Comedian and an Activist Walk into a Bar*, 41; Jerry H. Goldstein, Jerry M. Suls, and Susan Anthony, "Enjoyment of Specific Types of Humor Content: Motivation or Salience?" in *The Psychology of Humor: Theoretical Perspectives and Empirical Issues*, edited by Jeffrey H. Goldstein and Paul E. McGhee (New York: Academic Press, 1972), 159–72.

56 Daniel E. Berlyne, "Humor and Its Kin," in *The Psychology of Humor: Theoretical Perspectives and Empirical Issues*, edited by Jeffrey H. Goldstein and Paul E. McGhee (New York: Academic Press, 1972), 43–60.

57 Rod A. Martin, *The Psychology of Humor: An Integrative Approach* (Burlington, MA: Academic Press, 2007), 8; Borum Chattoo and Feldman, *A Comedian and an Activist Walk into a Bar*, 41.

58 Borum Chattoo and Feldman, *A Comedian and an Activist Walk into a Bar*, 38. Also, a similar framework for comedy's influence was proposed in Caty Borum Chattoo, "A Funny Matter: Toward a Framework for Understanding the Function of Comedy in Social Change," *HUMOR: The International Journal of Humor Research* (2018), https://doi.org/10.1515/humor-2018-0004.

59 Borum Chattoo and Feldman, *A Comedian and an Activist Walk into a Bar*; Lauren Feldman and Caty Borum Chattoo, "Comedy as a Route to Social Change: The Effects of Satire and News on Persuasion about Syrian Refugees," *Mass Communication and Society* 22, no. 3 (2019): 277–300, https://doi.org/10.1080/15205436.2018.1545035; Caty Borum Chattoo and Lauren Feldman, "Storytelling for Social Change: Leveraging Documentary and Comedy for Public Engagement in Global Poverty," *Journal of Communication* 67 (2017): 678–701, https://doi.org/10.1111/jcom.12318.

60 William V. Flores and Rina Benmayor (eds.), *Latino Cultural Citizenship: Claiming Identity, Space, and Rights* (Boston: Beacon Press, 1998).

61 Rebecca Krefting, *All Joking Aside: American Humor and Its Discontents* (Baltimore, MD: Johns Hopkins University Press, 2014), 17.

62 Flores and Rina Benmayor, *Latino Cultural Citizenship*, 43.

63 Edward Schiappa, Peter B. Gregg, and Dean E. Hewes, "The Parasocial Contact Hypothesis," *Communication Monographs* 72, no. 1 (2005): 92–115; Borum Chattoo and Feldman, *A Comedian and an Activist Walk into a Bar*, 28–29.

64 Priya Arora, "Mindy Kaling's New Show Tells a New Story: One Like Hers," *New York Times*, April 27, 2020, www.nytimes.com.

65 Gloria Calderón Kellett, phone interview with the author, November 20, 2020.

66 Kathryn VanArendonk, "*Nate* Is the Most Astonishing Special of 2020," *Vulture*, December 1, 2020, www.vulture.com.

67 Emily Stewart, "Wonder What Michelle Wolf Said to Make Everyone So Mad? Read It Here," *Vox*, April 30, 2018, https://www.vox.com.

68 Henry Jenkins et al., *By Any Media Necessary: The New Youth Activism* (New York: NYU Press, 2016), 29.

69 Borum Chattoo and Feldman, *A Comedian and an Activist Walk into a Bar*, 24–25.

70 Devon Ivie, "Dan Levy Explains Why *Schitt's Creek* Has No Homophobia," *Vulture*, November 18, 2018, www.vulture.com.

71 Ivie, "Dan Levy Explains Why."

72 Jeff Hiller, phone interview with the author, November 20, 2020.

73 Pamela J. Downe, "Laughing When It Hurts: Humor and Violence in the Lives of Costa Rican Prostitutes," *Women's Studies International Forum* 22, no. 1 (January 1999): 63–78, https://doi.org/10.1016/S0277-5395(98)00109-5.

74 Sabine Damir-Geilsdorf and Stephan Milich (eds.), *Creative Resistance: Political Humor in the Arab Uprisings* (New Rockford, ND: transcript publishing, 2020), 24.

75 Gloria Calderón Kellett, phone interview with the author, November 20, 2020.

76 Molly Gaebe, phone interview with the author, November 20, 2020.

77 Sabine Damir-Geilsdorf and Stephan Milich, *Creative Resistance*, 23.

78 Tomi Obaro, "Dave Chapelle Doesn't Need to Punch Down," *BuzzFeed*, August 27, 2019, www.buzzfeednews.com.

CHAPTER 2. "IT'S ALL ABOUT WHO YOU KNOW"

1 Seth Abramovitch, "How to Appear Smart in Meetings without Really Trying," RedBull.com, April 26, 2018, https://www.redbull.com.

2 Andrea Marks, "'I Have to Pinch Myself': Sarah Cooper's Rapid Rise from Trump TikToker to Netflix Star," *Rolling Stone*, October 27, 2020, www.rollingstone.com.

3 Nellie Andreeva and Denise Petski, "Sarah Cooper Comedy 'How to Be Successful without Hurting Men's Feelings' from PatMa Lands at CBS with Penalty," *Deadline*, August 20, 2020, https://deadline.com.

4 Paige Leskin, "Inside the Rise of TikTok, the Viral Video-Sharing App Wildly Popular with Teens and Loathed by the Trump Administration," *Business Insider*, August 7, 2020, www.businessinsider.com.

5 Stuart Cunningham and David Craig, *Social Media Entertainment: The New Intersection of Hollywood and Silicon Valley* (New York: NYU Press), 4.

6 "Archived: WHO Timeline—COVID-19," World Health Organization, accessed February 10, 2021, www.who.int.

7 "A Timeline of COVID-19 Developments in 2020," *American Journal of Managed Care*, accessed February 10, 2021, www.ajmc.com.

8 Alan Feuer and Andrea Saledo, "New York City Deploys 45 Mobile Morgues as Virus Strains Funeral Homes," *New York Times*, April 2, 2020, www.nytimes.com.

9 Megan McCluskey, "Comedian Sarah Cooper Doesn't Need Donald Trump Anymore," *Time*, October 27, 2020, https://time.com.

10 Aaron Rupar, "Trump Just Mused about Whether Disinfectant Injections Could Treat the Coronavirus. Really," *Vox*, April 23, 2020, www.vox.com.

11 Yohana Desta, "How Sarah Cooper Trumped Donald Trump—Without Saying a Word," *Vanity Fair*, July 20, 2020, www.vanityfair.com.

12 McCluskey, "Comedian Sarah Cooper Doesn't Need Donald Trump Anymore."

13 Sarah Cooper, Twitter post, April 23, 2020, 8:04 p.m., https://twitter.com/sarahcpr /status/1253474772702429189?lang=en.

14 Regina R. Robertson, "Meet the Comedian behind the 'How to Medical' TikTok Everyone Is Sharing," *Essence*, November 4, 2020, www.essence.com.

15 McCluskey, "Comedian Sarah Cooper Doesn't Need Donald Trump Anymore."

16 Anya van Wagtendonk, "Trump Dismisses His Daily Coronavirus Press Briefings as 'Not Worth the Time and Effort,'" *Vox*, April 26, 2020, www.vox.com.

17 "How to Bible," YouTube, Sarah Cooper, June 3, 2020, www.youtube.com/watch?v =bOCcThLYdEQ.

18 "How to Water," YouTube, Sarah Cooper, June 13, 2020, www.youtube.com/watch ?v=3LAS-1x9K7Y.

19 "How to Mask," YouTube, Sarah Cooper, July 6, 2020, www.youtube.com/watch?v =bMKgX3V3Y_k.

20 "How to Bunker," YouTube, Sarah Cooper, June 6, 2020, www.youtube.com/watch ?v=1iJA2cVXUAA.

21 Desta, "How Sarah Cooper Trumped Donald Trump."

22 McCluskey, "Comedian Sarah Cooper Doesn't Need Donald Trump Anymore."

23 Peter White, "Rising Comedian and TikTok Trump Impersonator Sarah Cooper Signs with WME," *Deadline*, June 11, 2020, https://deadline.com.

24 McCluskey, "Comedian Sarah Cooper Doesn't Need Donald Trump Anymore."

25 Todd Spangler, "Netflix CEO and Co-founder Reed Hastings' Memoir Is Titled *No Rules Rules: Netflix and the Culture of Reinvention*," *Variety*, February 19, 2020, https://variety.com.

26 Rebecca Rubin, "Sarah Cooper Hopes Donald Trump Gets Fired, Even If It Means the End of Her Impersonations," *Variety*, October 7, 2020, https://variety.com.

27 Ryan Cunningham, phone interview with the author, January 11, 2021.

28 Jack Sharf, "'I May Destroy You' Golden Globes Shutout Ignites Hollywood Outrage: 'Racism Is the Only Explanation,'" *IndieWire*, February 4, 2021, www.indiewire.com.

29 Esther Zuckerman, "HBO's 'I May Destroy You' Is the Most Astonishing Show on TV Right Now," *Thrillist*, July 7, 2020, www.thrillist.com.

30 Caroline Framke, "How Michaela Coel Processed Trauma and Fought to Own Her Story with 'I May Destroy You,'" *Variety*, August 19, 2020, https://variety.com.

31 Deborah Copaken, "I'm a Writer on *Emily in Paris*. *I May Destroy You* deserved a Golden Globe Nomination," *Guardian*, February 3, 2021, www.theguardian.com.

32 Sharf, "'I May Destroy You' Golden Globes Shutout."

33 Sharf, "'I May Destroy You' Golden Globes Shutout."

34 Janet Wasko, *Hollywood in the Information Age: Beyond the Silver Screen* (Cambridge, UK: Polity Press, 1994), 4.

35 Mary Kate McGrath, "Ava DuVernay Just Took the Golden Globes to Task for Their Lack of Black Inclusion," *Bustle*, February 22, 2021, www.bustle.com.

36 Todd Gitlin, *Inside Prime Time* (Los Angeles: University of California Press, 2000), 31.

37 Dino-Ray Ramos, "New Study Finds Hollywood Studios Could Lose Money from Movies That Lack Diversity," *Deadline*, October 6, 2020, https://deadline.com.

38 Adrienne Gibbs, "Top Tweets: Black Twitter Keeps Appointment TV Alive," Ipsos Future, accessed February 15, 2021, https://future.ipsos.com.

39 "Being Seen on TV: Diverse Representation and Inclusion on TV," Nielsen, December 2, 2020, www.nielsen.com.

40 "2020 Diverse Intelligence Series: Inclusion on TV," Nielsen, accessed February 15, 2021, www.nielsen.com.

41 Eric Deggans, "More Evidence TV Doesn't Reflect Real Life Diversity," NPR, December 4, 2020, www.npr.org.

42 Jessica Wolf, "Diversity Improves among TV Actors, but Executives Still Overwhelmingly White and Male," UCLA, October 22, 2020, https://newsroom.ucla.edu; Darnell Hunt and Ana-Christina Ramón, "Hollywood Diversity Report 2020: A Tale of Two Hollywoods (Part 2: Television)," UCLA, 2020, https://socialsciences.ucla.edu.

43 Wolf, "Diversity Improves among TV Actors"; Hunt and Ramón, "Hollywood Diversity Report 2020."

44 Gitlin, *Inside Prime Time*, xii.

45 Wolf, "Diversity Improves among TV Actors"; Hunt and Ramón, "Hollywood Diversity Report 2020."

46 Gitlin, *Inside Prime Time*, viii.

47 Aymar Jean Christian, *Open TV: Innovation beyond Hollywood and the Rise of Web Television* (New York: NYU Press, 2018), 4.

48 Amanda Lotz, *We Now Disrupt This Broadcast: How Cable Transformed Television and the Internet Revolutionized It All* (Cambridge, MA: MIT Press, 2018), x.

49 Lotz, *We Now Disrupt This Broadcast*, 103.

50 Lotz, *We Now Disrupt This Broadcast*, x.

51 Lotz, *We Now Disrupt This Broadcast*, 5.

52 Stuart Cunningham and David Craig, *Social Media Entertainment: The New Intersection of Hollywood and Silicon Valley* (New York: NYU Press, 2019), 5.

53 "Tops of 2020: Television," Nielsen, December 14, 2020, www.nielsen.com.

54 Lotz, *We Now Disrupt This Broadcast*, 177.

55 John Caldwell, *Production Culture: Industrial Reflexivity and Critical Practices in Film and Television* (Durham, NC: Duke University Press, 2008), 52.

56 Gitlin, *Inside Prime Time*, 14.

57 Caldwell, *Production Culture*, 91.

58 Ryan Cunningham, phone interview with the author, January 11, 2021.

59 Pierre Bourdieu, "Cultural Reproduction and Social Reproduction," in *Inequality: Classic Readings in Race, Class, and Gender*, edited by D. B. Grusky and S. Szelényi (Boulder, CO: Westview Press, 2006), 257–71.

60 Caldwell, *Production Culture*.

61 Kathy Le Backes, phone interview with the author, November 20, 2020.

62 Caldwell, *Production Culture*, 97.

63 Kesila Chambers, phone interview with the author, December 8, 2020.

64 Deniese Davis, phone interview with the author, January 29, 2021.

65 Vicki Mayer, *Below the Line: Producers and Production Studies in the New Television Economy* (Durham, NC: Duke University Press, 2011), 179.

66 Erika Soto Lamb, phone interview with the author, January 12, 2021.

67 Mahyad Tousi, phone interview with the author, January 28, 2021.

68 Caldwell, *Production Culture*, 81.

69 Gitlin, *Inside Prime Time*, 129.

70 Josh Church, phone interview with the author, January 12, 2021.

71 Jose Acevedo, phone interview with the author, December 8, 2020.

72 Mamoudou N'Diaye, phone interview with the author, January 19, 2021.

73 Deniese Davis, phone interview with the author, January 28, 2021.

74 Ryan Cunningham, phone interview with the author, January 11, 2021.

75 Josh Church, phone interview with the author, January 12, 2021.

76 Caldwell, *Production Culture*, 211.

77 Matt Ruby, "The Inside Scoop on the Jon Stewart Packet and How to Get Hired as a Comedy Writer," The Rubesletter (Substack), February 16, 2021, https://mattruby.substack.com.

78 Chelsea Devantez, Twitter post, February 23, 2021, 12:43 p.m., https://twitter.com/chelseadevantez/status/1364269687446540297?s=09.

79 Devantez, Twitter post.

80 Niles Abston, phone interview with the author, November 20, 2020.

81 Sasha Stewart, phone interview with the author, November 30, 2020.

82 Sasha Stewart, phone interview with the author, November 30, 2020.

83 Peter White, "'The Amber Ruffin Show' Gets NBC Slot, Replacing 'A Little Late with Lilly Singh' Repeats," *Deadline*, February 19, 2021, https://deadline.com.

84 Sasha Stewart, phone interview with the author, November 30, 2020.

85 A similar set of challenges exist for stand-up comedy and live stand-up shows. See Zahra Noorbakhsh, *Funny Is Funny: Development Models for Diverse Comedians in Stand-Up Comedy*, Pop Culture Collaborative, 2020, https://popcollab.org.

86 Joel Church-Cooper, phone interview with the author and Lauren Feldman, November 7, 2018, for Caty Borum Chattoo and Lauren Feldman, *A Comedian and an Activist Walk into a Bar: The Serious Role of Comedy in Social Justice* (Oakland: University of California Press, 2020).

87 Ryan Cunningham, phone interview with the author, January 11, 2021.

88 Deniese Davis, phone interview with the author, January 28, 2021.

89 Jandiz Cardoso, phone interview with the author, December 10, 2020.

90 Cunningham and Craig, *Social Media Entertainment*, 191.

91 Makiah Green, phone interview with the author, December 8, 2020.

92 Prashanth Venkataramanujam, phone interview with the author, December 20, 2020.

93 Deniese Davis, phone interview with the author, January 28, 2021.

94 Gloria Calderón Kellett, phone interview with the author, November 20, 2020.

95 Chauncey Alcorn, "Netflix Says It Needs More Latinx Programming after an Internal Diversity Audit," CNN, February 26, 2021, www.cnn.com.

96 Jose Acevedo, phone interview with the author, December 8, 2020.

97 Jandiz Cardoso, phone interview with the author, December 10, 2020.

98 Caldwell, *Production Culture*, 226.

99 Makiah Green, phone interview with the author, December 8, 2020.

100 Deniese Davis, phone interview with the author, January 28, 2021.

101 Gloria Calderón Kellett, phone interview with the author, November 20, 2020.

102 Rick Porter, "Taika Waititi-Sterlin Harjo Comedy Series a Go at FX," *Hollywood Reporter*, December 22, 2020, www.hollywoodreporter.com; Peter White, "'Rutherford Falls': Sierra Teller Ornelas Lauds Comedy for Native American Representation as Peacock Series Scheduled to Shoot in Three to Four Weeks," *Deadline*, August 10, 2020, https://deadline.com; Zoe Tennant, "'Rutherford Falls' Brings Indigenous Writers Together for New NBC Sitcom," CBC, February 7, 2020, www.cbc.ca.

103 Bobby Wilson, phone interview with the author, January 20, 2021.

104 Rick Porter, "Chuck Lorre Comedy about Afghanistan War Veterans Lands at CBS," *Hollywood Reporter*, October 10, 2019, www.hollywoodreporter.com.

105 Mahyad Tousi, phone interview with the author, January 28, 2021.

106 Dino-Ray Ramos, "Ava DuVernay, Tilane Jones, and Mercedes Cooper Celebrate 10 Years of ARRAY, Talk ARRAY Crew and Impact of Narrative Change Collective," *Deadline*, February 1, 2021, https://deadline.com.

CHAPTER 3. "HOLLYWOOD WON'T CHANGE UNLESS IT'S FORCED TO CHANGE"

1 Evan Hill, Ainara Tiefenthaler, Christiaan Tiebert, Drew Jordan, Haley Willis and Robin Stein, "How George Floyd Was Killed in Police Custody," *New York Times*, May 31, 2020, www.nytimes.com.

2 Elliott C. McLaughlin, "How George Floyd's Death Ignited a Racial Reckoning That Shows No Signs of Slowing Down," CNN, August 9, 2020, www.cnn.com.

3 Lindsay McKenzie, "Words Matter for College Presidents, but So Will Actions," *Inside Higher Education*, June 8, 2020, www.insidehighered.com; "After Years of Marginalizing Black Employees, Corporate America Says Black Lives Matter," *Washington Post*, June 13, 2020, www.washingtonpost.com.

4 McLaughlin, "How George Floyd's Death Ignited a Racial Reckoning."

5 Keeanga-Yahamatta Taylor, *From #BlackLivesMatter to Black Liberation* (Chicago: Haymarket Books, 2016), 2.

6 Taylor, *From #BlackLivesMatter to Black Liberation*, 2.

7 Michelle Alexander, *The New Jim Crow: Mass Incarceration in the Age of Colorblindness*, 10th anniversary ed. (New York: New Press, 2020), 3.

8 Meredith D. Clark, "White Folks' Work: Digital Allyship Praxis in the #Blacklivesmatter Movement," *Social Movement Studies* 18, no. 5 (2019): 519–34, https://doi.org/10.1080/14742837.2019.1603104.

9 Jonathan Berr, "Hollywood Responds to the Senseless Death of George Floyd, Riots," *Forbes,* May 31, 2020, www.forbes.com.

10 Leia Idliby, "A Growing Number of Media Outlets Make Juneteenth a Paid Holiday," *Mediaite,* June 19, 2020, www.mediaite.com.

11 Patrick Hipes and Denise Petski, "Juneteenth Programming Lineup: 'Black Panther' and 'Just Mercy,' HBO's 'Watchmen,' Apple's 'The Banker,' FX's 'Atlanta,' 'Selma,' and More," *Deadline,* June 19, 2020, https://deadline.com.

12 Mikey O'Connell, "Inside Color of Change's Renewed Fight against Police Procedurals: 'These Shows Have an Agenda,'" *Hollywood Reporter,* June 25, 2020, www .hollywoodreporter.com.

13 Mary Beth Oliver, "Portrayals of Crime, Race, and Aggression in 'Reality-Based' Police Shows: A Content Analysis," *Journal of Broadcasting & Electronic Media*, 38, no. 2 (1994): 179–92, https://doi.org/10.1080/08838159409364255; Mary Beth Oliver, "African American Men as 'Criminal and Dangerous': Implications of Media Portrayals of Crime on the 'Criminalization' of African American Men," *Journal of African American Studies* 7, no. 2 (2003): 3–18, www.jstor.org/.

14 O'Connell, "Inside Color of Change's Renewed Fight against Police Procedurals."

15 Ryan Cunningham, phone interview with the author, January 11, 2021.

16 Brian Welk, "Netflix Sets Up $100 Million Fund to Help Underrepresented Communities in Entertainment," *TheWrap,* February 26, 2021, www.thewrap.com.

17 Katie Kilkenny, "Diverse Representation Organization Launches Black Entertainment Executives Pipeline Initiative (Exclusive)," *Hollywood Reporter,* December 7, 2020, www.hollywoodreporter.com.

18 Dino Day-Ramos, "MTV Entertainment Group Launches Initiative to Bolster Content from BIPOC and Women-Owned Production Companies," *Deadline,* December 3, 2020, https://deadline.com.

19 "CBS Announces Diversity Overhaul of Writers Rooms and Script Development Program," *Los Angeles Times,* July 13, 2020, www.latimes.com.

20 Dino Day-Ramos, "Disney TV Studios Execs Address Inclusion, How Difficult Conversations about Race Will Incite Change and Accountability of White Decision Makers—TCA," *Deadline,* February 25, 2021, https://deadline.com.

21 Jandiz Cardoso, phone interview with the author, December 10, 2020.

22 Makiah Green, phone interview with the author, December 8, 2020.

23 Kristen Marston, phone interview with the author, January 22, 2021.

24 Gloria Calderón Kellett, phone interview with author, November 20, 2020.

25 Henry Jenkins, Gabriel Peters-Lazaro, and Sangita Shresthova, *Popular Culture and the Civic Imagination: Case Studies of Creative Social Change* (New York: NYU Press, 2020), 5.

26 Michael Kantor and Laurence Maslon, *Make 'Em Laugh: The Funny Business of America* (New York: Hachette Book Group, 2008), 276.

27 Norman Lear, foreword to Caty Borum Chattoo and Lauren Feldman, *A Comedian and an Activist Walk into a Bar: The Serious Role of Comedy in Social Justice* (Oakland: University of California Press, 2020), xi.

28 Martin Schneider, "Movin' on Up: How the Black Panthers Invented 'The Jeffersons,'" Dangerous Minds, May 5, 2016, https://dangerousminds.net.

29 Norman Lear, *Even This I Get to Experience* (New York: Penguin, 2014), 176.

30 Lear, *Even This I Get to Experience*, 176.

31 Schneider, "Movin' on Up."

32 Lear, *Even This I Get to Experience*, 176–77.

33 Lear, *Even This I Get to Experience*, 176–77.

34 Kathryn Montgomery, *Target Prime Time: Advocacy Groups and the Struggle over Entertainment Television* (New York: Oxford University Press, 1989), 71–72.

35 Nicole Sperling, "TV Titan Norman Lear Opens Up to 'Black-Ish' Creator Kenya Barris about Storied Career," *Entertainment Weekly*, March 31, 2017, https://ew.com.

36 Ibram X. Kendi, *Stamped from the Beginning: The Definitive History of Racist Ideas in America* (New York: Bold Type Books, 2016), 323.

37 Thomas Streeter, "What Is an Advocacy Group, Anyway?," in *Advocacy Groups and the Entertainment Industry*, edited by Michael Suman and Gabriel Rossman (Westport, CT: Praeger, 2000), 76.

38 Vincent Doyle, *Making Out in the Mainstream: GLAAD and the Politics of Respectability* (Quebec, Canada: McGill-Queen's University Press, 2016), 13.

39 William A. Donohue, "A Catholic Look at the Entertainment Industry," in *Advocacy Groups and the Entertainment Industry*, ed. Suman and Rossman, 19.

40 Vicki Mayer, *Below the Line: Producers and Production Studies in the New Television Economy* (Durham, NC: Duke University Press, 2011), 12.

41 Montgomery, *Target Prime Time*, 8.

42 Gabriel Rossman, "Hostile and Cooperative Strategy," in *Advocacy Groups and the Entertainment Industry*, ed. Suman and Rossman, 86.

43 Doyle, *Making Out in the Mainstream*, 4.

44 William Horn, as interviewed by Gabriel Rossman, "The Proactive Strategy of GLAAD," in *Advocacy Groups and the Entertainment Industry*, ed. Suman and Rossman, 23.

45 Guy Aoki, "Strategies of the Media Action Network for Asian Americans," in *Advocacy Groups and the Entertainment Industry*, ed. Suman and Rossman, 29–30.

46 Montgomery, *Target Prime Time*, 14.

47 See Montgomery, *Target Prime Time*, 198.

48 "Out of the Picture: Hispanics in the Media," National Council of La Raza (UnidosUS), 1994, 1, http://publications.unidosus.org.

49 Doyle, *Making Out in the Mainstream*, 8–10.

50 Lauren Berlant, *The Queen of America Goes to Washington City: Essays on Sex and Citizenship* (Durham, NC: Duke University Press, 1997), 9.

51 Doyle, *Making Out in the Mainstream*, 21–22.

52 Rossman, "Hostile and Cooperative Strategy," 89–90.

53 Rossman, "Hostile and Cooperative Strategy," 92–93.

54 Rossman, "Hostile and Cooperative Strategy," 95.

55 Sue Obeidi, phone interview with the author, January 21, 2021.

56 "Call for Nominations for 2020 MPAC Awards," MPAC, accessed June 17, 2021, www.mpac.org.

57 Sue Obeidi, phone interview with the author, January 21, 2021.

58 Kuang Keng Kuek Ser, "Data: Hate Crimes against Muslims Increased after 9/11," *The World* (Public Radio International), September 12, 2016, www.pri.org.

59 Shawna Ayoub Ainslie, "20 Ways 9/11 Changed My Life as an (American) Muslim," *Huffington Post*, December 6, 2017, www.huffpost.com.

60 Noura Alalawi, "How Do Hollywood Movies Portray Muslims and Arabs after 9/11? Content Analysis of *The Kingdom* and *Rendition* Movies," *Cross-Cultural Communication* 11, no. 11 (2015): 58–62, http://dx.doi.org/10.3968/7642.

61 Sue Obeidi, phone interview with the author, January 21, 2021.

62 Sue Obeidi, phone interview with the author, January 21, 2021.

63 Kristen Marston, phone interview with the author, January 22, 2021.

64 Henry Jenkins, Sangita Shresthova, Liana Gamber-Thompson, Neta Kligler-Vilenchik, and Arely Zimmerman, *By Any Media Necessary: The New Youth Activism* (New York: NYU Press, 2016), 17.

65 Stuart Cunningham and David Craig (eds.), *Creator Culture: An Introduction to Global Social Media Entertainment* (New York: NYU Press, 2021).

66 Henry Jenkins, *Participatory Culture Interviews* (Medford, MA: Polity Press, 2019), 3.

67 Sarah J. Jackson, Moya Bailey, and Brooke Foucault Welles, *#HashtagActivism: Networks of Race and Gender Justice* (Cambridge, MA: MIT Press, 2020). xxv–xxxiii.

68 Michael Curtin, "Gatekeeping in the Neo-Network Era," in *Advocacy Groups and the Entertainment Industry*, ed. Suman and Rossman, 71.

69 Robert Pekurny, "Advocacy Groups in the Age of Audience Fragmentation: Thoughts on a New Strategy," in *Advocacy Groups and the Entertainment Industry*, ed. Suman and Rossman, 110.

70 Caty Borum Chattoo, "Entertainment-Education as Social Justice Activism in the United States: Narrative Strategy in the Participatory Media Era," in *Entertainment-Education behind the Scenes: Case Studies for Theory and Practice*, edited by P. Falzone and L. Frank (London: Palgrave Macmillan, Cham, 2021), https://doi.org/10.1007/978-3-030-63614-2_4.

71 Borum Chattoo, "Entertainment-Education."

72 A. Farley, "This Activist Organization Wants to Transform the Criminal Justice System—Starting with Prosecutors," *Fast Company*, March 7, 2020, www.fastcompany.com,

73 "Color of Change," YouTube, https://www.youtube.com/playlist?list=PLtsktHeFUJfS9cOXwwprz-jHt_Zl98DQY.

74 "MTV Entertainment Group Launches 'Culture Code,' a Comprehensive DE&I Orientation for Its Entire Creative Community, including Staff, Talent, and Production Partners," *Business Wire*, November 19, 2020, www.businesswire.com.

75 Erika Soto Lamb, phone interview with the author, January 12, 2021.

76 "Welcome to America—Alternatino," YouTube, August 6, 2019, https://www.youtube.com/watch?v=S_IfXmKmg9o.

77 Erika Soto Lamb, phone interview with the author, January 12, 2021.

78 Arturo Castro, "Why Random Mass Shootings Make Absolutely No Sense to Hispanic Immigrants," *Washington Post*, August 6, 2019, www.washingtonpost .com.

79 Erika Soto Lamb, phone interview with the author, January 12, 2021.

80 Matt Donnelly, "CAA Launches Initiative to Improve Representation in Entertainment (EXCLUSIVE)," *Variety*, April 13, 2021, https://variety.com.

81 Donnelly, "CAA Launches Initiative."

82 "The Black List, IllumiNative, and Sundance Institute Announce Inaugural Indigenous Screenwriting List," *Native News Online*, December 9, 2020, https: //nativenewsonline.net; Manuel Betancourt, "Call for Submissions: 'The 2020 Latinx TV List' Hopes to Uplift Underrepresented Voices on TV," *Remezcla*, February 18, 2020, https://remezcla.com; Dino Day-Ramos, "The Black List Partners with MPAC and Pillars Fund for First-Ever Muslim List," *Deadline*, September 1, 2020, https://deadline.com.

83 Josh Church, phone interview with the author, January 12, 2021.

84 Deniese Davis, phone interview with the author, January 29, 2021.

85 William Horn, as interviewed by Gabriel Rossman, "The Proactive Strategy of GLAAD," in *Advocacy Groups and the Entertainment Industry*, ed. Suman and Rossman, 26.

86 Kristen Marston, phone interview with the author, January 22, 2021.

87 Sue Obeidi, phone interview with the author, January 21, 2021.

CHAPTER 4. "YOU LEARN TO BE RACIST FROM PEOPLE YOU LOVE"

1 Corey Ryan Forrester, phone interview with the author, June 4, 2021. Direct quotations from Forrester in this chapter, unless noted with other sources, come from this interview.

2 Ally Mutnick and Melanie Zanona, "House Republican Leaders Condemn GOP Candidate Who Made Racist Videos," *Politico*, June 17, 2020, www.politico.com; John Bowden, "Schiff: Marjorie Taylor Greene's Actions 'A Sign of the Greater Rot in Her Party,'" *The Hill*, May 25, 2021, https://thehill.com.

3 Michelle Lou, "When He Heard a Georgia Venue Wouldn't Do Same-Sex Marriages, He Offered His Own Yard," CNN, June 15, 2019, www.cnn.com.

4 *The Liberal Redneck Manifesto* (New York: Simon & Schuster, 2016).

5 Bethany Hall, phone interview with author, March 11, 2021. Direct quotations from Hall in this chapter, unless noted with other sources, come from this interview.

6 Denise Petski, "Daniel Powell and Alex Bach's Irony Point Inks Overall Deal with Netflix," *Deadline*, May 12, 2021, https://deadline.com.

7 "Comedy ThinkTanks," Center for Media & Social Impact, accessed May 25, 2021, https://cmsimpact.org.

8 P. E. Plsek, *Creativity, Innovation, and Quality* (New York: Irwin Professional Publishing, 1997), viii.

9 Kat Cizek and William Uricchio, "Co-Creating Media within Communities, across Disciplines and with Algorithms," Collective Wisdom, MIT Press, accessed May 25, 2021, https://wip.mitpress.mit.edu.

10 Terri R. Kurtzberg and Teresa M. Amabile, "From Guilford to Creative Synergy: Opening the Black Box of Team-Level Creativity," *Creativity Research Journal* 13, no. 3–4 (2001): 290.

11 Bernard De Koven with Holly Gramozio, *The Infinite Playground: A Player's Guide to Imagination* (Cambridge, MA: MIT Press, 2020), 150.

12 De Koven with Gramozio, *The Infinite Playground*, 2.

13 Kelly Leonard and Tom Yorton, *Yes, And: How Improvisation Reverses "No, But" Thinking and Improves Creativity and Collaboration* (New York: HarperCollins, 2015), 213.

14 Leonard and Yorton, *Yes, And*, 12–18.

15 "Creativity," *New World Encyclopedia*, accessed January 15, 2020, www.newworld encyclopedia.org.

16 Mark A. Runco and Acar Selcuk, "Divergent Thinking as an Indicator of Creative Potential," *Creativity Research Journal* 24, no. 1 (2012): 66–75, https://doi.org/:10 .1080/10400419.2012.652929.

17 Margaret A. Boden, *The Creative Mind: Myths and Mechanisms*, 2nd edition (New York: Routledge, 2004), 1.

18 Boden, *The Creative Mind*, 3–5.

19 P. B. Paulus and B. A. Nijstad, *Group Creativity: Innovation through Collaboration* (Oxford: Oxford University Press, 2003), vii.

20 Paulus and Nijstad, *Group Creativity*, 6.

21 Plsek, *Creativity, Innovation, and Quality*, 3.

22 Plsek, *Creativity, Innovation, and Quality*, 10–13.

23 J. P. Guilford, "Creativity," *American Psychologist* 5 (1950): 446, in Terri R. Kurtzberg and Teresa M. Amabile, "From Guilford to Creative Synergy: Opening the Black Box of Team-Level Creativity," *Creativity Research Journal* 13 (2001): 3–4, 285.

24 Mark A. Runco and Selcuk Acar, "Divergent Thinking as an Indicator of Creative Potential," *Creativity Research Journal* 24, no. 1 (2012): 66, https://doi.org/10.1080 /10400419.2012.652929.

25 "J. P. Guilford," *New World Encyclopedia*, accessed June 1, 2021, www.newworld encyclopedia.org.

26 Sasha Stewart, phone interview with the author, November 30, 2020.

27 Terri R. Kurtzberg and Teresa M. Amabile, "From Guilford to Creative Synergy: Opening the Black Box of Team-Level Creativity," *Creativity Research Journal* 13, no. 3–4 (2001); 287–90, https://doi.org/10.1207/S15326934CRJ1334_06.

28 Plsek, *Creativity, Innovation, and Quality*, 83–85.

29 Miguel Sicart, *Play Matters* (Cambridge, MA: MIT Press, 2017), 15.

30 Roger Silverstone, *Why Study the Media?* (London: Sage, 1999), 66.

31 Sicart, *Play Matters*, 5.

32 Kurtzberg and Amabile, "From Guilford to Creative Synergy," 289–90.

33 Noam Schuster, phone interview with the author, November 30, 2020.

34 Prashanth Venkataramanujam, phone interview with the author, December 7, 2020.

35 De Koven with Gramozio, *The Infinite Playground*, 144.

36 Tegand Wendland, "With Lee Statue's Removal, Another Battle of New Orleans Comes to a Close," NPR, May 20, 2017, www.npr.org.

37 Mitch Landrieu, "Mitch Landrieu's Speech on the Removal of Confederate Statues from New Orleans," *New York Times*, May 23, 2017, www.nytimes.com.

38 Ryan Berni, phone interview with the author, June 7, 2021. Direct quotations from Berni in this chapter, unless noted with other sources, come from this interview.

39 "About: E Pluribus Unum Fund," E Pluribus Unum, accessed June 2, 2021, www .unumfund.org.

40 "About: E Pluribus Unum Fund."

41 Scott Hutchison, phone meeting with the author, as noted in author field notes, January 2021.

42 E Pluribus Enum, internal audience research strategy document. Shared with the author in January 2021.

43 E Pluribus Unum internal audience research strategy document, shared confidentially with the author by the E Pluribus Unum team.

44 Josie Thaddeus-Johns, "The New Guard of Female Twitter Comedians," *Wall Street Journal*, June 23, 2020, www.wsj.com.

45 Clare Martin, "The Rise—and Limitations—of Front-Facing Camera Comedy," *Paste*, January 31, 2020, www.pastemagazine.com.

46 "About Jay Jurden," Jay Jurden, accessed June 1, 2021, www.jayjurden.com.

47 Jay Jurden, phone interview with the author, May 18, 2021.

48 Author field notes, March 23, 2021.

49 Author field notes, March 23, 2021.

50 David Perdue, phone interview with the author, May 17, 2021.

51 Author field notes, March 24, 2021.

52 "Comedian Corey Ryan 'Buttercream Dream' Forrester Has a Message for Racism #RacismIsNoJoke," YouTube, E Pluribus Unum, May 27, 2021, www.youtube.com /watch?v=ex2mNcEkAqg.

53 "#RacismIsNoJoke," E Pluribus Unum Fund, accessed July 1, 2021, www.unumfund .org/racismisnojoke.

54 "It's Your Money and You Need It Now," YouTube, Corey Ryan Forrester, June 3, 2021, www.youtube.com/watch?v=3jw_Xs5gkzk.

55 De Koven with Holly Gramozio, *The Infinite Playground*, 59.

CHAPTER 5. "INVISIBILITY IS NOT A SUPERPOWER"

1 Crystal Echo Hawk, phone interview with the author, August 9, 2021. Unless otherwise indicated, direct quotations from Echo Hawk come from this interview.

2 "Reclaiming Native Truth," IllumiNative, 2018, accessed August 15, 2021, https: //illuminatives.org.

3 "Reclaiming Native Truth," 8.

4 "Reclaiming Native Truth."

5 Rebecca Nagle, "Research Reveals Media Role in Stereotypes about Native Americans," Women's Media Center, July 18, 2018, www.womensmediacenter.com.

6 Nagle, "Research Reveals Media Role."

7 "About IllumiNative," IllumiNative, accessed August 15, 2021, https://illuminatives .org.

8 Nicholas A. Kuiper, "Humor and Resiliency: Towards a Process Model of Coping and Growth," *Europe's Journal of Psychology* 8, no. 3 (2012): 475–91, https://doi.org /10.5964/ejop.v8i3.464.

9 Crystal Echo Hawk, phone interview with the author, September 6, 2019.

10 I conducted this search (simply "Native Americans") on Google.com on September 10, 2021. According to IllumiNative, this scenario has been true for years, so it is safe to say these search results were not unusual.

11 Philip J. Deloria, *Indians in Unexpected Places* (Lawrence: University Press of Kansas, 2004), 6.

12 "Reclaiming Native Truth," 8.

13 "Reclaiming Native Truth," 9.

14 Deloria, *Indians in Unexpected Places*, 35.

15 Deloria, *Indians in Unexpected Places*, 49–50.

16 Deloria, *Indians in Unexpected Places*, 50.

17 Deloria, *Indians in Unexpected Places*, 74.

18 Deloria, *Indians in Unexpected Places*, 107.

19 Kliph Nesteroff, *We Had a Little Real Estate Problem: The Unheralded Story of Native Americans and Comedy* (New York: Simon & Schuster, 2021), 98–99.

20 Nesteroff, *We Had a Little Real Estate Problem*, 99.

21 Philip J. Deloria, *Playing Indian* (New Haven, CT: Yale University Press, 1998), 189–91.

22 Peter A. Leavitt, Rebecca Covarrubias, Yvonne A. Perez, and Stephanie A. Fryberg, "'Frozen in Time': The Impact of Native American Media Representations on Identity and Self-Understanding," *Journal of Social Issues* 71, no. 1 (2015): 39–53, https://doi.org/10.1111/josi.12095.

23 Kathryn Nagle, "Lessons Learned from Standing Rock," IllumiNative/First Nations Development Institute, July 2018, 6, www.firstnations.org.

24 Nagle, "Lessons Learned from Standing Rock," 4.

25 Nagle, "Lessons Learned from Standing Rock," 6.

26 Leah Donnella, "The Standing Rock Resistance Is Unprecedented (It's Also Centuries Old)," NPR, November 22, 2016, www.npr.org.

27 "Sterlin Harjo," Sterlin Harjo, accessed September 1, 2021, www.sterlinharjo.com.

28 Jana Schmieding, "Jana Schmieding on the Native Joy of *Rutherford Falls*," *Vanity Fair*, June 21, 2021, www.vanityfair.com.

29 Schmieding, "Jana Schmieding on the Native Joy of *Rutherford Falls*."

30 Schmieding, "Jana Schmieding on the Native Joy of *Rutherford Falls*."

31 Sarah McCammon, "'Reservation Dogs' Creator Talks New FX Series," NPR, August 7, 2021, www.npr.org.

32 Elaine Low, "How the All-Native Writers' Room for Netflix's 'Spirit Rangers' Was Assembled," *Variety*, March 1, 2021, https://variety.com.

33 Mia Galuppo, "LeBron James to Produce Netflix Native American Basketball Feature 'Rez Ball,'" August 5, 2021, www.hollywoodreporter.com.

34 "Sundance Institute's Native American and Indigenous Program Kicks Off Its 20th Anniversary," Sundance Institute, February 12, 2014, www.sundance.org/blogs /Sundance-Institute-8217-s-Native-American-and-Indigenous-Program-Kicks-off -its-20th-Anniversary.

35 Peter Gilstrap, "'We're Not Stoic': Book Traces the History of Native Americans in Comedy," KQED, July 30, 2021, www.kqed.org; N. Bird Runningwater, "Sundance Institute's Bird Runningwater Announces Departure after 20 Years (Guest Column)," *Hollywood Reporter*, September 22, 2021, www.hollywoodreporter.com.

36 "New Moon Wolf Pack Auditions!" YouTube, Sterlz501, December 1, 2009, www .youtube.com/watch?v=BmFxJYFSXy0.

37 "The 1491s," 1491s, accessed September 10, 2021, www.1491s.com.

38 "The 1491s," 1491s, accessed September 10, 2021, www.1491s.com.

39 Kelly Boutsalis, "'This Is What We Should Have Had All Along,'" *New York Times*, April 9, 2021, www.nytimes.com; Zoe Tennant, "*Rutherford Falls* Brings Indigenous Writers Together for New NBC Sitcom," Canadian Broadcasting Corporation, February 2, 2020, www.cbc.ca.

40 Nesteroff, *We Had a Little Real Estate Problem*, 169.

41 "The Ladies of Native Comedy," Ladies of Native Comedy, accessed September 15, 2021, https://ladies-of-native-comedy.com.

42 "The Jackie Show," *The Jackie Show Podcast*, accessed September 15, 2021, https: //keliiaa.podbean.com; "First Nations Comedy Experience," FNX, accessed March 28, 2020, https://fnx.org.

43 "Joey Clift Highlights 25 Native American Comedians for Indigenous Peoples' Day," The Comedy Bureau, October 12, 2020, https://thecomedybureau.com.

44 Jackie Kaliiaa, words on stage during the 2021 Yes, And . . . Laughter Lab NYC Comedy Pitch Showcase, held on September 17, 2021.

45 Vine Deloria Jr., *Custer Died for Your Sins: An Indian Manifesto* (New York: Macmillan, 1969), 146.

46 Deloria Jr., *Custer Died for Your Sins*, 2.

47 Deloria Jr., *Custer Died for Your Sins*, 147.

48 Deloria Jr., *Custer Died for Your Sins*, 147.

49 Nesteroff, *We Had a Little Real Estate Problem*, 111.

50 Nesteroff, *We Had a Little Real Estate Problem*, 111.

51 Nesteroff, *We Had a Little Real Estate Problem*, 112.

52 Nesteroff, *We Had a Little Real Estate Problem*, 112.

53 Ryan RedCorn, phone interview with the author, July 11, 2019. Unless otherwise indicated, quotations from RedCorn in this chapter come from this interview.

54 David Grann, *Killers of the Flower Moon: The Osage Murders and the Birth of the FBI* (New York: Doubleday, 2017).

55 Adrianne Chalepah, phone interview with the author, July 12, 2019.

56 Bobby Wilson, phone interview with the author, July 22, 2019.

57 Shannon O'Neill, phone interview with the author, July 12, 2019.

58 Joey Clift, phone interview with the author, July 11, 2019.

59 Johnny McNulty, phone interview with the author, July 11, 2019.

60 Sebastian Conelli, phone interview with the author, July 11, 2019.

61 *You're Welcome, America!* (Cultural Appropriation episode), script, 2021.

CHAPTER 6. "MAYBE THEY THINK BEAUTY CAN'T COME FROM HERE"

1 Deirdre "Mama D" Love, phone interview with the author, January 6, 2020.

2 "Hip Hop Caucus: Our Story," Hip Hop Caucus, accessed January 10, 2020, https://hiphopcaucus.org.

3 Rodney D. Green, Marie Kouassi, and Belinda Mambo, "Housing, Race, and Recovery from Hurricane Katrina," *Review of Black Political Economy* 40, no. 2 (2013), https://doi.org/10.1007/s12114-011-9116-0; Sherrow Pinder, "Notes on Hurricane Katrina: Rethinking Race, Class, and Power in the United States," *Twenty-first Century Society* 4, no. 3 (2009): 241–56, https://doi.org/10.1080/17450140902988883.

4 "Think 100%," Think 100%, accessed January 10, 2020, https://think100.info.

5 Rev. Lennox Yearwood Jr., phone interview with the author, January 23, 2020.

6 Author field notes, October 26, 2019.

7 See *Ain't Your Mama's Heat Wave* at aintyourmamasheatwave.com.

8 "Hip Hop Caucus, Climate Strike," Hip Hop Caucus, accessed January 10, 2020, https://hiphopcaucus.org.

9 Donald P. Moynihan, "The Response to Hurricane Katrina," International Risk Governance Council, 2009, 1–2, https://irgc.org; National Weather Service, "Extremely Powerful Hurricane Katrina Leaves a Historic Mark on the Northern Gulf Coast," 2005, www.weather.gov.

10 Moynihan, "The Response to Hurricane Katrina."

11 Donna Young, "Hurricane Katrina," Oxford American Studies Center, 2009, 1, https://oxfordaasc.com.

12 Jean Rhodes et al., "The Impact of Hurricane Katrina on the Mental and Physical Health of Low-Income Parents in New Orleans," *American Journal of Orthopsychiatry* 80, no. 2 (2010): 237–47, https://doi.org/10.1111/j.1939–0025.2010.01027.x.

13 Rhodes et al., "The Impact of Hurricane Katrina."

14 Green, Kouassi, and Mambo, "Housing, Race, and Recovery from Hurricane Katrina," 147.

15 Moynihan, "The Response to Hurricane Katrina," 1–2; National Weather Service, "Extremely Powerful Hurricane Katrina."

16 Pinder, "Notes on Hurricane Katrina," 245.

17 Pinder, "Notes on Hurricane Katrina," 245.

18 Green, Kouassi, and Mambo, "Housing, Race, and Recovery from Hurricane Katrina," 146.

19 Pinder, "Notes on Hurricane Katrina," 245.

20 Young, "Hurricane Katrina," 1, 3.

21 Green, Kouassi, and Mambo, "Housing, Race, and Recovery from Hurricane Katrina," 145.

22 Green, Kouassi, and Mambo, "Housing, Race, and Recovery from Hurricane Katrina," 145.

23 T. Ralli, "Who's a Looter? In Storm's Aftermath, Pictures Kick Up a Different Kind of Tempest," *New York Times*, September 5, 2005; Young, "Hurricane Katrina."

24 Pinder, "Notes on Hurricane Katrina," 252.

25 Shannon Kahle, Nan Yu, and Erin Whiteside, "Another Disaster: An Examination of Portrayals of Race in Hurricane Katrina Coverage," *Visual Communications Quarterly* 14, no. 2 (2007): 75–89, https://doi.org/10.1080/15551390701555951.

26 Terry W. Cole and Kelli L. Fellows, "Risk Communication Failure: A Case Study of New Orleans and Hurricane Katrina," *Southern Communication Journal* 73, no. 3 (2008): 215–16, https://doi.org/10.1080/10417940802219702.

27 Mike Tidwell, "Will Norfolk Be the Next New Orleans?," *Virginian-Pilot*, June 2, 2013, www.pilotonline.com.

28 Mike Tidwell, *Bayou Farewell: The Rich Life and Tragic Death of Louisiana's Cajun Coast* (New York: Vintage Books, 2004).

29 Tidwell, *Bayou Farewell.*

30 "Naval Station Norfolk Base Guide," Military.com, accessed March 28, 2022, www.military.com.

31 "Norfolk, Virginia: Identifying and Becoming More Resilient to Impacts of Climate Change," Natural Resources Defense Council, July 2011, 2,

32 Thomas R. Allen, Thomas Crawford, Burrell Montz, Jessica Whitehead, Susan Lovelace, Armon D. Hanks, Ariel R. Christensen, and Gregory D. Kearney. "Linking Water Infrastructure, Public Health, and Sea Level Rise: Integrated Assessment of Flood Resilience in Coastal Cities," *Public Works Management & Policy* 24, no. 1 (January 2019): 111, https://doi.org/10.1177/1087724X18798380.

33 Quick Facts: Norfolk, Virginia, United States Census Bureau, accessed March 28, 2022, www.census.gov.

34 Nicholas Kusnetz, "Norfolk Wants to Remake Itself as Sea Level Rises, but Who Will Be Left Behind?," *Inside Climate News*, May 21, 2018, https://insideclimatenews.org.

35 Sierra C. Woodruff, Sara Meerow, Missy Stults, and Chandler Wilkins, "Adaptation to Resilience Planning: Alternative Pathways to Prepare for Climate Change," *Journal of Planning Education and Research* (2018): 2, https://doi.org/10.1177/0739456X18801057.

36 "Coastal Resilience Strategy," City of Norfolk, accessed March 28, 2020, 10, www.norfolk.gov.

37 Kusnetz, "Norfolk Wants to Remake Itself."

38 Kusnetz, "Norfolk Wants to Remake Itself."

39 "St. Paul's Transformation Project," City of Norfolk, accessed March 28, 2020, www.norfolk.gov.

40 Kusnetz, "Norfolk Wants to Remake Itself"; "Cooperation Agreement for St. Paul's Area Development," City of Norfolk, 3, www.norfolk.gov.

41 Kusnetz, "Norfolk Wants to Remake Itself."

42 Michael Paolisso, Ellen Douglas, Ashley Enrici, Paul Kirshen, Chris Watson, and Matthias Ruth, "Climate Change, Justice, and Adaptation among African American Communities in the Chesapeake Bay Region," *Weather, Climate, and Society* 4, no. 1 (2012): 34, https://journals.ametsoc.org.

43 Paolisso et al., "Climate Change, Justice, and Adaptation," 34–35.

44 Paolisso et al., "Climate Change, Justice, and Adaptation," 36.

45 David J. Hess and Lacee A. Satcher, "Conditions for Successful Environmental Justice Mobilizations: An Analysis of 50 Cases," *Environmental Politics* 28, no. 4 (2019): 663, https://doi.org/1080/09644016.2019.1565679.

46 Hess and Satcher, "Conditions for Successful Environmental Justice Mobilizations," 663–64.

47 Hess and Satcher, "Conditions for Successful Environmental Justice Mobilizations," 681.

48 Hess and Satcher, "Conditions for Successful Environmental Justice Mobilizations," 681.

49 Aaron M. McCright and Riley E. Dunlap, "The Politicization of Climate Change and Polarization in the American Public's Views of Global Warming, 2001–2010," *Sociological Quarterly* 52, no. 2 (2011): 176, https://doi.org/10.1111/j.1533-8525.2011.01198.x.

50 Ted Nordhaus and Michael Shellenberger, "Global Warming Scare Tactics," *New York Times*, April 9, 2014.

51 Caty Borum Chattoo and Lauren Feldman, *A Comedian and an Activist Walk into a Bar: The Serious Role of Comedy in Social Justice* (Oakland: University of California Press, 2020), 85.

52 Yale Program on Climate Change Communication and George Mason University Center for Climate Change Communication, "Politics and Global Warming," 2018, https://climatecommunication.yale.edu.

53 P. Sol Hart and Erik C. Nisbet, "Boomerang Effects in Science Communication: How Motivated Reasoning and Identity Cues Amplify Opinion Polarization about Climate Mitigation Policies," *Communication Research* 39, no. 6 (December 2012): 701–23, https://doi.org/10.1177/0093650211416646.

54 Ed Begley Jr., Suzanne Yeagley, Timothy Brennan, Nicol Paone, "Climate Change Denial Disorder with Ed Begley Jr.," Funny or Die, April 15, 2015, www.funnyordie.com.

55 Borum Chattoo and Feldman, *A Comedian and an Activist Walk into a Bar*, 170.

56 Borum Chattoo and Feldman, *A Comedian and an Activist Walk into a Bar*, 171.

57 Montse Reyes, "'The North Pole' Freezes the Issues of North Oakland in Comedic Web Series," *San Francisco Chronicle*, October 8, 2019, https://datebook.sfchronicle.com.

58 Reyes, "'The North Pole' Freezes the Issues."

59 Martina Jackson Haynes et al., "Coal Blooded Action Toolkit," Energy Justice Network, 4, www.energyjustice.net.

60 Ben Jervey, "NAACP Reveals Tactics Fossil Fuel Industry Uses to Manipulate Communities of Color," DeSmog Blog, April 1, 2019, https://www.desmogblog .com/2019/04/01/naacp-report-fossil-fuel-industry-manipulative-tactics -communities-color; Jacqueline Patterson, "Fossil Fueled Foolery," NAACP Environmental & Climate Justice Program, April 1, 2019, https://live-naacp-site .pantheonsite.io.

61 Hip Hop Caucus Comedy ThinkTanks brainstorm document (Google Docs), August 28, 2019.

62 Hip Hop Caucus Comedy ThinkTanks brainstorm document.

63 Jeffrey P. Jones, *Entertaining Politics: New Political Television and Civic Culture* (Lanham, MD: Rowman & Littlefield, 2004), 156–57.

64 Author field notes, October 26, 2019.

65 Rev. Yearwood, phone interview with the author, January 23, 2020.

66 Rev. Yearwood, phone interview with the author, January 23, 2020.

67 Keja Reel, phone interview with the author, December 23, 2019.

68 Charles "Batman" Brown, phone interview with the author, December 23, 2019.

69 Elijah Karriem, phone interview with the author, January 22, 2020.

70 Gayle Kanoyton, phone interview with the author, March 13, 2020.

71 Gayle Kanoyton, phone interview with the author, March 13, 2020.

72 Deirdre "Mama D" Love, phone interview with the author, January 6, 2020.

73 Pastor Dwight Riddick, phone interview with the author, March 3, 2020.

74 Charles "Batman" Brown, phone interview with the author, December 23, 2019.

75 *Ain't Your Mama's Heatwave*, 2020, aintyourmamasheatwave.com.

76 Clark Jones, phone interview with the author, March 18, 2020.

77 Liz Havstad, phone interview with the author, January 13, 2020.

78 Liz Havstad, phone interview with the author, January 13, 2020.

79 Charles "Batman" Brown, phone interview with the author, December 23, 2020.

80 Rev. Yearwood, phone interview with the author, January 23, 2020.

CHAPTER 7. "I'VE ALWAYS BEEN A SYRINGE-HALF-FULL KINDA GUY"

1 "It Takes a Village," Murf Myer Is Self-Medicated, March 16, 2021, https://podcasts .apple.com.

2 Edward L. Glaeser, Joshua D. Gottlieb, and Oren Ziv, "Unhappy Cities," National Bureau of Economic Research, July 2014, www.nber.org/papers/w20291.

3 "It Takes a Village," Murf Myer Is Self-Medicated, March 16, 2021, https://podcasts .apple.com.

4 Murf Meyer, phone interview with author, June 4, 2021.

5 "Opioid Manufacturer Purdue Pharma Pleads Guilty to Fraud and Kickback Conspiracies," US Department of Justice, November 24, 2020, www.justice.gov.

6 "It Takes a Village."

7 "It Takes a Village."

8 "Class Traitors and Bullies," Murf Meyer Is Self-Medicated, March 24, 2021, https: //podcasts.apple.com.

9 Steve Green, "'The Chris Gethard Show' Forever: An Emotional Finale Proves This Crazy Late Night Show Is Worth Renewing," *IndieWire*, May 30, 2018, www .indiewire.com.

10 Murf Meyer, phone interview with author, June 4, 2021.

11 "It Takes a Village."

12 See "Yes, And . . . Laughter Lab," https://yesandlaughterlab.com.

13 "The Great Schlep," YouTube, Schlep Labs, April 9, 2015, www.youtube.com/watch ?v=AEGFQR1u-Mk.

14 Sarah Larson, "'Halal in the Family': The Sitcom We Need," *New Yorker*, May 11, 2016, www.newyorker.com.

15 Aymar Jean Christian, *Open TV: Innovation beyond Hollywood and the Rise of Web Television* (New York: NYU Press, 2018), 20.

16 See, for example, Stacy L. Smith, Marc Choueiti, and Katherine Pieper, *Inclusion or Invisibility? Comprehensive Annenberg Report on Diversity in Entertainment*, University of Southern California–Annenberg, February 2017, https://annenberg .usc.edu; and Maureen Ryan, "Showrunners for New TV Season Remain Mostly White and Mostly Male," *Variety*, June 8, 2016, http://variety.com.

17 S. L. Smith, M. Choueiti, K. Pieper, A. Case, and J. Marsden, "Inequality in 800 Popular Films: Examining Portrayals of Gender, Race/Ethnicity, LGBT, and Disability from 2007 to 2015," University of Southern California Annenberg School for Communication and Journalism, September 2016, http://annenberg.usc.edu; S. L. Smith, K. Pieper, and M. Choueiti, "Inclusion in the Director's Chair? Gender, Race, and Age of Film Directors across 1,000 Films from 2007–2016 (Brief)," University of Southern California Annenberg School for Communication and Journalism, February 2017, http://annenberg.usc.edu; D. Hunt, A. Ramón, and Z. Price, "2014 Hollywood Diversity Report: Making Sense of the Disconnect," University of California–Los Angeles Ralph J. Bunche Center for African American Studies, February 2014, http://www.bunchecenter.ucla.edu; D. Hunt, A. Ramón, and M. Tran, "2016 Hollywood Diversity Report: Business as Usual?," University of California–Los Angeles Ralph J. Bunche Center for African American Studies, February 2016, http://www.bunchecenter.ucla.edu.

18 Stuart Cunningham, *Hidden Innovation: Policy, Industry, and the Creative Sector* (Brisbane, Australia: University of Queensland Press, 2013), 4, 7.

19 Cunningham, *Hidden Innovation*, 77.

20 Christian, *Open TV*, 101–55.

21 "Yes, And . . . Laugher Lab 2021 Winners and Finalists," Yes, And . . . Laughter Lab, accessed September 1, 2021, https://yesandlaughterlab.com.

22 Peter White, "Medical Comedy from Roy Wood Jr. and Carolyn Pierre-Outlar in the Works at NBC," *Deadline*, August 10, 2021, https://deadline.com.

23 Video remarks delivered at the Los Angeles 2021 pitch showcase of the Yes, And . . . Laughter Lab, September 30, 2021.
24 Carla Lee, phone interview with the author, December 5, 2019.
25 Mamoudou N'Diaye, phone interview with the author, December 11, 2019.
26 Joey Clift, phone interview with the author, December 5, 2019.
27 We are still experiencing a pop culture mirror in which nearly nine in ten scripted cable TV programs, for instance, are not created by any member of an under-represented group. Source: Hannah Giorgis, "Not Enough Has Changed since *Sanford and Son*: The Unwritten Rules of Black TV," *Atlantic*, September 13, 2021, www.theatlantic.com.

CONCLUSION. TAKING COMEDY SERIOUSLY

1 Rodney Lamkey Jr., "Laureano Márquez, Venezuela, International Press Freedom Awards 2010," Committee to Protect Journalists, accessed December 31, 2021, https://cpj.org.
2 "Laureano Márquez—N° 003 Honorary Member of Venezuelan Press," Venezuelan Press, accessed December 31, 2021, www.venezuelanpress.com.
3 Lamkey Jr., "Laureano Márquez."
4 Scott Neuman, "Venezuela's Maduro Wins Boycotted Elections amid Charges of Fraud," NPR, May 21, 2018, www.npr.org; "Venezuela: Maduro Looks to 'Sham' Re-Election," Freedom House, May 17, 2018, https://freedomhouse.org.
5 "Venezuela Humanitarian Crisis," UNHCR (the UN Refugee Agency), accessed December 31, 2021, www.unrefugees.org.
6 Teresa Romero, "Percentage of Households in Poverty and Extreme Poverty in Venezuela from 2002 to 2020," Statista, November 5, 2021, www.statista.com.
7 See, for example, John Otis, "The U.S. Predicted His Downfall but Maduro Strengthens His Grip on Power in Venezuela," NPR, December 8, 2021, www.npr.org.
8 "Pro-government Groups Attack Reporters Covering Juan Guaidó's Return to Venezuela," Committee to Protect Journalists, February 13, 2020, https://cpj.org; Lucy Westcott, "Caracas Full of Uncertainty for Journalists Covering Venezuela Crisis," Committee to Protect Journalists, May 15, 2019, https://cpj.org.
9 "TV Station Chief: We Are Not Afraid of Chavez," CNN, May 30, 2007.
10 Laureano Márquez, "Querida Rosinés, por Laureano Márquez," *Tal Cual*, November 25, 2005, https://talcualdigital.com.
11 Lamkey Jr., "Laureano Márquez."
12 Abby Prestin and Robin Nabi, "Media Prescriptions: Exploring the Therapeutic Effects of Entertainment Media on Stress Relief, Illness Symptoms, and Goal Attainment," *Journal of Communication* 70, no. 2 (2020): 145–70, https://doi.org/10.1093/joc/jqaa001.
13 Borum Chattoo and Feldman, *A Comedian and an Activist Walk into a Bar*.
14 Bobby Wilson, phone interview with the author, July 22, 2019.
15 Shannon O'Neill, phone interview with the author, July 13, 2019.

INDEX

Page numbers in *italics* indicate Figures

ABC, *Black-ish* on, 83, 212

Abston, Niles, 65; on social media, 70

Acevedo, Jose: on diversity, 62–63, 72; on social media, 71

ACLU, Rainbow benefiting, 29

activists, social justice: CAA collaboration with, 94–95; civic imagination of, 80–81; comedian collaboration with, 102–6, 109–10, 146, 178, 213; in entertainment industry, 82–87, 90–91, 92–93, 95–96, 190–91; groups of, 85, 89; as incognito, 142

addiction, 182–83, 185–87

Affleck, Ben, 3

AIDS crisis, 85

Ainslie, Shawna Ayoub, 88

Ain't Your Mama's Heat Wave (Hip Hop Caucus), 25, 158, 171–73, *177*, *181*; at Crispus Attucks Theater, 175–78; at festivals, 180

Alcatraz Island, 141

alcoholism, in Luzerne County, 182

Alexander, Kenny, 173

Alexander, Michelle, 76–77

Algeria, Bouteflika in, 36

Allen, Tom, 173

All in the Family (TV show), 81–82

allyship, 22, 117–18, 124

Alternatino (TV show), 93, *94*

The Amber Ruffin Show (TV show), 66

Amos 'n' Andy (TV show), 85

Aoki, Guy, 85

appropriation, of Native culture, 135

Arab Spring (2010), comedy during, 35

Aristotle, on comedy, 39

Array, 73

Aslan, Reza, Boomgen Studios of, 73

Associated Press, Hurricane Katrina coverage by, 160

audiences: comedian relation to, 40–41, 110; comedy effect on, 42; diversity among, 74

authoritarianism: comedy relation to, 31–32, 37; subtlety of, 30

The AzN PoP! (YALL project), 196–97

Bahrain, political satire in, 36

Bailey, Moya, 91

Baiocchi, Gianpaolo, 9

Barris, Kenya, *Black-ish* by, 83

al-Bashir, Omar, 36

Bayou Farewell (Tidwell), 161

BBC, on political satire, 35, 36

Begley, Ed, Jr., 166

Bendecidas ya Afortunadas (Blessed and Highly Favored) (YALL project), 197

Benmayor, Rina: on cultural citizenship, 42; on inequality, 9

Al-Bernameg (YouTube series), 35

Berni, Ryan, 111–12, 118, 210; on #RacismIsNoJoke success, 122

Black, Indigenous, People of Color (BIPOC): climate change threatening, 25, 157, 168–70, 173–74, 176, 179; comedy of, 42; cultural revolution of, 53, 74; demand for media of, 55, 67–68; gatekeeper relation to, 60, 65; MTV initiative for, 78–79; as showrunners, 56;

Black, Indigenous, People of Color (*cont.*) on social platforms, 70–71, 81; under-representation of, 23, 109, 192; in YALL, 193. *See also* marginalized groups

Black Entertainment Executives Pipeline, Diverse Representation, 78

Black-ish (TV show), 83, 212

Black Lives Matter: origination of, 10–11, 76; 2020 racial-justice uprisings relation to, 23

Black Panthers, Lear influenced by, 82–83

Boomgen Studios, 73

Bourdieu, Pierre, 86

Bouteflika, Abdelaziz, 36

Bread and Puppet Theater, creative deviance of, 33, 34–35

Breakthrough Institute, 165

Broad City (TV show), 53, 193

Brown, Charles "Batman," 172–73, 175, 179–80

Brown, Michael, 76

Bush, George W., 2

Buttercream Dream (Forrester), 100–101, *121*

By Us for Us (comedy production), 93

CAA. *See* Creative Artists Agency

Calderón Kellett, Gloria, 42–43; on comedy, 45; Glo Nation of, 73; on racial reckoning, 80; on Twitter, 70

California, Los Angeles, 1, 127, 195, *199*

CameronTown (YALL project), 197

Camp (YALL project), 196

Cane, Jená, Citizen University cofounded by, 8

Cardoso, Jandiz, 68; on racial-justice, 79; on social media, 71

Carter, Chaz, on social media, 70

Castell, Manuel, 18–19

Castro, Arturo, 93–94

Caveat, in New York City, 195, *196*

CBS: *All in the Family* on, 81–82; diversity initiatives of, 79; NAACP targeting, 85; *Old News* on, 47–48; *The United States of Al* on, 73

Center for Media & Social Impact, 22; co-creation process of, 103–6; Color of Change collaboration with, 93

Chalepah, Adrianne, 144, 146, 147; as cohost of *You're Welcome, America!*, 148–50, *149*, *150*

Chambers, Kesila, 59–60

Chapelle, Dave, 45

Charleston, Donnie, 119

Chasing Coral (documentary), 165

Chasing Ice (documentary), 165

Chauvin, Derrick, 75

Chavez, Hugo, 207; Márquez critique of, 205

Chesapeake Climate Action Network, 161

Choose or Lose, MTV, 2

The Chris Gethard Show (TV show), 102; Meyer on, 184

Christian, Aymar Jean, on "Open TV," 191

Church, Josh, 62; on activism in Hollywood, 95; on decision-maker risks, 64

Church-Cooper, Joel, 67

Citizen Change campaign, 2

Citizen University, founding of, 8

civic imagination: of entertainment activists, 80–81; in representation, 151; for social change, 12, 44, 211

civic power: of advocacy organizations, 15–16; for comedians, 124; comedy to build, 39–40, 41–42, 44–45, 46, 193, 212–13, 214; creative power relation to, 22, 25–26; creative process relation to, 7; democracy relation to, 10; for social change, 37–38

Civic Power (Ramhan and Gilman), 10

Clift, Joey, 145, 146, 198, 202

climate change: coastal storm relation to, 160–61; denial of, 165–66; grassroots organizations, 167; people of color threatened by, 25, 157, 168–70, 173–74, 176, 179; social justice relation to, 163–64, 178–79

climate justice: Hip Hop Caucus for, 7, 25, 174–75; racial justice relation to, 180

Clinton, Bill, 8

co-creation: Comedy ThinkTank process for, 103–6, 168–70; creative group ideation in, 146; in improv comedy, 107

Coel, Michaela, 53–54

Colbert, Stephen, *Old News* of, 47–48

Color Creative, Hoorae Productions, 72–73

Color of Change, 79; Center for Media & Social Impact collaboration with, 93; collaboration with ViacomCBS, 92–93; Diverse Representation collaboration with, 78; Hurricane Katrina relation to, 7, 89; *Normalizing Injustice* by, 77–78

Combs, Sean "P. Diddy," "Puffy," 156; Citizen Change campaign of, 2

comedians: activist collaboration with, 102–6, 109–10, 146, 178, 213; audience relation to, 40–41, 110; careers of, 47; civic power for, 124; creative deviance of, 105–7, 108; cultural power of, 209; as cultural watchdogs, 38–39; culture of, 42

comedy. *See specific topics*

Comedy Central: Declare Yourself in partnership with, 3–4; Soto Lamb in, 93–94; YALL collaboration with, 21

Comedy for Change network, Finger Awards of, 36–37

"Comedy for Social Change," 190

Comedy ThinkTank: comedy co-creation model of, 103–6, 168–70; EPU collaboration with, 115–16; Hip Hop Caucus collaboration with, 158, 168–70; IllumiNative collaboration with, 131–32, 143–47, 150–51; innovation process of, 101; social-justice initiatives of, 24;

YALL collaboration with, 21. *See also* Center for Media & Social Impact

commercial marketplace, comedy in, 188–90, 191, 203, 212

Committee to Protect Journalists, on Márquez, 205

Conelli, Sebastian, 144, 146

Convergence Culture (Jenkins), 18

Cooper, Sarah, 51, *51*; career path of, 47–48; COVID-19 response of, 49–50; on *Everything's Fine*, 52; lip syncs of, 23

Copaken, Deborah, 54

COPS (TV show), 77

Costanza-Chock, Sasha, 223n53

Covarrubias, Rebecca, 136

COVID-19 pandemic, 37; Cooper response to, 49–50; effect on EPU, 114–15; effect on YALL, 200; Rainbow show cut short by, 29; 2020 racial-justice uprisings relation to, 75

Craig, David, 69

Creative Artists Agency (CAA), social justice activist collaboration with, 94–95

creative culture, for social change, 38, 130

creative deviance: of comedians, 105–7, 108; comedy as, 32–35, 39, 104, 125

creative power: civic power relation to, 22, 25–26; in social justice organizations, 15, 17, 124

creative process, 15; between activism and comedy, 146, 178, 213; civic power relation to, 7; for comedy, 24, 106–7, 169; for grassroots organizations, 17

creativity theory: diversity in, 109; in innovation, 107–8, 124, 214; in participatory media, 105–6; in participatory politics, 7–8; in social change work, 16–17

Crispus Attucks Theater, Norfolk, 175–76

Cross, David, 3

Cross, Dejuan, 176

Crowder, Trae, 99

cultural citizenship, of marginalized groups, 41–42, 46

cultural power: of comedians, 209; of entertainment industry, 13, 46, 210–11; representation as, 137; social justice relation to, 7; on social media, 90

cultural strategy, in entertainment industry, 91–92

culture work: in participatory politics, 11–12; of YALL, 200

Cunningham, Ryan, 53; on change in Hollywood, 78; on networking, 59; on unique voices, 67–68; on women's point of view, 63–64

Cunningham, Stuart, 192; on social media entertainment, 69

Custer Died for Your Sins (Deloria, V.), 140–41

The Daily Show (TV show), 212; comedic public resistance on, 32; influence of, 20–21; Stewart, J., on, 2

Dances with Wolves (movie), 129

Davidson, Jack, 135

Davis, Deniese, 60; on activism in Hollywood, 95; on Color Creative, 72–73; on pitching, 63; on social media, 70; on underrepresented writers, 68

Dawson, Rosario, 167

DC Environmental Film Festival, 180

Declare Yourself campaign, 5, 221n9; Comedy Central in partnership with, 3–4; launching of, 1–2

Deep South (US): EPU work in, 112–14, 210; racism in, 119

Define American, 6–7, 89

De Koven, Bernard, 110, 124; on imagination, 106

Deloria, Philip J., 132, 148; on Native portrayals in media, 133–34; *Playing Indian* by, 135–36

Deloria, Vine, Jr., 140–41

democracy: Americans distrusting, 9; civic power relation to, 10; culture relation to, 38; demise of, 30–31; humor to strengthen, 209; journalist relation to, 43; social media relation to, 18–19; Trump as threat to, 32; in Venezuela, 208

Denver Post (publication), Echo Hawk story in, 126

Deol, Kiran, 166–67

Designing Women (TV show), 44

"Desperate Cheeto" (YouTube), 28–29, 29

Devantez, Chelsea, 64–65

Disney Television, diversity initiatives of, 79

divergent thinking, in creativity theory, 108

Diverse Representation, Color of Change collaboration with, 78

diversity: among audiences, 74; in creativity theory, 109; in entertainment industry, 6, 13–14, 19, 21, 25, 54–56, 64, 67, 72, 78–79, 145, 203; in gatekeeping positions, 62; Hollywood showcases of, 200–201; on social media, 69–71; in YALL, 193

Domestic Workers Alliance and Caring Across Generations, 11–12

Donohue, William, 84

Douyin, 48

Doyle, Victor, 86

Duncombe, Stephen: on artivism, 16; on public opinion, 38

DuVernay, Ava, 73, 92, 131

Dynasty Typewriter, Los Angeles, 199

Echo Hawk, Crystal, 126–28; on comedy, 142, 144; on Native American comedy, 131; Reclaiming Native Truth of, 129–30; on Standing Rock uprising, 137

Egypt, political satire in, 35

El Paso, Texas, mass shooting in, 93

Emily in Paris (TV show), 54

entertainment industry: activists in, 82–87,
90–91, 92–93, 95–96, 190–91; comedy as
microcosm of, 58; cultural power of, 13,
46, 210–11; cultural strategy in, 91–92;
diversity in, 6, 13–14, 19, 21, 25, 54–56,
64, 67, 72, 78–79, 145, 203; fetishization
in, 185; marginalized groups in, 23–24,
191–92, 200–201, 246n27; marketplace
of, 188–90, 191, 203, 212; participatory
culture relation to, 140; pitch to, 61–62,
203; social capital in, 193; social justice
relation to, 6–7, 13–14, 18, 74, 80, 92, 194;
streaming effect on, 17, 57; TikTok effect
on, 48, 52–53

environmental justice: coalitions for,
163–64; Hip Hop Caucus for, 156–57;
participatory culture relation to, 164,
166–67

E Pluribus Unum (EPU): Comedy
ThinkTank collaboration with, 115–16;
Deep South work of, 112–14, 210; social
media campaign of, 24

erasure, as racism, 129–30

"Even Supervillains Think Our Sexual
Assault Laws Are Insane," 15

Everything's Fine (comedy special), 52

Facebook, 19; during Arab Spring, 35

Fast Company (publication), 92

Feig, Paul, 59–60

Feldman, Lauren, 40, 41, 165

Finger Awards, Comedy for Change,
36–37

First Nations Development Institute,
Reclaiming Native Truth of, 129–30

Flores, William, 9, 42

Floyd, George: murder of, 75; protests
related to, 79

Foreign Policy (Popovic and Joksic), 31–32

Forrester, Corey Ryan, 97–99, 110, *123*, 124;
Buttercream Dream of, 100–101, *121*;
front-facing comedy of, 114–15; Jurden
collaboration with, 115–16, 117, 119–20

"The 1491s," 139–40

Freeland, Sydney, 138–39

French, Franqi, 68

Freud, Sigmund, 39

front-facing comedy: during COVID-19,
114–15; #RacismIsNoJoke as, 120–22

"Frozen in Time" (Leavitt, Covarrubias,
Perez, and Fryberg), 136

Fryberg, Stephanie A., 136

Full Story initiative, CAA, 94

Fund for Creative Equity, Netflix, 78

"Funniest Native Comedians to Watch"
list, Illuminative, 198

Funny or Die: *Climate Science Denier
Disorder* of, 166; Nguyen partnership
with, 14

Gaebe, Molly, on comedy, 45

gatekeeping positions: BIPOC, LGBTQ+
relation to, 60, 65; diversity in, 62

The Gay and Lesbian Alliance Against
Defamation (GLAAD), 85

gentrification, in Norfolk, 156, 162

Gethard, Chris, 184

Getting Schooled (YALL project), 196

Gilman, Hollie Russon, 9–11

Gitlin, Todd: on Hollywood norms, 62; on
politics of dis*play*, 34

GLAAD. *See* The Gay and Lesbian Alliance Against Defamation

Glazer, Ilana, 53

Glo Nation, 73

Golden Globe Awards (2021), 53–54

González, Gabe, *196*, 197

González, Marcos, *196*

Good Times (TV show), 82

Gore, Al, 164–65

grassroots organizations: climate change
work of, 167; creative process for, 17; as
engines for participatory politics, 11; of
Hip Hop Caucus, 171; of marginalized
people, 6; participatory culture in, 18

Grease (film), 28

Green, Makiah: on activism, 79; on diversity, 72; on social media, 69
Green, Rodney, 160
Greene, Marjorie Taylor, 97
Guardian (publication), 54
Guilford, J. P., on creativity, 108

Hall, Bethany, 20, 119; at Center for Media & Social Impact, 103–5; as comedy facilitator, 144, 168; social justice work of, 101–2; in YALL, 21
Hall, Stuart, on rights, 9
Hampton Roads, 161–62; climate change effect on, 163, 178–79
Harjo, Sterlin, 73, 138–39; on Native representation, 137
harm-reduction movement, for addiction, 185–86
#HashtagActivism (Jackson, S. J., Bailey, and Welles), 91
Hathout, Maher, 88
Havstad, Liz, 168–69, 179
Healey, Josh, 167
Held, David, 9
Help America Vote Act (2002), 2
Hess, David, 164
Hill, Charlie, 138; The 1491s compared to, 140
Hiller, Jeff, 44
Hilo (YALL project), 198
Hip Hop Action Summit, 2
Hip Hop Caucus, 152; *Ain't Your Mama's Heat Wave* of, 25, 158, 171–73, 175–78, *177*, 180, *181*; for climate justice, 7, 25, 174–75; Comedy ThinkTank collaboration with, 158, 168–70; Hurricane Katrina recovery by, 156–57
Hoffman, Abbie, 34
Hollywood: activism in, 84, 95; awards shows in, 36–37, 53–54, 86, 87, 100; climate change stories in, 165; comedy packaging in, 188–90; diversity showcases of, 200–201; MPAC relation to,

88–89; Native portrayals in, 133–36, 137, 139; norms in, 62, 67; power dynamics in, 58–59; social justice in, 77–79; social media effect on, 71, 96, 190
Hollywood Foreign Press Association, 53–54, 55
Hoorae Productions, Color Creative of, 72–73
Horn, Bill, 85
hostile humor, harm caused by, 45–46
housing policies, racist, 159, 169
How Democracies Die (Levitsky and Ziblatt), 30
How to Be Successful without Hurting Men's Feelings (Cooper), 47
"How to Medical" (Cooper), 50, *51*, 52
Hurricane Katrina: Color of Change relation to, 7, 89; destruction of, 158–60; Hip Hop Caucus recovery for, 156–57
Hurricane Maria, 28–29
Hutcheson, Scott, 113

IllumiNative: Comedy ThinkTank collaboration with, 131–32, 143–47, 150–51; "Funniest Native Comedians to Watch" list of, 198; mission of, 130; *You're Welcome, America!* by, 24–25, 132, 148–51, *149*, 150
Imani, Aminah, 176
I May Destroy You (TV show), 53–54, 55
improv comedy: principles of, 105, 107; in writers' room, 169
An Inconvenient Truth (documentary), 164–65
IndieWire (publication), 54
Indigenous People's Day (2021), 150
#InTheTimeItTakes, social media campaign, 5
innovation: Comedy ThinkTank process for, 101, 104–5; during COVID-19, 114; in creative industries, 191–92; creativity in, 107–8, 124, 214
Insecure (TV show), 53, 193

Inside Climate News (news outlet), 163
Intergovernmental Panel on Climate Change (IPCC), 164
International Press Freedom Award, Márquez winning, 205
IPCC. *See* Intergovernmental Panel on Climate Change
Iraq, political satire in, 36
Islamic State, comedic opposition to, 36
Islamophobia, in Hollywood, 88

Jackson, Sarah J., 91
Jackson, Shantira, 169
Jackson, Vanessa, 117, 119
Jacobsen, Abby, 53
The Jeffersons (TV show), 82–83
Jenkins, Henry, 18; on civic imagination, 44; on cultural power, 90; on participatory politics, 11
Johnson, Joyelle Nicole, as cohost of *You're Welcome, America!*, 148–50, *149*, *150*
Jokes and Their Relation to the Unconscious (Freud), 39
Joksic, Mladen, 31–32
Jones, Clark, 176–78, *177*
Jones, Jeffrey, 170
Jones, Leslie, 100
journalists: democracy relation to, 43; in Venezuela, 207–8
Juneteenth, 77
Jurden, Jay, *122*; Forrester collaboration with, 115–16, 117, 119–20; on racism, 118, 119, 123–24

Kaliiaa, Jackie, 140
Kaling, Mindy, 42
Kanoyton, Gaylene, 173–74
Karriem, Elijah, 153, 168
Kasem, Casey, 87
Kendi, Ibram X., 83–84
Kerry, John, 2
Kim, Roger, 169

King, Martin Luther, Jr., 117
Kristof, Nicholas, 32

Lakey, George, 36
Landrieu, Mitch, 24, 110; racial justice work of, 111–12
Lear, Norman, 194–95; Black Panthers influence on, 82–83; Declare Yourself by, 1–2, 5; sitcoms of, 81
Leavitt, Peter A., 136
Le Backes, Kathy, 59
LeBlanc, Judith, 136
Lee, Carla, 197; on YALL, 201
Levitsky, Steven, 30
Levy, Dan, 44
LGBTQ+ people: comedy of, 42; cultural revolution of, 53, 74; demand for media of, 55, 67–68; gatekeeper relation to, 60, 65; marriage equality for, 128; on social platforms, 70–71, 81; underrepresentation of, 23, 109, 192; in YALL, 193. *See also* marginalized groups
The Liberal Redneck Manifesto (Forrester, Crowder, and Morgan), 99
Lifeline (YALL project), 197
Lit Lounge (YALL project), 198
Little, Andrew, 32
A Little Late (TV show), 53
Liu, Eric: Citizen University cofounded by, 8; on democracy, 9
Live PD (TV show), 77
Locke, Alaine Leroy, 84
Los Angeles, California: Declare Yourself campaign in, 1; Echo Hawk in, 127; YALL pitch showcase in, 195, *199*
Louisiana, New Orleans, 25, 110–11, 156–57, 158–59, 171
Love, Deirdre "Mama D," 152–53, 155–56, 174; in *Ain't Your Mama's Heat Wave*, 173
LuPone, Panni, Rainbow singalong with, 29

Luzerne County, Pennsylvania, 182–83
Lyonne, Natasha, 52; on Coel, 54

Maduro, Nicolás, 207
MANAA. *See* Media Action Network for Asian Americans
Al-Marayati, Salam, 88
March for Our Lives, 10
marginalized groups: comedy used by, 41–43, 44–46, 189–90, 213; creative power in, 8; in entertainment industry, 23–24, 191–92, 200–201, 246n27; grassroots advocacy of, 6; Hollywood activism for, 84; narrative power of, 12; in popular culture, 83, 89, 128, 129, 130–31; social capital for, 60–61, 73–74
Márquez, Laureano, *207*; *Tal Cual* column of, 208; Venezuela relation to, 205–6
Marston, Kristen, 22, 79; on entertainment narratives, 89–90; on performative activism, 96
Martin, Clare, 114
Mary Poppins (film), 28
McCants, Thaddeus, 198
McNeal, Tim, 79
McNulty, Johnny, 146
Media Action Network for Asian Americans (MANAA), 85
#MeToo, 77
Meyer, Murf, *187*, 190; comedy of, 183–84; on Luzerne County, 182–83; *Murf Meyer is Self-Medicated* of, 186–87, 197–98; at YALL, 184–85, 188
Meyers, Seth, 66–67
Minhaj, Hasan, 19, *20*, 190
Mittal, Aditi, *20*
Modern Family (TV show), 41, 212
Momo's Amerika (YALL project), 197
Montgomery, Kathryn, 84
Moore, Michael, 225n26
Moore, Mik, 190

Moore + Associates: voter-engagement initiatives of, 190; YALL collaboration with, 21
Morse, David, 12
Movement for Black Lives, 10
MPAC. *See* Muslim Public Affairs Council
MTV Entertainment Group: Choose or Lose of, 2; diversity initiatives of, 78–79; Movie & TV Awards, 100
Murf Meyer is Self-Medicated (YALL project), *187*; OSF grant for, 185; podcast of, 186–87; second season of, 197–98
Musical.ly, 48
Muslim Public Affairs Council (MPAC), 87; Hollywood relation to, 88–89
"My Country 'Tis of Thee," 141

NAACP. *See* National Association for the Advancement of Colored People
Nagle, Mary Kathryn, 136
narrative power, political power contrasted with, 12
narrative strategy: activist collaboration with entertainment industry, 92–93; for social justice, 91–92
Nate (comedy special), 43
National Association for the Advancement of Colored People (NAACP), 85; in Norfolk, 173–74
National Bureau of Economic Research, "Unhappy Cities" report (2014) of, 182–83
The National Council of La Raza, 85
National Geographic, 165
National Organization for Women (NOW), 85
Native American Rights Fund, Echo Hawk work with, 127–28
Native Americans, Native peoples: Alcatraz Island seized by, 141; entertainment industry portrayals of, 130; Hollywood portrayals of, 133–37, 139; Osage Nation of, 132, 142–43; partici-

patory media used by, 142; in popular culture, 128, 129, 130–31; racism toward, 126–27; Standing Rock Sioux tribe of, 136; TV comedy about, 73
Native Comedy at the Rock (YALL project), 197
Native joy: in comedy development, 144, 146; in *Rutherford Falls*, 138; in *You're Welcome, America!*, 151
Native Organizers Alliance, 136
Natural Resources Defense Council, 161–62
NBCUniversal: Peacock of, 138; *Rhonda Mitchell, MD* sold to, 198–99
N'Diaye, Mamoudou, 63, 93, 176; on YALL, 202
Nesteroff, Kliph, 140, 141
Netflix: *Emily in Paris* on, 54; *Everything's Fine* on, 52; Fund for Creative Equity of, 78; *Nate* on, 43; *Never Have I Ever* on, 42; *Spirit Rangers* on, 138; *When They See Us* on, 92
networks, social capital building, 59–60
Networks of Outrage and Hope (Castells), 18–19
Never Have I Ever (comedy show), 42
"New Moon Wolfpack Auditions" (YouTube), 139
The New Negro (Locke), 84
New Orleans, Louisiana, 156; Landrieu as mayor of, 110–11; Norfolk compared to, 25, 157, 158, 161–62, 171; racial segregation in, 159
New York City: Bread and Puppet Theater in, 34; Caveat in, 195, *196*; Márquez in, 206; as pandemic epicenter, 49; Upright Citizens Brigade Theater in, 184
New York Post (newspaper), GLAAD response to, 85
New York Times (newspaper): Breakthrough Institute op-ed in, 165; Hurricane Katrina coverage of, 160
NextGen America, 166–67
Nguyen, Amanda, 14–15, 16–17

Nice Tan (YALL project), 197
Nielsen, TV study of, 55–56
9/11 terrorist attacks, 88–89
Nobel Peace Prize, 164
Norfolk, Virginia, 174; *Ain't Your Mama's Heatwave* in, 171–73, 175–78; New Orleans compared to, 25, 157, 158, 161–62, 171; public housing in, 162–63; shooting in, 155–56; Vivian C. Mason Art & Technology Center for Teens in, 152–54, *154*
Normalizing Injustice (Color of Change), 77–78
North Dakota, Standing Rock uprising in, 129, 132, 136–37
The North Pole (TV show), 167
Nossel, Suzanne, 16
NOW. *See* National Organization for Women

Obeidi, Suhad "Sue," 87, 88, 96; on popular culture, 89
Obergefell v. Hodges (2015), 128
Oklahoma: Comedy ThinkTank session in, 143; Pawhuska, 142
Old News (TV show), 47–48
100 Resilient Cities initiative, Rockefeller Foundation, 162
100 Tricks to Appear Smart in Meetings (Cooper), 47
One Day at a Time (TV show), 73
O'Neill, Shannon, 145, 213
Open Society Foundations (OSF), 185
"Open TV," 13, 191
Organization for Economic Cooperation and Development, on Norfolk, 161–62
Ornelas, Sierra Teller, 138
Osage Nation, 132, 142–43
#OscarsSoWhite, 77
OSF. *See* Open Society Foundations

Palamides, Natalie, 43
Paolisso, Michael, 163

Parks and Recreation (TV show), 129
participatory culture: entertainment
 industry relation to, 140; environmental justice relation to, 164, 166–67; in
 grassroots organizations, 18; in postmillennial media era, 5–6, 11; power in,
 25–26, 212–13; in social media, 90–91
participatory media: creativity theory in,
 105–6; marginalized voices in, 192; Native Americans using, 142
participatory politics: creativity in, 7–8;
 culture work in, 11–12; social media
 relation to, 90–91
patriarchy, in entertainment industry,
 54–55
Pawhuska, Oklahoma, 142
Pawnee Nation, 126
Peacock (NBCUniversal), 138
Pennsylvania, Luzerne County, 182–83
Pentagon, Yippies levitating, 33, 34
Perdue, David, 118–19; on allyship, 124
Perez, Yvonne A., 136
philanthropy: comedy funded by, 185–86,
 189, 191, 193, 194, 211–12; entertainment
 industry relation to, 25
Pierre-Outlar, Carolyn, 198–99
Pinder, Sherrow, 159
pitch, 61–63; YALL process for, 195–200,
 202–3
Playing Indian (Deloria), 135–36
Poehler, Amy, on Declare Yourself, 3
political power, narrative power contrasted with, 12
political satire: of Cooper, 50–51; in Egypt,
 35; in Iraq, 36
Polley, Sarah, 54
Poo, Ai-jen, 11–12
Popovic, Srdja, 31–32
Popps, Mpho, *20*
popular culture: marginalized groups in,
 83, 89, 128, 129, 130–31; as unifying, 210
postmillennial media era: concerns of, 19;
 participatory culture in, 5–6, 11

Powderkeg Media, 59–60
Powell, Dan, 103
public housing, in Norfolk, 162–63
Puerto Rico, Hurricane Maria in, 28–29

racial justice, 83, 101, 111; climate justice
 relation to, 180; EPU for, 112–13, 116; in
 Hollywood, 77–79; #RacismIsNoJoke
 for, 120–23; 2020 uprisings for, 23, 75
racism, 123–24; erasure as, 129–30; hous-
 ing policies as, 159, 169; in Hurricane
 Katrina media coverage, 160; toward
 Native Americans, 126–27, 128; sys-
 temic, 76–77, 113, 118, 119, 132–33, 135
#RacismIsNoJoke, social media cam-
 paign, 24, 120–23
Radical Optimist Collective, 118
Radio Caracas Televisión (RCTV), 208
Radio Rochela (sketch comedy show), 208
Rae, Issa: Davis relation to, 60; Hoorae
 Productions of, 72–73; *Insecure* of, 193;
 Tales of an Awkward Black Girl of, 53
Rahman, K. Sabeel, 9–11
Rainbow, Randy: comedy on Trump by,
 23, 27–28, 32; "Desperate Cheeto" of,
 28–29, *29*
Ramy (TV show), 212
The Randy Rainbow Show, 28–29
RCTV. *See* Radio Caracas Televisión
Reclaiming Native Truth, 129–30, 133, 144,
 147
Red Corn, Raymond, 142
RedCorn, Ryan, 145, 151; activism of,
 142–43
Reece, Stacy, 118
Reel, Keja, 172
Reform Media Group, 60
RE.Invest Initiative, 162
representation, media: civic imagina-
 tion in, 151; comedy combined with,
 42–43, 192–93; cultural citizenship
 through, 46; Native, 133–37; optimism
 through, 80; organizations for, 89;

social inequalities in, 84; social media amplifying, 87, 90–91

Reservation Dogs (TV show), 138

Rez Ball (TV show), 138–39

Rhonda Mitchell, MD (YALL project), 198–99

Riddick, Dwight, 173, 175

right-wing extremism, comedic response to, 36

Robinson, Rashad, 12

Rocha, Zack de la, 127

Rockefeller Foundation, 100 Resilient Cities initiative, 162

Rock the Vote, 2

Rodriguez, Favianna, 167

Rome, creative deviance in ancient, 33

Rossman, Gabriel, 85

Rubin, Jerry, 34

Ruby, Matt, 64

Rudolph, Maya, 52

Ruffin, Amber, 66–67

Runningwater, Bird, 139

Russi, Lorena, 198

Rutherford Falls (TV show), 138, 151

samizdat jokes, 33, 225n30

Satcher, Lacee, 164

Saturday Night Live (TV show), 32

Schitt's Creek (TV show), 44

Schmieding, Jana, 137–38

Schumann, Peter, Bread and Puppet Theater of, 34

Schuster, Noam, 110

Sexual Assault Survivors Bill of Rights (2016), 14

Sharf, Zach, 54

showrunners: comedy writing packet relation to, 64–65; cultural understanding of, 62–63; diversity among, 56

Silverman, Sarah, 3

Simmons, Russell, 156; Hip Hop Action Summit of, 2

Singh, Lilly, 53

Sivills, Kristen, 176

Smackdown Your Vote, 2

Smith, Antonique, 175

Smith, Kevin, 3

social capital: comedy writing packet relation to, 64, 66; in entertainment industry, 193; as holy grail, 147; for marginalized groups, 60–61, 73–74; networks built by, 59–60; social media relation to, 71; YALL building, 201–3

social change: civic imagination for, 12, 44, 211; civic power for, 37–38; creative culture for, 38, 130; creativity theory in, 16–17

social critique: comedy as, 39, 41–42, 43, 45–46; by Rainbow, 28; in Venezuela, 208

social justice, 98–99; allyship in, 22; climate change relation to, 163–64, 178–79; comedy for, 19–21, 38–39, 39–40, 42, 46, 180–81, 189–91, 202, 211–12, 213–14; Comedy ThinkTank initiatives for, 24; creative power for, 15; cultural power relation to, 7; entertainment industry relation to, 6–7, 13–14, 18, 74, 80, 92, 194; in Hollywood, 77–79; narrative strategy for, 91–92. *See also* activists, social justice

social justice organizations: comedy used by, 7, 15, 20–21, 96, 131, 211–12, 213; creative power in, 15, 17, 124; entertainment industry collaboration with, 194; in postmillennial media era, 5–6

social media, 35, 46; democracy relation to, 18–19; diversity on, 69–71; effect on Hollywood, 71, 96, 190; entertainment on, 13, 48; EPU campaign on, 24; Facebook as, 19; front-facing comedy on, 114; political satire on, 36; representation amplified by, 87, 90–91; TikTok as, 48, 50–53; Twitter as, 50–52, 70, 100, 121–22

social media campaign: #InTheTimeItTakes, 5; #RacismIsNoJoke, 24, 120–23

Soto Lamb, Erika, 60–61; Comedy Central work by, 93–94

Soviet Union, samizdat jokes in, 33, 225n30

spec scripts, 64

Spirit Rangers (TV show), 138

Spotlight California (YouTube series), 166–67

Spreadable Media (Jenkins), 18

Standing Rock Sioux tribe, 136

Standing Rock uprising, 129; visibility through, 132, 136–37

Stand Up Planet (documentary), 19, 20, 190

Stewart, Jon, 2; on comedy writing packets, 66

Stewart, Sasha, 65–66, 108–9

streaming networks: comedic agitation through, 35; effect on entertainment industry, 17, 57; Netflix as, 42, 43, 52, 54, 78, 92, 138; Peacock as, 138

Sudan, al-Bashir in, 36

Sundance Film Festival, 12; *An Inconvenient Truth* in, 164; MPAC relation to, 88–89

Sundance Institute's Native Program, 139

Swaney, Brooke, 148

Sykes, Wanda, 3

systemic racism, 76–77; as interdependent system, 119; toward Native Americans, 132–33, 135; White people relation to, 113, 118

Tal Cual (publication), 208

Tales of an Awkward Black Girl (YouTube series), 53

Target Prime Time (Montgomery), 84

Taylor, Breonna, protests related to, 79

Taylor, Keeanga-Yahamatta, 76

TED Talk, of Liu, 8

Teller Orenelas, Sierra, 73

Texas, El Paso, 93

Thanksgiving (TV show), 103

Think 100% campaign, 157, 168

30 Rock (TV show), 102

Three Kings (movie), 87

Tidwell, Mike, 160–61

TikTok, 48; Cooper on, 50–53

Till, Emmett, 75

Tousi, Mahyad, 61; Boomgen Studios of, 73

Travis, Yedoye, 169

Treaty of Fort Laramie (1968), 141

Trudell, John, 141

Trump, Donald, 43; comedy based on, 23, 27–28; COVID-19 response of, 49–50; Hurricane Maria response of, 28–29; as threat to democracy, 32

"20 Ways 9/11 changed My Life as an (American) Muslim" (Ainslie), 99

2020 racial-justice uprisings, 23, 75

Twitter: during Arab Spring, 35; Calderón Kellett on, 70; Cooper on, 50–52; Forrester on, 100; #RacismIsNoJoke response on, 121–22

"Unhappy Cities" report, National Bureau of Economic Research (2014), 182–83

UnidosUS, 85

United States (US), 34, 37; Deep South of, 112–14, 119, 210; democracy in, 30–32; Native story in, 133–34

The United States of Al (TV show), 73

Upright Citizens Brigade Theater, New York, 184

US presidential election (2004), 2, 4

US presidential election (2020), 29

US presidential primary (2016), 27–28

Valencia, Karissa, 138

Vanity Fair (publication): Cooper in, 51; Schmieding essay in, 137–38

Vargas, Jose Antonia, 89

Venezuela: humanitarian crisis in, 206–8; Márquez from, 205–6

Venkataramanujam, Prashanth: on joking, 110; on social media, 69–70

ViacomCBS, Color of Change collaboration with, 92–93
Vietnam War, 81
Virginia: Hampton Roads in, 161–62, 163, 178–79; Norfolk, 25, 152–54, *154*, 155–57, 158, 171–73, 175–78
Virginian-Pilot (newspaper), 160–61
Vivian C. Mason Art & Technology Center for Teens, Norfolk, 152–54, *154*
voter-engagement initiatives, 2; Declare Yourself as, 1; of Moore + Associates, 190

Wahid, Ahmed, on political satire, 36
Washington Post (newspaper), Castro article in, 94
We Had a Little Real Estate Problem (Nesteroff), 140
Welles, Brooke Foucault, 91
WellRED Comedy Tour, 99–100
When They See Us (TV show), 92
"White Folks' Work" (Clark), 22
White House Coronavirus Task Force, 49–50
White House Correspondents' Dinner (2017), 43, 209
White people: allyship of, 117–18, 124; systemic racism relation to, 113, 118
William Morris Endeavor, Cooper represented by, 52
Wilson, Bobby, 73, 145–46, 212
Wilson, Lisa Flick, 118
Wolf, Michelle, 209; on Trump, 43
Wood, Roy, Jr., 199
World Health Organization, 49
World Wrestling Entertainment, Inc. (WWE), 98, 100

World Wrestling Foundation, Smackdown Your Vote of, 2
"Wrestling with My Emotions" (comedy series), 100
writing packet, comedy, 64–66
WWE. *See* World Wrestling Entertainment, Inc.

YALL. *See* Yes, And . . . Laughter Lab
The Years of Living Dangerously (TV show), 165
Yearwood, Lennox, Jr. "Rev.," 168, 181; on *Ain't Your Mama's Heat Wave*, 171–72, 176; Hip Hop Caucus founded by, 156–57
Yes, And . . . Laughter Lab (YALL), 21; creation of, 25; culture work of, 200; Meyer at, 184–85, 188; model of, 193–94; participatory media relation to, 192; pitch showcase of, 195–200, *196*, *198*, 202–3; social capital built by, 201–3
Yippies, creative deviance of, 33, 34
You're Welcome, America! (IllumiNative), 24–25, 132, 148–51, *149*, *150*
Youssef, Bassem, *Al-Bernameg* of, 35
YouTube, 5, 57; *Al-Bernameg* on, 35; "New Moon Wolfpack Auditions" on, 139; political satire on, 36; Rainbow on, 27, 28–29, *29*, 32; *Spotlight California* on, 166–67; *Tales of an Awkward Black Girl* on, 53

Zapatista uprising, Echo Hawk work with, 127
Ziblatt, Daniel, 30

ABOUT THE AUTHOR

CATY BORUM is Executive Director of the Center for Media & Social Impact (CMSI), a creative innovation lab and research center based at American University that creates, showcases, and studies media designed for social change; and Associate Professor at the American University School of Communication in Washington, DC. She is an award-winning media producer and engaged scholar working at the intersection of entertainment storytelling, creative culture, and social justice. She is the coauthor of *A Comedian and an Activist Walk into a Bar: The Serious Role of Comedy in Social Justice*, with Lauren Feldman (2020). Her documentary book, *Story Movements: How Documentaries Empower People and Inspire Social Change* (2020), was recognized with the 2021 Broadcast Education Association Book Award. In 2020, she was named to DOC NYC's New Documentary Leaders list for her significant contributions to the documentary industry.

In 2019, she cofounded and launched, in partnership with cultural strategy agency Moore + Associates, the Yes, And . . . Laughter Lab, a creative incubator of subversive comedy that partners with the entertainment industry and leading social-justice organizations. Under her leadership, the Center for Media & Social Impact directs high-impact initiatives that bring professional comedians and social-justice organizations together as collaborators. As a documentary and media producer, she has produced films and TV programs that have premiered internationally and nationally across TV, festivals, and theaters. Previously, Borum was a senior communication agency executive specializing in social-change strategy, longtime collaborator with TV producer and philanthropist Norman Lear, program officer in the Kaiser Family Foundation's Entertainment Media & Public Health program, and civic journalism fellow at the *Philadelphia Inquirer*.

In the United States and around the world, Borum is an invited speaker on the topic of entertainment storytelling and social justice at film festivals and social-change convenings. Her peer-reviewed scholarship is featured in leading academic journals, and her research and creative media programs have been funded by the MacArthur Foundation, Ford Foundation, Atlantic Philanthropies, Gates Foundation, Open Society Foundations, Luminate, Doris Duke Foundation for Islamic Art, Comedy Central, Perspective Fund, Pop Culture Collaborative, National Endowment for the Arts, McNulty Foundation, Unbound Philanthropy, Argosy Foundation, and more.